BENGAL DISTRICT GAZETTEERS

BURDWAN

BENGAL DISTRICT GAZETTEERS

BURDWAN

BY

J. C. K. PETERSON

GYAN

ISBN : 978-81-212-1834-4 (HB)

First Published, 1910

Published, 2018

Published by

Gyan Publishing House
5, Ansari Road
Daryaganj, New Delhi-110002
Phone: 011-47034999, 9811692060
www.gyanbooks.com
E-mail: books@gyanbooks.com

Printed at: G. Print Process, Delhi.

PREFACE.

I DESIRE to acknowledge my obligations to Mr. W. B. Hoycock, I.C.S., Collector of Burdwan, and to Captain Mackworth, I.M.S., Civil Surgeon of Burdwan, for the assistance they have given me in the preparation of this volume. I am indebted to the former for having the proofs read and corrected in his office and to the latter for the greater part of the information contained in the Chapter on Public Health. The volume owes much to Mr. W. B. Oldham's pamphlet on the Historical and Ethnical Aspects of the Burdwan District, which is a mine of valuable and interesting information.

J. C. K. P.

PLAN OF CONTENTS.

TABLE OF CONTENTS.

CHAPTER I.

PHYSICAL ASPECTS.

PAGES

CHAPTER II.

HISTORY.

CHAPTER III.

THE PEOPLE.

CHAPTER IV.

PUBLIC HEALTH.

CHAPTER V.

AGRICULTURE.

CHAPTER VI.

NATURAL CALAMITIES.

CHAPTER VII.

RENT, WAGES, AND PRICES.

CHAPTER VIII.

OCCUPATIONS, MANUFACTURES, AND TRADES.

CHAPTER IX.

THE RĀNIGANJ COAL-FIELD.

CHAPTER X.

MEANS OF COMMUNICATION.

CHAPTER XI.

LAND REVENUE ADMINISTRATION.

CHAPTER XII.

GENERAL ADMINISTRATION.

CHAPTER XIII.

LOCAL SELF-GOVERNMENT.

CHAPTER XIV.

EDUCATION.

CHAPTER XV.

GAZETTEER.

GAZETTEER

OF THE

BURDWAN DISTRICT.

CHAPTER I.

PHYSICAL ASPECTS.

THE district of Burdwān, one of the western districts of the Burdwān Division, is situated between 22° 50′ and 23° 53′ north latitude and between 86° 48′ and 88° 25′ east longitude. It contains an area of 2,689 square miles as ascertained by the latest survey, and a population, according to the census of 1901, of 1,532,475 persons. Burdwān, the principal town and administrative head-quarters, is situated on the north bank of the Bānka, some 2 miles from the Dāmodar river, in 23° 14′ N. and 87° 51′ E. The name *Bārdhamāna* in the vernacular is a corruption of the Sanskrit *Vārdhamāna* (the present participle passive of the verb *vārdh*) and implies "the increasing or prosperous." GENERAL DESCRIPTION.

The district lies mainly between the Ajay, the Bhāgīrathi or Hooghly, and the Dāmodar rivers. It is bounded on the north by the Santāl Parganas, Bīrbhūm and Murshidābād; on the east by Nadiā; on the south by Hooghly, Midnapore and Bānkurā; and on the west by Mānbhūm. The Ajay separates it on the north from the Bīrbhūm and Murshidābād districts forming a natural boundary line till shortly before its junction with the Bhāgīrathi; while on the south the Dāmodar, running parallel to the Ajay for a considerable portion of its course, forms the main boundary. A small portion of the Kātwa subdivision lies to the north of the Ajay, and the Khandaghosh and Raina thānas of the head-quarters subdivision lie to the south of the Dāmodar, which here takes a sharp bend to the north-east. On the west the Barākar passes along the north-western boundary for a few miles before its junction with the Dāmodar and divides the Boundaries district from Mānbhum. On the east the Hooghly, known in its upper reaches as the Bhāgīrathi, forms the main boundary with Nadiā, but a small strip of land on the right bank of the river which contains the town of Nadiā belongs to that district. The south-eastern boundary marches with the Hooghly district and is formed by an irregular line drawn north-east from the Dhalkisor river, which for a few miles forms the boundary with Midnapore, to the Hooghly. The natural boundaries formed by the great rivers to the north, east and south are fairly constant, and there have been no important changes within recent times.

Configuration. In shape the district resembles a club or hammer, of which the handle consisting of the Asansol subdivision is some 60 miles in length. The head is formed by the delta to the east lying between the great rivers which form the main boundaries, and the greatest breadth here is about 70 miles. The total length of the district from the Barākár river to the Hooghly below Kālna is 130 miles. It falls naturally into two main divisions. The eastern portion, comprising the Burdwān, Kālna and Kātwa subdivisions with a total area of 2,071 square miles, is a wide alluvial plain enclosed by the Ajay, the Bhāgīrathi, and the Dāmodar on the north, east, and south, and bounded by the Asansol subdivision on the west. To the west the district narrows to a mere strip of rocky, undulating land, some 15 miles wide, lying between the Ajay and the Dāmodar rivers.

Natural divisions. These two tracts differ completely from each other in natural characteristics, scenery and population. That to the east, which contains more than two-thirds of the total area of the district, is a delta the southern edge of which approaches the sea-board and is of the most recent formation. The rivers which have worked to form it are the Ajay, the Dāmodar, and the Ganges, of which river the Bhāgīrathi is an ancient channel. The latter in its efforts to break eastwards has left long loops of disused channels all along its western banks and the soil here is water-logged and swampy. In the Ausgrām *thāna* a large tract of a hundred square miles is still covered with *sāl* jungle. Elsewhere the country is densely cultivated. Wide plains, green in their season with rice, and at other times patterned like a gigantic chess-board by the low embankments which divide the fields, stretch in unvarying monotony to an horizon dotted with trees and villages. The villages are situated on higher ground and are usually buried in tropical vegetation. Large trees are scarce, but the clumps of bamboos, the mango groves, and the date and other palms which encircle the houses have a quiet beauty of their own. One very noticeable feature of this portion of the district is the great number of tanks which cover its surface. Many of the more valuable lands are irrigated from them and in the villages there is hardly a family of any position which has not its own private tank for bathing and other domestic purposes. Unfortunately little care is taken to cleanse these depressions, and in many cases they become mere cess-pools receiving all the sullage water from the houses on their banks. The general drainage is from west and south-west to east. The course of the Dāmodar along the south-western boundary is higher than the Hooghly to the east and several channels run down this slope. The fall however is very slight, the average from the Dāmodar to the Hooghly being only 4 feet per mile. The Dāmodar itself drains but a small portion of the district, and its bed here is generally higher than the surrounding country.

The western portion of the district resembles a promontory jutting out from the hill ranges of Central India and consists of barren, rocky and rolling country with a laterite soil rising into rocky hillocks on the right bank of the Ajay river and shut in on the west, north and south by the hills of Chotā Nāgpur and the Santāl Parganas. The actual headland of this peninsula is formed by the *pargana* of Gopbhūm formerly by tradition the seat of a Sadgop dynasty, with the delta not only fencing it in on the east but edging round it on the south and north. This tract is practically treeless though a portion is still covered with *sāl* forest and before the discoveries of coal in the last century was a tremendous wilderness dotted at long intervals by tiny clearings and settlements and intersected by no great road or route. The surface is generally covered with clay, in some parts alluvial, but in others formed from the decomposition of the rocks, though in places the rocks are exposed and great stretches of land are wholly unfit for cultivation. It is chiefly in the depressions and along the edges of the numerous drainage channels that rice is cultivated in terraces banked up on the slopes. Along the Dāmodar to the south however there are narrow strips of land formed by alluvion which yield good harvests. The famous Rānīganj coal field is situated in this strip of undulating country enclosed by the Ajay and Dāmodar rivers and this corner of the district is one of the busiest industrial tracts in Bengal. The country is dotted with coal pits and factories, and its coal and iron fields are thronged by miners from the neighbouring districts. The drainage is chiefly into the Dāmodar, the water shed, a range of high ground which rises in places to over 300 feet, running some 5 miles south of the Ajay river. Rānīganj and Asansol, the two principal towns in the Asansol subdivision, are situated at an altitude above sea level of 303 and 257 feet respectively.

River system. The Bhāgīrathi, which in its lower reaches below the town of Nadiā and after its junction with the Jalangi, is known as the Hooghly, ultimately receives all the drainage of the district as is shown by the following table :—

Stream			Tributary of	Ultimately drains into
Kunur	...	...	Ajay	Bhāgīrathi or Hooghly.
Bānka	...	...	Ajay	Bhāgīrathi or Hooghly.
Kharī	...	...	Ajay	Bhāgīrathi or Hooghly.
Nunia	...	...	Dāmodar	Bhāgīrathi or Hooghly.
Singarān	...	...	Dāmodar	Bhāgīrathi or Hooghly.
Dhalkisor	...	...	...	Bhāgīrathi or Hooghly.

The Bhāgīrathi is navigable by large boats all the year round, but the channel is gradually silting up and, in February and March below Kātwa, is only with great difficulty kept open. The Dāmodar is only navigable during the rains and in the dry weather dwindles to an insignificant stream, in many places not a foot deep. Before the construction of the East Indian Railway all the coal from the Rānīganj coal field was sent down this river on barges, but the traffic on it is now of little importance. The larger streams within the district are the Kunur, a tributary of the Ajay, the Nunia and Singarān which drain the Asansol subdivision, and the Bānka and Khāri which flow into the Bhāgīrathi. The Bānka and Kharī were originally offshoots of the Dāmodar, and the old beds up to their junction with the parent stream can still be traced. Throughout their courses these rivers receive numerous smaller tributaries which are merely drainage channels for the superfluous water collected in the rice fields during the rains. There are also a large number of small creeks and water-courses interlacing with the larger streams which are almost entirely dry during the greater part of the year.

Cases of alluvion and diluvion are frequent in the larger rivers but no extensive changes in their course have recently taken place though the Bhāgīrathi is now said to be threatening the town of Kātwa. It is clear however that such changes were frequent in former times. The Bhāgīrathi has left long loops of disused channels all along its western bank and, at the beginning of the last century, by a sudden change of course, swung eastwards and left the town of Nadiā and a considerable strip of land north and south of that city on its right bank. The Dāmodar after flowing till comparatively recent times in different channels due east through the silt, has broken violently to the south and is now attempting to break a course back to the south-west. As has already been noted the Kharī and Bānka, though now separated from it, were originally spill-channels of this river.

The banks of the rivers are generally low and their beds sandy and cultivation is only carried on along the edges of the larger rivers where the fields are protected by embankments. The Bhāgīrathī is fordable below Kātwa in February and March. The Dāmodar and Ajay are deep streams in the rains but at other seasons are passable on foot at any part of the district. The Kharī is never fordable for the last few miles of its course before its junction with the Bhāgīrathi, while the other streams are fordable at all seasons except after heavy rain. The following is a brief description of the principal rivers.

Bhāgīrathi or Hooghly.

The Bhāgīrathi or Hooghly forms the whole eastern boundary of the district with the exception of a short distance where it enters the Nadia district near the town of Nadiā. This river is one of the many channels which the Ganges in its progress eastwards has abandoned, and, although still regarded as one of the mouths of the sacred river, now receives but little water from it. For Hindus the Bhāgīrathi just above Kātwa possesses an especial sanctity even rivalling the Ganges at Benares in this respect; according to tradition the great Vikramaditya used to transport himself daily from his palace at Ujain in Rājputāna to Kātwa to bathe in its purifying waters. The bed is gradually silting up and in its upper reaches in the dry season there is hardly any current. A large river-borne trade is carried on it, and there is a regular service of river steamers from Calcutta during the rains which competes not unsuccessfully with the railways both for goods and passenger traffic. The average breadth is about a mile, but in the hot weather the main channel above Kālna is often less than a hundred yards across, and the river is fordable in many places in the Kātwa subdivision. The Bhāgīrathi first touches Burdwān a little south of the battle field of Plassey, which is on the opposite bank. Thence it flows southwards as far as Kātwa where it is joined by the Ajay. After an exceedingly winding course in a south-easterly direction it enters the district of Nadiā a little north of the town of that name, but again forms the boundary of Burdwān from Samudragarh, where it receives the Kharī, and continues its southward course past Kālna till it leaves the district opposite the town of Santipur and forms the eastern boundary of the adjoining district of Hooghly. The principal places on its banks are Kālna, Kātwa and Dāinhāt. A large trade in salt, jute and cloth was formerly carried on at these places which were regarded as the ports of the district. With the advent of the railway, however, their importance has greatly decreased.

Ajay. The Ajay takes its rise in the hills of the Santāl Parganas and drains a large portion of their southern and western slopes. It first touches the district near Gaurangdi station ten miles north-west of Asansol, and flowing thence due east forms the northern boundary for about eighty miles until it enters the Kātwa subdivision near the village of Kumārpur some fifteen miles above its confluence with the Bhāgīrathi at Kātwa. In the western portion of its course the channel is comparatively straight and the banks are well defined, but after issuing from its rocky bed the river flows in an extraordinarily serpentine course which has been formed by the oscillations of the current through the deltaic silt. The bed is sandy and the banks low. The East Indian Loop Line crosses the river at Bhedia and at Baidyanathpur, a recently constructed bridge carries the line connecting Andal and Suri over it. Formerly this river was the only route through the dense jungle that once covered this part of Bengal and its importance is evidenced by the line of forts planted along its banks. The rapidity of the current and the sudden freshets to which, like other hill-fed streams, it is liable, render navigation hazardous, and there is practically no river-borne traffic of any importance on it. The Ajay has been identified by Wilford as the Amystis of Arrian with Kātwa (Sanskrit Katadvipa) as his Katadupa. Hunter derives the name Ajay from the Sanskrit A-jaya, "not without victory, unconquered." It is, however, more probably the ordinary contracted form of the Sanskrit Ajāvati.

Damodar. The Dāmodar, the sacred river of the Santāls, rises in the Chotā Nāgpur water-shed and, after a south-easterly course of about 350 miles, falls into the Hooghly just above the ill-famed "James and Mary Sands," a shoal which it has helped to deposit at its mouth. Together with its tributaries it forms the great line of drainage of the country stretching north-west from Calcutta to the fringe of the Central Indian plateau. The river first touches upon the Burdwān district at its junction with the Barākar a few miles south of the Barākar police station. It then flows in a south-easterly direction, past Rānīganj and Andāl, forming the boundary between Burdwān and Bānkurā for about 45 miles, and enters the district near Khandaghosh. The river here takes a sharp bend to the north-east and after passing close to the town of Burdwān turns, due south and eventually leaves the district near the village of Mohanpur. The principal places on its banks are Kasba

Gohagrām, Gopalpur, Jamālpur and Salimābād, situated at its junction with the Kāna river which here flows out of the parent stream. The course of the river is tolerably straight, but it is full of sand banks with a fall of 3·40 feet per mile. During the rains it is navigable by country boats and before the construction of the railway, which runs parallel to it along its north bank, large quantities of coal were sent down it from the Rānīganj mines in boats of 20 tons burden and upwards to the depôt at Mahishabha in Hooghly, and were thence transhipped and forwarded *viā* the Uluberiā canal and the Hooghly river to Calcutta. The river-borne traffic is now, however, of little importance and consists mainly of rafts of timber which are floated down the stream during the rains. The rafts formed are sometimes 50 to 60 yards long and generally flotillas of 10 or 12 rafts are launched together from the forests higher up. Shortly before entering the Hooghly district the river assumes the usual deltaic type and instead of receiving affluents throws off distributaries, the best known being the Kāna which branches from the parent stream at Salimābād. In the hot season the current dries up almost completely. The maximum discharge below Rānīganj has been proved to be about 500,000 cusecs, but by October and November this may fall to 1,500 cusecs or even less.

The river is a hill-fed stream deriving its water from the Hāzaribagh plateau and is liable in the lower part of its course to sudden floods which have caused much damage in the past. In 1770 the town of Burdwān was practically destroyed by a rising of this river, and immense damage and loss of life was also caused by the floods of 1823 and 1855. The right bank is now thoroughly protected by embankments and in consequence floods are frequent in the portion of the Burdwān subdivision which lies to the south of the river. They do not however last long, and as the quality of the silt which this river carries is good the inundation does good as well as harm and is certainly not a serious evil. Considerable damage and loss of life is however occasionally caused by the bore or head-wave which sweeps down the channel after heavy rain, rising sometimes to a height of 5 feet. Wilford has identified the Dāmodar as the Andômatis of Arrian.

Barākar

The Barākar, though not properly speaking a river of Burdwān, flows for some 5 miles along its north-western boundary before its junction with the Dāmodar and separates the district from Mānbhūm. At Barākar it is spanned by the bridge which carries the Grand Trunk Road and by the railway bridge recently constructed for the Grand Chord line of the East Indian Railway.

Dhalkisor. The Dhalkisor (Dwārkeswar) passes for a few miles along the southern boundary of the district.

Kunur. The Kunur, a tributary of the Ajay, rises in the undulating country north of Kāksa police station and receives the drainage of the eastern slopes of the Rānīganj water-shed. Thence it flows almost due west for some 50 miles past Ausgrām and Guskhārā till it falls into the Ajay near Mangalkot. During the rains it is liable to sudden freshets and occasionally overflows its banks, but the volume of water brought down by it is not large enough to do any very great damage. In its lower reaches it presents all the usual characteristics of a deltaic river, and its course through the silt is a constant succession of sharp curves caused by the oscillation of the current. The river is fordable everywhere and is practically dry in the hot season. It is not navigable.

Khari. The Kharī river takes its rise in an excavated hollow beside the Grand Trunk Road near the police-station of Bud-bud in the west of the district. Its bed is a wide and deep valley which bears all the appearance of having once been the channel of a great river, and there is little doubt that the stream was formerly one of the many offshoots of the Dāmodar. The old bed to its junction with the parent stream can still be traced. After flowing eastwards for some 30 miles in a circuitous course through the Galsi and Sāhibganj thānas the river bends sharply to the north and enters the Kālna subdivision a little south of the Manteswar police-station. Some seven miles north of Manteswar after an extraordinarily winding course through that thāna it again turns southwards, and forms the boundary between the Manteswar and Purbasthālī *thānas* till, after its confluence with the Bānkā near the village of Nādanghāt, it falls into the Bhāgīrathi at Samudragarh. The river is navigable for country boats as far as Gopālpur in the rains, but at other times of the year navigation above Nādanghāt is blocked by the numerous dams or weirs which are constructed across it for irrigation purposes. The banks are well defined and there has been no recent change of course of any importance. Floods are not frequent except after very heavy rain.

Bānka. The Bānka, the principal tributary of the Kharī, rises in a rice swamp near Silla in the Galsi thāna. The river was formerly in its origin a spill channel of the Dāmodar and its present source lies within a few miles of that river. The connecting channel is now completely silted up, but the bed which was formerly scoured out by the action of the main river now serves as a drainage channel for the south of the district where the land is generally lower than the bed of the Dāmodar. A connection still exists between the Bānka and the parent river at Jujuti where a sluice and feeding channel have been constructed in order to admit an adequate supply of drinking water for the town of Burdwān. Unfortunately of late years the main channel of the Dāmodar has shifted to the southern bank and a high sand bank or *chur* has been thrown up in front of the sluice, with the result that the supply of water from the Dāmodar is occasionally entirely cut off. The river flows in an easterly course parallel to the Dāmodar and at a short distance from it, and after passing through the town of Burdwān, which is situated on the north bank, crosses the railway and flows north of it as far as Saktigarh station, where it turns north-east and finally joins the Kharī a few miles above the junction of that river with the Bhāgīrathi. The stream is practically dry during the hot season, and even in the rains is only navigable for a few miles above its confluence with the Kharī. There is little or no current except after heavy rain and in consequence the river exercises but little action on its banks. Floods do occur but generally do little damage.

The Nunia enters the district from the north-west flowing like a hill stream in a deep ravine and after passing to the north of Sītārāmpur and Asansol eventually enters the Dāmodar at Rānīganj. In the hot season the river dwindles to a series of pools with little or no current. **Nunia.**

The Singarān, also a tributary of the Dāmodar, rises a little to the north of Ikda junction on the Ondal Loop line of the East Indian Railway and, after a course of some 20 miles in a south-easterly direction, falls into the Dāmodar below Andāl at the village of Srirampur. **Singarān.**

The Tamla rises a little to the west of the large village of Ukhra and thence flows south-east till it enters the Dāmodar near the boundary of Shergarh *pargana*. These three rivers, which drain the southern slopes of the Rānīganj watershed, all present the same characteristics. There are few springs and for the greater part of the year they are mere *nullahs* or channels consisting of a series of rocky pools unconnected by any flow of water. In the rains, however, there is a considerable flow of water which is used for the irrigation of the rice fields on their banks. **Tamla.**

The principal offshoot of the Dāmodar is the Kāna which branches off from the parent stream at Salimābād. Thence it flows for a few miles south-eastwards through the Salimābād thāna before it leaves the district. **Kāna.**

Brāmhain. The Brāmhain, a tributary of the Bhāgīrathi, rises in the rice fields to the south of Mangalkot police station. Thence it flows eastwards in a circuitous course and eventually enters the Bhāgīrathi at Dāinhāt. Its bed is of clay and the banks being low it is liable to flood after heavy rain. It is fordable everywhere.

Bābla. The Bābla enters the district north-east of the Ketugrām police-station and flowing south-east falls into the Bhāgīrathi near Kātwa.

EMBANKMENTS. An embankment starting at Silla 20 miles west of Burdwān protects the left or northern bank of the Dāmodar. Another important embankment runs along the right bank of the Ajay in the Asansol subdivision extending 7 miles from Gaur Bazar to Kajlādihi, 4 miles from Bishnupur to Arjunbāri and 7 miles from Sātkahaniā to Sāgarpostā, a total length of 22 miles.

MARSHES, FORESTS AND CANALS. There are no lakes in the district, but in the eastern portion, more particularly in the Kātwa and Kālna subdivisions, small *jhils* or swamps in which water remains throughout the year abound. The more extensive of these marshes lie on the right bank of the Bhāgīrathi and have plainly been caused by the overflow of that river, while a few similarly caused border the Ajay and Dāmodar. The smaller internal rivers and streams are very often embanked for purposes of irrigation; these embankments form a considerable obstruction to the natural drainage of the district, and are supposed to have largely contributed towards the outbreaks of malaria which have been such a scourge in recent times. In some of the smaller rivers a thick variety of reed called *sar* grows wild which is largely used in roofing houses. Long-stemmed rice is not grown in the district and there are no marshes or swamps suitable for its cultivation. The alluvial plain to the east is covered with an enormous number of tanks which have been excavated for the supply of drinking water or for irrigation, but almost without exception they have been long neglected and many are now overgrown with weeds and filled up with silt. There are no forests properly so called in the district, but a large tract of about 100 square miles in the Ausgrām police-station and the western uplands of the Asansol subdivision are covered with young *sāl* (*Shorea robusta*). The forests yield but slight revenues and no trees of any size are found. They were cut down when the railway was under construction, but attention has recently been drawn to their value and some of them are now closely preserved. The *sāl* saplings are chiefly used as rafters and beams and have an especial value for this purpose on account of their immunity from the attacks of white-ants. There are no large uncultivated pastures in the deltaic portion of the district, all the available ground being taken up for tillage. In the undulating country to the west there are vast stretches of waste land the herbage on which dries up in the hot season.

The only artificial waterway is the Eden Canal called after Sir Ashley Eden, an irrigation channel 22 miles in length reaching from Kānchannagar, the western suburb of Burdwān, to Jāmalpur where the Kāna river and the Kāna Damodār join it. The canal takes its supply from the Dāmodār at Jujuti where there are two head sluices connecting with the Bānkā river. The maximum discharge of the canal in the rainy season is 700 cubic feet per second, but in the winter the supply falls very low and sometimes in April and May dwindles to 50 cubic feet per second. The water admitted through the sluices flows along the Bānka for about seven miles to Kānchannagar, where it is held up by a weir across the channel and admitted into the canal proper by an anicut. After passing through Kānchannagar, the canal runs parallel to the left embankment of the Dāmodar for about 20 miles; the supply is then divided, about one-third flowing down the old channel of the Kāna Dāmodar which falls into the Hooghly above Ulubaria, while the remainder flows by the Kāna river into the Saraswati.

The canal was originally constructed for sanitary purposes. The Dāmodar embankments having closed all the old side channels of the river, it was excavated in order to supply drinking water to the town of Burdwān and to scour out the old channels leading from the Damodār, the silting up of which was supposed to be one of the principal causes of the outbreak of the Burdwān fever. At present about 33 square miles in the Burdwān and Jamālpur thānas and in the Memāri outpost are irrigated from it.

GEOLOGY.

The district is covered by alluvium except in the Asansol subdivision where Gondwāna rocks are exposed. The deposits which cover the immense alluvial plain of the Ganges and the Brāhmāputrā and their tributaries belong in part to an older alluvial formation, which is usually composed of massive argillaceous beds of a rather pale reddish-brown hue often weathering yellowish, disseminated throughout which occur *kankar* and pisolitic ferruginous concretions. The soil is partly a laterite clay more or less altered and partly a red-coloured coarse-grained sand, characteristic of the eastern ranges of the Vindhya formation, large surfaces composed of which are to be found in the beds of the Dāmodar and Ajay rivers.

The Gondwāna system is represented in the Rājmahāl hills, the Dāmodar valley, several of the Chotā Nāgpur districts, and in Orissa. The system is divisible into an upper and lower series, characterised by marked stratigraphical discordance and an utter change in the type of the fossil flora, cycads and conifers prevailing in the upper, and equisetaceous plants in the lower subdivision, ferns being found commonly in both. The following table shows the probable correlation of the Gondwāna groups as developed in the different Bengal areas:—

General sequence.	Rājmāhāl hills.	Bīrbhūm, Deogarh and Kār-hārbāri.	Dāmodar valley.	Darjeeling district.	Tālcher field.
Upper Gondwana: Umia and Jabalpul (Oalite)	...	...	...	...	...
Upper Gondwana: Rājmāhal (Lias).	Rājmāhāl	...	Mahadeva	...	Mahadeva.
Upper Gondwana: Mahadeva (Rhoetie)	Dubrājpur	...	...	...	...
Pānchet (Trias)	...	...	Pānchet	...	...
Dāmodar ... (Pirmian and Permocar-boniferos.)	Barākar...	Barākar	Rānīganj	Rānīganj	...
			Iron stone shales.	...	...
			Barākar	...	Barākar.
Tālchers ... (U. Carboni-feros.	Tālcher	Kārhār-bāri.	Kārhār-bāri.	...	...
		Tālcher...	Tālcher...	...	Tālcher.

The Tālcher group, which forms the basis of the Gondwāna system, consists of silty shales usually of a greenish, grey and olive colour weathering into minute, thin, angular fragments and of fine, soft sandstones composed chiefly of quartz and of undecomposed pink felspar. The most striking feature in connection with these rocks is the occurrence amongst them of unusually well-rounded pebbles and conglomerates, the transport of which to their present position is ascribed to the agency of ice. The rocks of the Kārhārbāri group consist almost solely of sandstones, grits and conglomerates with seams of coal.

The Tālcher Kārhārbāri groups are superposed by a great series of beds known as the Dāmodar series which consists of three subdivisions known in ascending order as the Barākar group the ironstone shales and the Rānīganj beds.

The Barākars consist of conglomerates, sandstones (which are often coarse and felspathic), shales and coal seams of a somewhat irregular character thinning out at short distances. Above the Barākar group in the Rānīganj and a few other coal fields of the Dāmodar valley, there is found a great thickness of black or grey shales with bands and nodules of clay ironstone. The Rānīganj beds comprise a great thickness of coarse and fine sandstones mostly false bedded and felspathic, with shales and coal seams which are frequently continuous over considerable areas. The Pānchets consist chiefly of thick beds of coarse felspathic and micaceous sandstones often of a white or greenish white colour with subordinate bands of red clay. All these groups have yielded plant fossils; and the Pānchet rocks contain, in addition, reptilian and fish remains. In the Rājmahāl hills the Lower Gondwānas are overlaid by coarse sandstones and conglomerates for the most part ferruginous which are comprised under the Dubrājpur group. They are overlaid by the rocks of the Rājmahāl group which consist of a succession of bedded basaltic traps with interstratifications of contemporaneous shales and sandstones. Dykes believed to be of Rājmahāl age are abundant in the coal fields of the Dāmodar valley. The Gondwāna strata have a general southern dip varying from 5° to 25°, and along the southern boundary, they are turned up and cut off by a great fault. Their total thickness in the Rānīganj field is estimated at about 11,000 feet. The area known as the Rānīganj coal field comprises not only the Gondwāna formation as developed in the Rānīganj subdivision, but also a small coal area immediately adjoining it in the districts of Bānkurā, the Santāl Parganas and Mānbhūm. The area of the field over which the coal-bearing rocks are exposed is some 500 square miles: but the total Gondwāna area may be even double that since on the east side the rocks dip under and are concealed by alluvium.

The district lies almost in the centre of the province of Western Bengal which stretches westward from the Bhāgīrathi and Hooghly to the eastern base of the Chotā Nāgpur hills. "Quite narrow at its northern extremity this province widens gradually southwards to where it passes with hardly a break into the low lands of Orissa. Along its eastern edge it forms a rather narrow belt of deltaic alluvium, with all the patterns characterising Central Bengal. West of this belt lies a non-alluvial plain, possessing many of the patterns of Behar, and passing BOTANY.

(Blanford, "The Raniganj coal field"; Memoirs, Geological Survey of India, Vol. III, part 1; Manual of the Geology of India, part III; Economic Geology by V. Ball; Annual Report of the Chief Inspector of Mines for 1901; Report on the Administration of Bengal for 1901-1902.)

gradually into the submontane forests below the eastern ghāts of Chotā Nāgpūr with all the transitions encountered as we pass southwards through Behar to the northern edge of the same table-land. Our knowledge of the northern half of this non-alluvial tract is fairly adequate, and perhaps the most interesting feature in its flora is the fact that here we find growing side by side a few species characteristic of the Punjāb and Rājputānā that have managed to find their way through Bundelkand and Behar thus far to the east; and a few equally characteristic of Coromandel and the Circars that have succeeded in spreading through the lowlands of Orissa and Midnapore thus far to the north. One of the most interesting members of the latter category is, perhaps, the intrinsically insignificant monotypic genus Sphæromorphæa."*

In itself the district presents most of these characteristics. The eastern portion forms part of the great Gangetic delta and here, in land under rice cultivation, are found the usual marsh weeds of the Gangetic plain and many sedges. On ponds and in ditches and still streams float aquatic plants and many submerged water-weeds. The villages and towns are surrounded by the usual shrubberies of semi-spontaneous and sub-economic shrubs and small trees which often cover a considerable area. The more characteristic shrubby species are *Glycosmis*, *Polyalthia suberosa*, *Clerodendron infortunatum*, *Solanum torvum* and various other species of the same genus, besides *Trema*, *Streblus* and *Ficus hispida*. Other species of figs, notably the *pīpal* and banyan with the red cotton tree (*Bombax malabaricum*) mango (*Magnifera indica*), and jiyal (*Odina Wodier*) make up the arborescent part of these thickets in which *Phœnix dactylifera* and *Borassus flabellifier* are often present. Hedges and waste places are covered with climbing creepers and various milk weeds and also harbour quantities of *Jatropha gossypifolia*, *Urena*, *Heliotropium*, *Sida* and similar plants. Road-sides are often clothed with a sward of short grasses and open glades with tall coarse grasses. The district contains no forest but the laterite country and the uplands of the Asansol subdivision are in places clothed with coppices of *sāl* (*Shorea robustea*).

FAUNA. The carnivora of the district comprise leopard, wolf, hyæna, jackal and other smaller species. Leopards are not common but are occasionally found in the villages near Dāinhāt in the Kātwa subdivision. They destroy cattle and goats and have been known to attack men. A leopard was quite recently killed close to the town of Burdwân, and in 1909 a good deal of

* D. Prain, *Bengal Plants*.

damage was done by one in Kâlna town. Tigers were formerly common in the district, especially in the jungles of the Asansol subdivision adjoining the Sāntal Parganas, but have now entirely disappeared. Wolves are scarce and are mostly met with in the jungles north of Kāksa; they have been known to carry off children. Hyænas do not commit much mischief as they content themselves with carrion but they occasionally carry off goats and sheep. Wild pig are numerous throughout the district and do considerable damage to the crops; monkeys also abound. Poisonous snakes are very common and include several kinds of cobra, the karait and the deadly Russell's viper. Snipe are very numerous in the rice fields during the months of September, October and November and afford excellent sport, while among other game birds are grey and black partridges, pea-fowl, and jungle-fowl which are plentiful in the *sāl* jungles of the Asansol subdivision. On the Dāmodar and in the marshes and *jhils* east of the Hooghly, goose, duck and teal are found in fair numbers but are not so plentiful as in other parts of Bengal. Green pigeon are also occasionally to be found. Other common birds are those usually met with in Bengal.

Fish is consumed in large quantities by almost all classes of the people excepting the widows of high-caste Brāhmans, Baidyas and Kayasths to whom it is forbidden by religious custom. The supply is mainly drawn from the Bhāgīrathi, the Dāmodar and the internal rivers and channels in which a large variety of freshwater fish are found. A considerable portion of the supply is also derived from the numerous tanks in the eastern portion of the district, but in many tanks the water has become poisonous in consequence of the decomposition of rank vegetation and the fish as a result are diseased. The practice of salting fish is very little resorted to, but in some parts the Muhammadans are in the habit of drying fish for home consumption, and the lower classes eat it with avidity even in a putrid state. Hunter enumerates six different methods of catching fish which are practised in the district—netting, there are twelve distinct varieties of nets; fishing by traps which are usually small cages of split bamboo placed in a current; fishing by *Polus*, a conical basket; fishing by rod and line; spear fishing; and fishing by *huri* and *sikti*. The *huri* is a bunch of twigs and thorns tied together and thrown into the river where there is little or no current. Small fish and prawns take shelter among the twigs and are captured by means of a net called *sikti*. Fishing with rod and line is the favourite sport of the Bengali and it is rare to pass a tank without seeing one or more fishermen thorns without FISH.

their tiny floats. Breeding fish are largely taken in the district for consumption but are not wastefully destroyed and young fry are also captured in large quantities principally for the purpose of stocking tanks, as it is generally believed that large fish cannot spawn in tanks.

The most common fish are the *rui*, *katla* and *mirgel* which are found everywhere in the rivers and tanks and the *magur* which are found in the tanks only, but there are a great number of other varieties which form an important part of the people's daily food. *Hilsa* are also taken in the Dāmodar.

CLIMATE. In Burdwān, like some of the more western districts of south-west Bengal where the surface soil is of the red laterite character and the hot westerly winds from Central India penetrate at times, exceptionally high day temperatures are a feature of the hot weather months. The mean maximum temperature, which is on an average below 80° in December and January, rises to 84° in February, 94° in March and 101° in April. Thereafter there is a steady fall until the monsoon is established when the average day temperature remains steady at about 90° up till October. Night temperature, which increases from 55° in January to 79° in June, remains almost unchanged until September when it begins to fall, and is 75° in October, 64° in November and 56° in December. Rainfall for the month is less than one inch between November and February, and between one inch and two inches in March and April, after which there is a rapid increase owing to the occasional incursion of cyclonic storms in May. During the monsoon season weather conditions in Burdwān are very similar to those in other parts of south-west Bengal. The rainfall is maintained chiefly by cyclonic storms which form in the north-west angle of the Bay and influence the weather over the whole of the south-west of the province, and by inland depressions which form over the central districts of Bengal and move slowly westward. As the district of Burdwān is more in the line of advance of these latter disturbances, rainfall is not appreciably lighter, as might be expected from its inland position. The average fall in June is 10, July 12, August 11·5, September 8·6 and in October 4 inches. The total average fall between May and November is 53 inches. The highest temperature recorded for Burdwān is 113° 7 in May 1889. The heaviest annual rainfall is 99 inches in 1861 and the lightest 40·5 in 1870. Since the latter year the following light falls have occurred: 42·2 inches in 1884, 40·8 in 1892 and 45·8 in 1895.

The district for many years suffered from a fever of a very fatal type to which it gave its name. The real "Burdwān fever," which often proved fatal within one or two days, appears to have died out, though the district is still subject to fevers especially those of a remittent type, the water-logged tract along the Bhāgīrathi being particularly unhealthy. Statistics of the rainfall for the various recording stations are given below for the cold weather (November to February), the hot weather (March to May) and the rainy season (June to October), the figures shown being the averages recorded: —

Station.	Years recorded.	November to February.	March to May.	June to October.	Annual Average
Burdwān ...	40-41	2.04	9·00	46·50	57·54
Kālna ...	30-31	2·58	9·62	43·06	55·26
Kātwa ...	30-31	2·21	8·26	43·86	54·33
Rāniganj ...	31-33	2·10	6·12	47·91	56·13
Mānkar ...	15-16	1·65	7·12	48·26	57·03

CHAPTER II.

HISTORY.

PREHISTORIC PERIOD.

By reason of its position and natural advantages the district of Burdwān must, from the earliest times, have been the seat of a settled civilisation. The town itself has been identified with the Parthalis or Portalis which, according to the Greek geographers, was the royal city of the Gangardæ or Gangarides. Mr. Wilford also identifies the Dāmodar river as the Andômatis of Arrian and the Ajay as his Amystis with Kātwa (Sanskrit Katadvipa) as his Katadupa. The early Aryan invaders, thrown back at first by the Rājmahāl hills and the deadly jungle which lay on their western slopes, soon found their way into the plain of Bengal by the Ganges, which then as now was the sacred river of the Hindus, and had long before the time of the Greek geographers founded the great city of Tamralipta (Tāmluk) near its mouth. Their numbers, however, were not sufficiently strong to enable them to drive out the original Dravidian inhabitants whom they found settled in possession of the country. Nor indeed could the invaders have done without them. Serfs and labourers must have been needed to till the ground; menials must have been required for domestic services. These classes of the community were naturally recruited from the conquered and subject races who formed by far the larger part of the population. The usual process by which the subject races were admitted within the pale of Hinduism followed, and probably in a few generations the original population of the country had accepted the status allotted to it under the Brāhminical system and was included among the lower castes.

THE GANGARDÆ.

The Gangardæ were undoubtedly Hindus, and Mr. Oldham* has conjectured that they were mainly composed of the Bāgdis who can still be identified as the original stratum of the population in the deltaic portion of the district, and who are allowed by the Hindus of pure Aryan race to represent the great aboriginal

* W. B. Oldham, *Some Historical and Ethical Aspects of the Burdwan District*, Calcutta, 1894.

section which was admitted within the pale of Hinduism in distinction from all the rest who are classified as Chuars. He further conjectures that this caste or tribe is in its origin sprung from the same stock as the Sauria Malér of the hills of Rājmahāl and of north Godda and Pakur and the Māl Pāhāriā of the Santāl Parganas.

Both these races, in his opinion, are derived from the Malli and the Sabaræ or Suari or Suaræ who are mentioned by all the Greek geographers. They lay to the east of the Prasii of Palibothra (Patna): their boundary was the Ganges, and they lay about Mount Maleus or Mallus which threw so portentous a shadow, and which has been identified with the Mandar hill in South Bhagalpur:—"In the forest tracts of Shergarh", Mr. Oldham writes, "and the adjoining jungle, pargana Senpahāri, chiefly in villages on the Ajay, are still to be found nearly 2,300 Māls—Rājbansi Māls they call themselves—who can be clearly identified as members of the great Māl race. Between these Māls and the Bāgdis there is an intimate connection. To this day they partake of the same *hookah* and admit a common origin, and in the case of Bishtupur a common sovereign; and my observation of both people leads me to conjecture that the Bāgdis are the section of the Māl who have accepted civilization and life in the cultivated country as serfs and co-religionists of tho Aryans: while those Māls who are still found scattered through the Bengal delta, and who are not, like the Rājbansi Māls of Burdwān, clearly traceable to the Malér of the hills, are either the descendants of isolated and conservative fragments of the race, or of those members of it who tried to follow the example of the Bāgdi after the latter had become constituted as a recognised and exclusive caste and therefore failed. In the Malér we have an undoubtedly autocthonous race. To them are easily and certainly traced the Māl Pāhāris, and through these the Māls of at all events all western and deltaic Bengal, and, as I conjecture, the Bāgdis."

THE MALLI.

If however this conjecture is correct, there is little doubt that the Bāgdis of the Greek geographers' time had already adopted the status under the Brāhminical system which they now occupy, and that the Gangardæ, while mainly composed of them, included also their Brāhman priests and masters. If then the Bāgdi were the most numerous among the Gangardæ and if Portalis was Burdwān and their chief city, it must have occupied

n more recent
dom held by a
self.

THE BAURIS.

The other great stratum of the population, the Bauri caste, is to be found in the western portion of the district. But the Bauris though semi-Hinduised and calling themselves Hindus, and so-called by their low caste neighbours, are not admitted to be Hindu by the Hindu Aryans but are pronounced by them to be unmitigated Chuars. Although undoubtedly Dravidian, it is impossible to connect them with any other tribe or caste. They are, however, plainly the lowest large stratum now to be found in the non-deltaic portion of the district, which may be called Bauri land, while the remaining large deltaic portion is still more distinctly Bāgdi land. The typical Bauri tract is pargana Shergarh, the stretch of rolling rocky country which lies between the Ajay and Dāmodar rivers to the west. Before the coal discoveries of the last century, it was a tremendous wilderness, dotted at long intervals by tiny clearings and settlements, and intersected by no great road or route. Here there are few remains of any importance, except the ruins of the forts at Dighi east of Faridpur police-station, at Churulia on the Ajay, and at Dihi Shergarh, the old capital of the pargana. The forts at Churulia and Dighi are by local tradition assigned to the Burdwān family, but the stonework at Dighi is far more ancient than any remains of theirs and resembles the Katauri remains in the Santāl Parganas. The fort at Churulia is said to have been built by Raja Narottam, but nothing further is known of him. The Dihi Shergarh fort is comparatively modern.

THE CHUARS OF THE JHARKHAND.

Owing to its physical character and situation, this tract was for long a sort of debateable land, and served as the high-road and harbour of the Chuars or jungle-tribes of the Jharkhand the great western forest, in their descents upon the settled country to the east. It is probable that it had no settled population, and that the Māls already mentioned are its real aborigines. The Bauris however are by far the largest section of its population of a primitive character. They do not claim to be autocthonous as do the Māls, and as they have all the characteristics of a broken race with no cohesion, it is possible that they are, as has been conjectured, a portion of some such people as the Uberræ of Megasthenes, the Bhārs of Behar, who poured or drifted into the country as it became open to them. They have no traditions of kings, or leaders, or gods, or indeed of any state anterior to their present degraded serfdom, and though clearly Dravidian, it is impossible beyond this to connect them with any other tribe or caste. "There is," Mr. Oldham writes in 1894, "no other considerable section of the population of Burdwān of undoubtedly Dravidian origin. The inexplicable Dōms are over

50,000 strong: the Kolārians have no more numerous representatives than the Santāls some 6,000 strong, the side drift of the great northern immigration of that race increased by immigrants whom the coal mines have attracted. There are some 3,000 or 4,000 Kaoras and some 35,000 Chandals. Some individuals of the former tribes claim affinity with the Maghs of the Sunderbans, and it is quite possible that both people came up the delta from the coast and are comparatively modern Mongolian or low Indo-Chinese in contrast to the old Mongolian Kolārians or to the Dravidians who came down towards the sea."

In the dawn of history therefore we find the greater part of Burdwān included in a great Māl or Bāgdi kingdom which stretched far into Bīrbhum, and up to the modern Dāmin-i-Kōh with its chief town at Burdwān or more possibly at Bishnupur itself. While the wild rolling country to the west which lay at the foot of the impenetrable hills and forests of Central India was still a vast unsettled wilderness, the haunt and refuge of thieves and robbers, of demon-worshippers and those "eaters of raw flesh" who were so abhorred by the early Aryans.

THE GUPTA KINGS.

In the seventh century under the Gupta kings the district formed part of a kingdom known as Karna Suvarna, which lay to the west of the Bhāgīrathi and comprised the districts of Burdwān, Bānkurā, Murshidābād and Hooghly. Its king, Sashanka or Narendra, the last of the Guptas, was a fanatical worshipper of Siva, and early in the seventh century invaded Magadha and cut down the sacred Bodhi tree. The capital of this country has been identified by Colonel Waddell with a suburb of the town of Burdwān. Mr. Beveridge, however, places it at Rāngamati in Murshidābād, and this is probably the more correct view. Later the district came under the rule of the Sen kings, of whom the most famous is Ballal Sen who re-organized the caste system and introduced Kulinism amongst the Brāhmans, Baidyas and Kayasthas. To him is attributed the division of Bengal into four parts—Bārendrā, Bāgri, Bānga, and Rārh to the west of the Bhāgīrathi which included Burdwān. The last king, Lakshmana Sen, was still ruling when Bakhtyar Khilji invaded Bengal at the end of the 12th century.

THE SEN KINGS.

The Sadgop dynasty of Gopbhūm.

In more recent times the first settlement of which a glimpse can be obtained is that of the Sadgop dynasty of Gopbhūm, the farthest cape or headland of the promontory of rocky land which juts out into the district from Central India. The neck of this promontory is pargana Shergarh lying between the Ajay and the Dāmodar. Between it and Gopbhūm in the same formation are the recently formed parganas Salīmpur and Senpahāri which probably belonged to Gopbhūm. The actual headland is formed by Gopbhūm, with the delta not only fencing it in on the east, but coming round it on the south and edging in on the north. Beyond lay the country formed by the uncertain and ever-changing courses through the silt of the Dāmodar, the Ajay and the Ganges, which on the British accession was found to be the richest tract in Bengal and the area of its oldest and most settled cultivation.

Gopbhūm with part of the debateable land between it and Pānchet now included in the parganas Salīmpur and Senpahāri was formerly, according to the universally current tradition of the tract, the seat of a Sadgop dynasty, some traces of which are still extant. The only Rājā of the race whose name still survives was Mahendra Nath, or, as he is locally called, Mahindi Rājā. His seat was Amrārgarh, close to the station and town of Mānkur, and the long lines of fortification which enclosed his walled town are still visible. How far the Sadgop power extended to the east can be surmised from the local prevalence of the members of the modern caste, the Aguris. The line of marshes which lies south of Kātwa to the west of the Bhāgīrathi is still held by this caste who occupy the old deltaic soil between this line and the present boundary of Gopbhūm in which the Sadgops are still the most prominent caste. The Aguris, by their own admission, are the product of unions between the Khetris of the house of Burdwān and the Sadgops of the Gopbhūm dynasty, and the caste arose within the last two hundred years. This recent formation of the Aguri caste indicates that the Sadgop kingdom of Gopbhūm existed in however curtailed a state till almost modern times, first as subject to the Mughals, and then under the shadow of the house of Burdwān itself. Its south-western extremity, now pargana Salīmpur, was apparently held by two Sadgop kinglings, probably mere cadets of the house of Gopbhūm, one stationed at Bharatpur on the Dāmodar, and the other at Kānkeswar or Kāksa. The latter was attacked and overthrown, and his lands taken by a Bokhāriot partisan named Sayad Sayad Bokhāri, whose descendant Sayads still hold the Kāksa lands in *aimma* to this day. A similar fate probably overtook the Bharatpur chief. The remains of the tiny forts at Bharatpur and Kāksa are still to be seen, and old Hindu images carved in black basalt are frequently found in the neighbouring tanks. Mangalkot on the Ajay, which is rich in Hindu remains, similar to those found at Kāksa, may also have been an outpost of the Sadgop kingdom. It can however only be said for certain that the Sadgop dynasty held the present Gopbhūm and Salīmpur parganas, and it is here only that any remains of them are found : nor does tradition assign to it any wider domain. The prevalence of the Aguris, who undoubtedly sprang from it, in such numbers to the east of Gopbhūm indicates that its extent may have been wider, but in any case its undoubted seat was on the high pasture lands and at the edge of the forest of Gopbhūm. It is highly probable that though originally the Sadgops came with the higher Aryans to Bengal and attended them as serfs or menials in their successive progresses, they ultimately worked their way up through the Bāgdi country to the pleasant pastures of Gopbhūm, and finding themselves undisturbed and alone there, since the non-pastoral Bāgdis had deserted its barren and shallow soil for the richer delta, founded their kingdom which was of no great antiquity or duration, and could not have existed without the protection or neutrality of the neighbouring Bāgdi sovereign of Bishnupur.*

THE MUHAMMADAN INVASIONS.

The Muhammadan invaders early fixed on Burdwān as one of their seats, and have left in it several interesting relics of those times, of which the most notable is the splendid military road from Gaur and Rājmahāl to Midnapore and Cuttack. Close by was their great settlement at Pandua, and due north of it near Manteswar thāna was Mahmudpur: while the fine strategic position of Kātwa had soon attracted them. In 1199 A.D., Bakhtyār Khilji, the Pathan general of Muhammad Ghori who conquered Behar, possessed himself of Nabadwip or Nadiā, and his followers spread over Burdwān. The whole district is sprinkled over with numberless *aimma* tenures, and the history of Kāksa and the Muhammadan settlement at Churulia under Raja Narottam's fort show how some of the Muhammadan villages were formed. Subsequently the greater part of Bengal gradually came under the control of the governors who ruled at Gaur or Laknanti until 1338 when Muhammad Tughlak declared himself independent. From that date till 1574, in which year Akbar defeated Daud and annexed Bengal, the country was ruled by various lines of independent kings, mostly of Pathan origin.

THE MUGHALS.

Burdwān is first mentioned in Muhammadan histories in 1574 in which year, after Daud Khān's defeat and death at Rājmahāl, his family were captured in the town of Burdwān by Akbar's troops. Some ten years later the district formed the scene of several engagements between Daud's son Kuttu and the imperial forces. The conquest

* This account of the Sadgop dynasty is condensed from that given by Mr. Oldham.

of the district must however have been complete and rapid, as in 1590 we find Burdwān mentioned in the *Ain-i-Akbari* as a *mahal* or *pargana* of Sarcar Sharifabād assessed at 1,876,142 *dams*.

SHER AFGAN.

In 1606 the famous Sher Afgan, then superintendent of the district under the Subahdār of Bengal, was attacked and slain by order of the Emperor Jehangir just outside the town. The unmerited misfortunes of this nobleman, his lofty character and courage, and the beauty and exalted destiny of his wife Mihr-ul-nissa, "the sun of women," render their story perhaps the most romantic in all the romantic history of the Mughal Emperors. Mihr-ul-nissa, afterwards the Empress Nur Jahān (light of the world), was the daughter of Chaja Aiass, a native of Western Tartary who with his wife had left that country to push his fortune at the court of the Emperor of Hindustan. "In the midst of the great solitudes through which they had to pass, his wife was taken in labour and was delivered of a daughter. They had fasted three days: no house was there to cover them from the inclemency of the weather; no hand to relieve their wants. To carry the child was impossible. A long contest began between humanity and necessity: the latter prevailed, and they agreed to expose the child on the highway. The infant, covered with leaves, was placed under a tree; and the disconsolate parents proceeded in tears. When they had advanced about a mile from the place, and the eyes of the mother could no longer distinguish the solitary tree under which she had left her daughter, she gave way to grief; and throwing herself from her horse on the ground exclaimed 'my child, my child.' Aiass was pierced to the heart. He prevailed upon his wife to sit down: he promised to bring her the infant. He arrived at the place. No sooner had his eyes reached the child, than he was struck almost dead with horror. A black snake, it is said, was coiled around it; and Aiass believed he beheld him extending his fatal jaws to devour the infant. The father rushed forward: the serpent alarmed at his vociferation retired into the hollow tree. He took up his daughter unhurt and returned to the mother. He gave her child into her arms, and as he was informing her of the wonderful escape of the infant, some travellers appeared and soon relieved them of all their wants. They proceeded gradually and came to Lahore. The advancement of Aiass at the court of Akbar was rapid, and he eventually attained the office and title of Actimad-ul-Dowla, or High-Treasurer of the Empire. Meanwhile the child who had been so miraculously preserved, grew in beauty and learning. She was educated with the utmost care and attention. In music, in dancing, in poetry, in painting, she had no equal among her sex. Her disposition was volatile, her wit lively and satirical, her spirit lofty and uncontrolled. Selim the prince royal visited one day her father, and the ladies according to custom were introduced in their veils. The ambition of Mihr-ul-Nissa aspired to a conquest of the prince. She sung, he was in raptures: she danced, he could hardly be restrained by the rules of decency to his place. Her stature, her shape, her gait had raised his ideas of her beauty to the highest pitch. When his eyes seemed to devour her, she as by accident dropt her veil, and shone upon him at once with all her charms."

Selim distracted with his passion, knew not what course to take. Mihr-ul-Nissa had been betrothed by her father to Aly Cooly Sher Afgan, a Turkomanian nobleman of great renown. Selim applied to his father Akbar, who sternly refused to commit a piece of injustice, though in favour of the heir to his throne. The prince retired abashed, and Mihr-ul-Nissa became the wife of Sher Afgan, who shortly after left the Court of Agra and retired to Burdwān.

The passion for Mihr-ul-Nissa which Selim had repressed from a respect and fear of his father, returned with redoubled violence when he himself mounted the throne of India. He recalled Sher Afgan from his retreat. He was afraid however to go so much against the current of public opinion as to deprive that Amir of his wife. His incredible strength and bravery had rendered Sher extremely popular. His family and his former reputation were high. Born of noble parents in Turkomania, he had spent his youth in Persia; and had served with uncommon renown Shaw Ismail, the third of the Sufoiye line. His original name was Asta Jillo; but having killed a lion, he was dignified with the title of Sher Afgan or the Overthrower of the Lion. In the wars of Akbar he had served with great reputation. Jehangir kept his court at Delhi when he called Sher Afgan to the presence. He received him graciously and conferred new honours upon him. Sher Afgan naturally open and generous, suspected not the Emperor's intentions. Time he thought had erased the memory of Mihr-ul-Nissa from Jehangir's mind. He was deceived: the monarch was resolved to remove his rival: but the means he used were at once ungenerous and disgraceful. On one occasion he enticed Sher Afgan to attack a tiger unarmed: on another he gave private orders that one of the elephants should waylay him in a narrow street and then tread him to death. Both attempts failed: Sher Afgan killed both tiger and elephant. The doomed nobleman now retired to Bengal, but even there security was denied him.

Kutb-ud-din, the Subahdār of Bengal and foster brother of the Emperor, hired forty assassins to attack and murder the Emperor's rival when an opportunity should offer. The attempt was made one night when Sher was asleep. Roused by one of his assailants who thought it shame that forty men should fall on one, he defended himself so vigorously that he slew many of the ruffians and put the band to ignominious flight. Despairing of safety, the unfortunate nobleman retired from the capital of Bengal to his old residence at Burdwān, hoping to live there in obscurity with his wife. Shortly after his retirement Kutb-ud-din paid a state visit to Burdwān. He made no secret to his principal officers that he had the Emperor's orders for despatching Sher. The Amir hearing that the Subahdār was entering the town, rode out with two servants only to meet him. One of the pikeman insulted him and on the insult swords were drawn, and Sher Afgan realising that his fate was come attacked Kutb-ud-din, who had mounted his elephant, and breaking down the howdah, cut him in two. Five other nobles fell by his hand, but he was at length overpowered by numbers. It is said that Jehangir in grief at the death of his foster-brother swore a vow that he would never see Mihr-ul-Nissa again. But her beauty and his former love conquered, and for many years she, conjointly with him, ruled the empire of India. A circumstance so uncommon in an Asiatic government is thus recorded on the coin of that period: "By order of the Emperor Jehangir, gold acquired a hundred times additional value by the name of the Empress Noor Jahān (Light of the World)."*

Death of Sher Afgan and Kutb-ud-din.

The tombs of Sher Afghan and Kutb-ud-din lie side by side within the town of Burdwān and tradition still points out the scene of their encounter.

Prince Khurram's rebellion.

In the year 1624, Prince Khurram, afterwards the Emperor Shāh Jahān, in his rebellion against his father the Emperor Jehangir, after passing through Central India, seized upon Orissa and moving northwards attacked the district. The fort of Burdwān after a short resistance was surrendered by its commander, Sālik.

THE RISE OF THE BURDWAN RAJ.

Shortly afterwards the great Burdwān house whose history from this period onwards is identical with that of the district was founded. According to tradition the original founder of the house, was one Sangam Rai, a Khattri Kāpur of Kotli in Lahore, who, on his way back from a pilgrimage to Puri, being much taken with the advantages of Baikunthapur, a village near the town, settled there and devoted himself to commerce and money

* Stewart, *History of Bengal.*

lending. Abu Rai, who was appointed Chaudhuri and Kotwāl of Rekhābi Bazar in the town in 1657 under the Faujdār of Chakla Burdwān, is said to have been his grandson, and he is the first member of the house of whom there is any historical record. He owed his appointment to the good service rendered by him in supplying the troops of the Faujdār with provisions at a critical time.* His son Babu Rai, who owned pargana Burdwān and three other estates, was succeeded in his turn by his son Ghana Shyam Rai. Upon the death of Ghana Shyam Rai, his son Krishna Ram Rai succeeded to the zamindāri, and among other new estates acquired the pargana of Senpahāri. In 1689, he was honoured with a *farman* from the Emperor Aurangzeb in the 38th year of his reign confirming his title as Zamindār and Chaudhuri of pargana Burdwān.

REBELLION OF SUBHA SINGH.

During the reign of this emperor, in 1696 A.D., Subha Singh, zamindār of Chituā and Bardā, then a part of Burdwān, with the aid of Rahim Khān, an Afghan chief, raised the standard of rebellion against the empire. Having united their forces they advanced to Burdwān, and in a pitched battle slew the Rājā and captured all the members of his family, except his son Jagat Rām Rai who escaped to Dacca and sought assistance from the governor. The rebels encouraged by their success which drew a large number of soldiers of fortune and other vagabonds to their standards, succeeded in capturing the important town of Hooghly, and possessed themselves of most of the country west of the Bhāgīrathi. Amongst the captives taken in Burdwān was the Rāj Kumāri Satyabati, the daughter of the Rājā whom Subha Singh kept in confinement until an opportunity should offer of sacrificing her to his lust. Entering her apartment secretly, he endeavoured to outrage her, but the heroic girl as he approached drew from her clothes a dagger which she had concealed as the last defence of her honour and stabbed him, killing him almost immediately. Feeling herself polluted by his touch, she then turned the weapon on herself and pierced her own heart. On the death of Subha Singh, the insurgents elected the Afghān chief Rahim Khān to be their commander, and under his leadership the rebellion assumed so threatening an aspect that the emperor appointed his own grandson Azim-u-Shān to the government of Bengal, Behar and Orissa. In the meantime Zubbadust Khān, son of the Nawāb, had taken the field against the rebels, and had by a series of successful movements driven them back upon Burdwān. They were finally defeated just outside the town by Azim-u-Shān, and

* (B. K. Mukerjee "Annals of Burdwan Raj," *The Calcutta Review*, January, 1910).

their leader Rahim Khān was killed. The revolt of Subha Singh is of special interest, as it indirectly led to the foundation of the towns of Calcutta, Chandernagore and Chinsura. The English at Sutanuti, the French at Chandernagore and the Dutch at Chinsura, alarmed at the progress of the rebels, applied to the Nawāb Nazim for permission to put their factories into a state of defence. The Nawāb ordered them in general terms to defend themselves, and interpreting his orders in accordance with their inclinations they transformed the settlements into fortified cities which were the first which the Indian emperors suffered foreigners to build in any part of their dominions. After his defeat of the rebels Azim-u-Shan continued to reside for nearly three years in the town of Burdwān during which time he built the great mosque which bears his name.*

Fortification of Calcutta.

Kirti Chandra Rai.

Jagat Rām Rai, who had been restored to the estate and honours of his father, the deceased Rājā Krishna Rām Rai, after the revolt of Subha Singh, made further additions to the family estates of the Burdwān house, and was honoured with a *farman* by the Emperor Aurangzeb. He was treacherously murdered in 1702 A.D., and left two sons, Kirti Chandra Rai and Mitra Sen Rai. The elder brother, Kirti Chandra Rai, inherited the ancestral zamindari, and added to it the parganas of Chitua, Bhursut, Bardā and Manoharshāhi. Kirti Chandra was a man of bold and adventurous spirit. He fought with the Rājās of Chandrakonā and Bardā near Ghatal, and dispossessed them of their petty kingdoms. He also seized the estates of the Rājā of Balgharā, situated near the celebrated shrine of Tārakeswar in Hooghly. He subsequently proceeded to Murshidābād and got his name registered as proprietor of the new properties. But the boldest achievement of Kirti Chandra was his attacking and defeating the powerful Rājā of Bishnupur. The end of the seventeenth century had left the Birbhūm and Bishnupur Rājās at the summit of their fortunes. Their territory lay beyond the direct control of the Musalman power, and as frontier chiefs they were of so much importance in keeping the border, that the Muhammadan viceroys treated them rather as allies than as subjects. The Burdwān Rājās dwelt nearer to the Murshidābād Court, and were from time to time squeezed accordingly. Nevertheless they prospered, from a money point of view, as a clever Hindu family almost always did prosper in contact with indolent Musalman administrators.

THE MARATHAS.

But with the beginning of the eighteenth century, an entirely new set of conditions came into play in Western Bengal. A

* Stewart, *History of Bengal.*

new and more powerful enemy appeared, in whose presence all local dissensions were for the time forgotten. Year after year the inexhaustible Marāthā horse overflowed upon the border. Under the Muhammadan system, a family was secure in proportion as it was near the frontier and distant from court; but now safety could be found only in the heart of the Province. The Marāthās fell with their heaviest weight upon the border principalities of Birbhūm and Bishnupur. Tribute, free quarters, forced services, exactions of a hundred sorts, reduced the once powerful frontier houses to proverty; and their tenantry fled from a country in which the peasant had become a mere machine for growing food for the soldier. Burdwān not only lay farther inland, but its marshy and river-intersected surface afforded a less tempting field for cavalry, and a better shelter for the people. The Marāthās spent their energy in plundering the intervening frontier tracts where the dry soil and fine undulating surface afforded precisely the riding ground which their cavalry loved. There they could harry the villages exhaustively, and in detail, by means of small parties. But in Burdwān the nature of the country compelled them to be more circumspect. They could act safely only in considerable bodies; and the cultivators soon became accustomed to fly, as a matter of course, to some swamp-protected village whenever the Marāthā horse appeared, leaving very little to eat, and nothing to destroy, behind them.*

Ali Vārdi Khān repels the Marāthās.

In 1741 forty thousand horse under Ragoji Bhonsla, the Marāthā chief of Berār, overran Orissa and the western districts of Bengal, plundering and laying waste the country as far north as Kātwa. The Nawāb Ali Vārdī Khān, who was encamped at Midnapore, fell back before the invaders on Burdwān, and thence retired to Kātwa. But the retreat soon became a rout, and it was only with the greatest difficulty and with the loss of most of his baggage and artillery that he gained the shelter of that fortress. Encouraged by his reverse, the raiders possessed themselves of all the country west of the Bhāgīrathi. Their ravages have been graphically described in the *Riyazu-s-Salatin*: "Sacking the villages and towns of the surrounding tracts, and engaging in slaughter and captures, they set fire to granaries and spared no vestige of fertility. And when the stores and granaries of Burdwān were exhausted, and the supply of imported grains was also completely cut off, to avert death by starvation, human beings ate plantain roots, whilst animals were fed on the leaves of trees. Even these

* Hunter's *Statistical Account of Burdwan.*

gradually ceased to be available. For breakfast and supper, nothing except the disc of the sun and the moon feasted their eyes. The whole tract from Akbarnagar (Rājmahāl) to Midnapur and Jaleswar (Jalasore) came into the possession of the Marāthās. Those murderous freebooters drowned in the rivers a large number of the people, after cutting off their ears, noses and hands. Tying sacks of dirt to the mouth of others, they mangled and burnt them with indescribable tortures."* In the next year Ali Vārdi Khān defeated Bhaskar Rao, the Marathā general, at Kātwa, and after a short but successful campaign drove the raiders out of his dominions. The Marāthā general retreated to the passes of Pānchet, and eventually making good his retreat to Chandrakonā, emerged in the open country round Midnapore.† This was, however, but the first of many such raids, and although frequently defeated the Marāthās returned again and again until in 1751 the Nawāb, worn out by the struggle, ceded the province of Cuttack to them, and agreed to pay an annual tribute of 12 lakhs of rupees as the *chaut* or tribute of Bengal.

CLIVE TAKES KATWA.

Ali Vārdi Khān died in 1756, and within two years his successor, the weak and dissolute Suraj-ud-Doulah, was a fugitive, and the province of Bengal was virtually in the hands of the East India Company. In 1757 Clive in his march up the western bank of the Bhāgīrathi, before the battle of Plassey, seized the fort of Kātwa which was abandoned by the garrison at the first assault. The governor of the fort, who was an adherent of Mir Jafar Khān and implicated in his conspiracy, had promised to surrender, but when Major Coote, who had been sent forward with a small force, summoned the fort, he found that its commandant had again changed sides, and he was therefore compelled to attack it. As soon however as the garrison saw the troops advancing, they set fire to the mat buildings in the fort and absconded. The English army encamped in the town and the neighbouring villages, and Clive halted here for two days while he continued his negotiations with Mir Jafar Khān. Dissatisfied with the assurances of the latter, he determined to consult his officers on the situation. Having called a council of war, he proposed two plans for their consideration, either that the army should at once cross the river and attack the Nawāb who was advancing from Murshidābād, or that availing themselves of the large supply of stores which they had taken in Kātwa they should halt there during the rains and await reinforcements. The council by a

* *Riyazu-s-Salatin*—Translation by Maulavi Abdus Salām, Calcutta, 1904.

† *Seir-ul-Mutakharin*, Raymond's translation.

majority of twenty to seven decided in favour of delay, but Clive, after an hour's meditation in a grove near the town, decided to attack at once, and acting on his own responsibility gave orders for the advance which led to the decisive battle of Plassey.*

Three years afterwards the Marāthās again appeared in the district. During the invasion of Shāh Alam, the Marāthā chief Sheobhat, who supported the cause of the Emperor, suddenly advanced to Midnapore, and after making himself master of the country, pushed forward a detachment to Bishnupur and theatened Burdwān. The Emperor marched south towards Murshidābād and the Marāthā general advanced to Bishnupur, but was unable to prevent the Nawāb, Mīr Jafar Khān, from effecting a junction with a British force under Major Caillaud in the neighbourhood of Burdwān. Finding it impossible to force his way to Murshidabad in the face of the combined forces, Shāh Alam withdrew with the Marāthās to Bishnupur, and thence marched with them to Patna. A small force was left at Bishnupur, but at the close of the year was driven out by an English force.†

Meanwhile the Burdwān house had continued to prosper. Kirti Chandra died in the year 1740, and was succeedeed by his son Chitra Sen Rai, who added the parganas of Mandalghat, Arshā and Chandrakonā to the paternal estate, and was invested with the title of Rājā by the Delhi Emperor. The fort at Rājgarh, which still exists, was built by him as an outpost against his enemies of Birbhūm, Pānchet and Bishnupur, with all of whom he and his father had waged successful war. North-west of it on the Ajay there lies a small table-land clothed with dense forest on which he built another and still stronger fort. His cannon with his name in Persian deeply graved on them lie there to this day. The sorrounding tract, part of which lies across the Ajay in the present Birbhūm district he called after himself and his new stronghold, Senpahāri.‡ He died in the year 1744 without issue, and was succeeded by his cousin, Tilak Chandra Rai. In 1753, Tilak Chandra Rai was honoured by the Emperor Ahmad Shāh with a *farman* recognising and confirming his right to the *rāj*, and a few years afterwards was invested by Shāh Alam with the titles of Mahārāj Ādhirāj Bahādur, and Pānj Hazāri, or commander of five thousand troops. In 1755, in retaliation for the attachment of his property in Calcutta by order of the Mayor's Court, he put an embargo on the Company's trade

Chitra Sen Rai.

* Stewart's *History of Bengal.*

† Broome's *History of the Rise and Progress of the Bengal Army.*

‡ *Some Historical and Ethnical Aspects of the Burdwan District.*

within his estates, stopping it completely. The dispute was only settled by the intervention of the Nawāb.

Burdwan ceded to the East India Company. Three years after the battle of Plassey, on the 27th September 1760, "the enlarged compact and fertile zamindary of Burdwan, which is like a garden in the wilderness"* was, together with the districts of Midnapore and Chittagong, ceded to the East India Company by Nawāb Mīr Muhammad Kasim Khān, Governor of Bengal. At this time Burdwān contained an area of 5,174 square miles, and is described as being the most productive district within the whole province or *Subah* of Bengal. But the country was in a very unsettled state, and the Company did not find their new acquisition so profitable as they had hoped. The early days of their rule were troubled ones. The Mahārājā had not accepted the new order of things without opposition, and the records of the time are full of complaints of his "insolence" and "rebellion." That these were not uncalled for may be inferred from the fact that in July 1760 his troops actually defeated two hundred sepoys in an engagement that had arisen out of an attempt to arrest one of his servants. Soon after the transfer of government the Mahārājā broke out in open revolt, and in November 1760 we find the Nawāb informing the British authorities that the Birbhūm and Burdwān Rajas have made common cause, have collected ten or fifteen thousand peons and robbers and are preparing to fight. The insurrection was short-lived. Major White was at once sent to take possession of Burdwān, and on the 29th December 1760 completely defeated the allies who had endeavoured to resist his passage of the river Damodar at Sanghatgola.†

But civil war even when successfully waged is not likely to improve the revenues. The zamīndāri of Burdwān when ceded to the Company was estimated to yield a net revenue of 31,75,391 sicca rupees, and within three years the assessment was raised to Rs. 41,72,000 by the resumption of lands formerly held as bāze-zamīn without payment of revenue. But for many years afterwards the Company's officers had the greatest difficulty in collecting even a portion of this sum. The first "Superintendents" appointed were Mr. Johnstone, Mr. Hay and Mr. Bolts. Dissatisfied with the collections of revenue for 1760-61, they farmed out the estate at public auction for a period of three years, a procedure which was directly opposed to the financial

* Fifth Report from the the Select Committee on the Affairs of the East India Company.

† Selections from the Unpublished Records of Government. Revd. J. Long, Calcutta, 1869.

practice of the Mughal Empire. The needy adventurers who became contractors at the sale, as might have been expected, failed in their agreements, and matters went steadily from bad to worse. The Superintendents were charged with every sort of corruption, and apparently they did as a matter of fact hold a considerable part of the district in their own hands.

The district still suffered from the ravages of the Marāthā raiders, and the Mahārājā took full advantage of the fact to avoid the payment of revenue. A letter from him to the English authorities describes the ruin caused by these raids:—"How can I relate to you," he writes, "the present deplorable situation of this place? Three months the Marāthās remained here, burning, plundering and laying waste the whole country; but now, thank God! they have all gone, but the inhabitants are not yet returned. They have lost almost all they were worth. You are well acquainted with the bad situation of this place at present, but I hope I shall soon be able to pay you the money in the time that I agreed. It has been my bad fortune to have my country burned, plundered and destroyed by the Marāthās, which is the reason that there is now a balance due to the Company; and to reinstate my country again must be attended with great difficulties, which gives me much uneasiness."*

Terrible however as the depredations of the Marāthās had been, the records prove that the permanent injury inflicted on a deltaic district in the last century was comparatively slight. The dry, undulating territory on the frontier returned to jungle, and the ancient houses of Bishnupur and Bīrbhūm were ruined; but the moist lands of Burdwān yielded their yearly harvests, and, excepting the tract to the north of Kātwa, which was in a state of chronic devastation, even received an increase of cultivators, by the general flight of the peasantry from the western borders. A more dreadful calamity was impending, and before the country had recovered from the ravages of the invaders it was plunged in all the horrors of widespread famine.

The famine of 1769 did for the Burdwān Rājās what the Marāthā horse had under Muhammadan rule done for the great frontier houses of Bishnupur and Bīrbhūm. A graphic account of this terrible visitation is given in Hunter's "Annals of Rural Bengal." Famine of 1770.

"The distress continued to increase at a rate that baffled official calculations, and in the second week of May the Central Government awoke to find itself in the midst of universal and irremediable starvation. 'The mortality, the beggary,' they then wrote, 'exceed all description. Above one-third of the

* Hunter's Statistical Account of Burdwān.

inhabitants have perished in the once plentiful province of Purneah, and in other parts the misery is equal.' All through the stifling summer of 1770 the people went on dying. The husbandmen sold their cattle; they sold their implements of agriculture; they sold their sons and daughters, till at length no buyer of children could be found; they ate the leaves of the trees and the grass of the field; and in June 1770 the Resident at the Durbar affirmed that the living were feeding on the dead. Day and night a torrent of famished and disease-stricken wretches poured into the great cities. At an early period of the year pestilence had broken out. In 1770 the rainy season brought relief, and before the end of September the province reaped an abundant harvest. But the relief came too late to avert depopulation. Starving and shelterless crowds crawled despairingly from one deserted village to another, in a vain search for food or a resting place in which to hide themselves from the rain. Millions of famished wretches died in the struggle to live through the few intervening weeks that separated them from the harvest, their last gaze being probably fixed on the densely covered fields that would ripen only a little too late for them. 'It is scarcely possible,' writes the Council at the beginning of the September reaping, 'that any description could be an exaggeration.'

Before the commencement of 1771, one-third of a generation of peasants had been swept from the face of the earth, and a whole generation of once rich families had been reduced to indigence. Every district reiterated the same tale. The revenue farmers—a wealthy class who then stood forth as the visible government to the common people—being unable to realize the land-tax, were stripped of their office, their persons imprisoned, and their lands, the sole dependance of their families, re-let. The ancient houses of Bengal, who had enjoyed a semi-independence under the Moghuls and whom the British Government subsequently acknowledged as the lords of the soil, fared still worse. From the year 1770 the ruin of two-thirds of the old aristocracy of Lower Bengal dates. The Mahārājā of Burdwān, whose province had been the first to cry out and the last to which plenty returned, died miserably towards the end of the famine, leaving a treasury so empty that the heir had to melt down the family plate, and, when this was exhausted, to beg a loan from the Government, in order to perform his father's obsequies."

EARLY ADMINISTRATION. In 1776, the administration of the district and of the Burdwān estates was taken out of the hands of Tej Chandra, and placed in those of his mother, the Mahārāni Bishtu Kumāri, the widow of Mahārājā Tilak Chandra, one of the principal opponents of

Warren Hastings. From the proceedings in Council of the 16th January 1775, we find that she charged Mr. Graham with embezzling 11 lakhs of rupees alleged to be the property of her infant son. Graham was a friend of Warren Hastings who defended him warmly, and the Governor-General's opponents in Council fastened on the charge, and even went so far as to insinuate that Hastings had himself profited by his subordinate's dishonesty. The charge against Mr. Graham was never proved, and there is little reason to doubt that it was totally false. The Mahārāni retained control over the estate and district till 1779, after which date Mahārājā Tej Chandra resumed the management.

The records of 1782 disclose the house sinking steadily into ruin. The Government forced the Rājā, as zamīndār, to discharge in some fashion his duties towards his people, and many of the earliest documents contain articles of agreement for the repair of the embankments and bridges at his expense. Until after the permanent settlement, the family still maintained a considerable body of troops as bodyguard, the annual cost of which was estimated at four lakhs of rupees, besides other costly paraphernalia of native pomp, without the income necessary to pay for them. A long series of painful personal degradations followed: imprisonments of the Rājā in his palace, forced sales of his lands, the foreclosures of mortgages, the swooping down of his private creditors, and a hundred miserable evasions and struggles. Our officers were not very patient, and they were constantly provoked. Not only was there a vast mass of 'arrears,' which the Collector was ordered, under pain of high displeasure, to levy, and of which he found it absolutely impossible to recover a single rupee; but four times each year, at the quarterly instalments, the Rājā sank deeper and deeper into our debt.* Of other features of our administration in these early days we hear little but here and there in the old records we get glimpses of the state of the country. From a letter written in 1788 we find that the Collector maintained on his own responsibility a small standing army. It consisted of a Subahdār, a Jemadar, and a Havildar Major, eight Havildars and seven *naeks*, seventy-seven sepoys and five drums and fifes: the total cost of the establishment was Rs. 619 a month. That such a force was necessary can be seen from the same letter. "I had had occasion," the Collector writes, "to send out a force to arrest a notorious dakait named Jeebna, who has assembled under him upwards of four hundred men armed, and with whose assistance he committed the most atrocious depredations in the pargana of Shergarh and St. Pahary, laying waste with fire whole

* Hunter's Statistical Account of Burdwān.

villages, levying contributions and plundering the inhabitants." The country in fact was overrun with these banditti, and a few years later the Magistrate of Bīrbhūm estimated that there were two thousand dacoits in Burdwān, Bīrbhūm and Rājshahi alone. Disbanded soldiers, thieves, and broken and lawless men of every class, collected in formidable bands, roamed the countryside plundering and burning at their will. On one occasion the officer charged with the duty of arresting the leader of one of these bands actually asked for a howitzer and a battalion of sepoys. And the head-quarters of the British officers were only too often surrounded by a ring of blazing villages whose fate they could neither prevent nor avenge.

Except the Collector and his assistant, there were practically no Europeans in the district. The Company were very jealous of any interference with their trade, and in 1788 strict orders were issued that no European being a British subject not in their service would be allowed to reside in the district without a license. Much of the Collector's time seems to have been occupied in bitter and acrimonious correspondence with the various commercial residents, including the well known Mr. Cheap of Bīrbhūm. The insolence and oppression of their servants was proverbial, and there were constant disputes between them and the peasantry. "I imagine," writes the Collector to one of the residents, "it would be attended with less trouble to you in case of future references that you forward them by dāk instead of peons the insolence of whom in many instances requires chastisement."

But in fact the chief object of the administration at this time seems to have been to make the Mahārājā pay his revenue, and all other considerations were subordinated to this. The very earliest letter preserved in the records of the Burdwān Collectorate contains a suggestion that his property should be attached, and a few months afterwards in 1788 we find the threat executed. "Besides the peons which you have placed over me for the balance of the Māgh kist," the Mahārājā writes in a tone of dignified remonstrance to the Collector, "you are now increasing my distress and disgrace by proceeding to attach my house and property." Remonstrance however availed little with the Board in Calcutta. On one occasion the Collector held over an attachment and was promptly censured. It was useless to plead that the district had suffered from a flood such as that of 1787 when "every house in Burdwān and every village contiguous to it fell down, and nothing but the banks of tanks remained for the reception of every living creature." The Board insisted on payment, and regarded such pleas as mere equivocations.

The Company was, moreover, only one of a host of claimants; and what between the stringent demands of the Revenue Committee, the piteous requests for pension by female members of the family, and the clamorous private duns and usurers who thronged the Rājā's palace, the Collector had a very unhappy time of it. "The Ranee," he writes in 1787, "is at her old tricks again." Severities did but little good. The Government might summon the impoverished Rājā to Calcutta, imprison him in a wing of his palace, and turn his own bodyguard into his jailers; but such measures produced little money and much popular discontent. Whenever the Board of Revenue had been specially hard upon the Rājā, a thousand annoyances and interruptions somehow took place in the Company's trade. The commercial resident complained of 'obstructions,' and the Salt Department deplored an outbreak of "opposition to the business of the Aurangs." While the Revenue authorities could make the Rājā's life miserable, the Rājā could render his territory a very unprofitable one to the British Government.*

THE PERMANENT SETTLEMENT.

The Permanent Settlement substituted a reign of law for these endless bickerings and quarrels, and the new order of things which it brought about rescued Burdwān. Under Regulation I of 1793, Mahārājā Tej Chandra entered into an agreement with Government to pay regularly the revenue, amounting to *Sicca* Rs. 40,15,109, and also *Sicca* Rs. 1,93,721 for *pulbandhi* or repairs of embankments. But in spite of the Permanent Settlement the affairs of the estate did not fully recover, and the disastrous effects of the scarcity of 1769 and the bond of debt and arrears which it had left in its train were still felt. The estate fell into arrears, and the mismanagement became so pronounced that the Mahārājā's mother compelled him to execute a deed of sale assigning the entire estate to her. She was a woman of considerable business capacity, and she might ultimately have succeeded in saving the whole estate if her life had been prolonged. Many of the lands had been parcelled out among a large number of farmers or *ijārādārs*, most of whom withheld payment. And the Mahārājā found it impossible to realise his rents with the same punctuality with which he was compelled to pay his revenue. The inevitable result of this system of sub-infeudation was the accumulation of arrears in the Government demand. The Mahārājā was summoned to attend the Board of Revenue, and was threatened with the forfeiture of his zamīndāri, but to no purpose. Munshi, afterwards Rājā, Naba Krishna Deb was appointed *kruk*

* Hunter's Statistical Account of Burdwān.

sazawal, or attaching officer, but he could do nothing. The Collector of Burdwān suggested the sale of the zamīndāri in lots, as the only way of recovering the arrears of revenue; and in 1797 the Board commenced selling portions of the estate. Each lot consisted of several villages. The principal purchasers were Dwarkanath Singh of Singur, Chhaku Singh of Bhastara, the Mukharjis of Janai, and the Banarjis of Telinipara.

Thus was laid the foundation of the present landed aristocracy of the Burdwān and Hooghly districts. These sales went on regularly every three months; and in order to prevent the entire dismemberment of the estate, Mahārājā Tej Chandra bought up several lots in the names of his officials and dependants. About this time Mahārāni Bishnu Kumāri died. On her death, Mahārājā Tej Chandra resumed the management of the estate and one of his first acts was to endeavour to arrest its ruin by giving away portions of his zamīndāri in perpetual leases, or *patnīs*, a form of tenure, which is described amongst the land tenures of the district. After half a century of poverty and ruin, the Burdwān house at last found itself under the guidance of a singularly prudent Rājā: the creation of under-tenures, and the various other machinery for improving an estate which the Permanent Settlement introduced, have now rendered it the most prosperous house in Bengal.

SUBSEQUENT HISTORY.

The subsequent history of Burdwān is of little interest. Mahārājā Tej Chandra had a son, Pratap Chandra, who disappeared during the lifetime of his father, and was never heard of afterwards. It is supposed that he went forth incognito either through some petty annoyance or in search of adventure. Several years afterwards a pretender personating him appeared, but his claim, after a searching investigation, was dismissed by the Civil Court. In 1832 Mahārājā Tej Chandra died, leaving to an adopted son, Mahtāb Chānd, his great landed and funded estates. On the latter succeeding to the rāj in 1833, the English Government honoured him with a *khillat*, and he afterwards became one of the most enlightened representatives of the landed aristocracy of the province. At the time of the Santāl rebellion in 1855, the Mahārājā aided the military authorities by forwarding and supplying stores and means of transport. During the Sepoy Mutiny in 1857, he did everything in his power to strengthen the hands of Government. He placed elephants and bullock-carts at the disposal of the authorities, and kept open the roads between Burdwān and Bīrbhūm and between Burdwān and Kātwa, so that there was no interruption of intelligence between the seat of Government and the anxiously watched stations of Bīrbhūm and

Berhampur. In 1864 the Mahārājā was appointed an additional Member of the Viceregal Legislative Council, being the first native gentleman of Bengal who was so honoured. He died in 1881, and was succeeded by his adopted son, Aftāb Chānd, who only lived till 1885, when on his decease and according to his will the estate was taken charge of by the Court of Wards. Aftāb Chānd left a widow whom he had empowered to adopt, and she exercised the right in July 1887 in favour of Sir Bijay Chānd Mahtāb Bahadur, K.C.I.E., the present Mahārāj Adhiraj Bahādur. The Mahārājā has recently obtained from Government a *sanad*, dated the 1st May 1903, conferring upon him as zamīndār of Burdwān the hereditary title of Mahārāj Adhirāj to be attached to the estate.

CHANGES OF JURISDICTION. When ceded to the East India Company in 1760 the district or *chakla* of Burdwān, as then constituted, comprised besides the present district the whole of the present district of Bānkurā formerly known as Western Burdwān, together with parts of Hooghly and Bīrbhūm. In 1805, the western parganas of Senpahāri and Shergarh which now form part of the Asansol subdivision, together with the territory now included in Bānkurā, were made into a new district, called the Jungle Mahals. These parganas was afterwards restored to Burdwān when the district of Bānkurā was formed in 1833, but their criminal jurisdiction fluctuated for many years later between the Magistracies of Bīrbhūm and Bānkurā. In 1820, Hooghly was formed into a separate district, and numerous minor transfers to and from the district were afterwards made. In 1872, the district area was increased from 2,825 square miles to 3,588 square miles, including river circuits, by transfer from Mānbhūm, Bānkurā and Hooghly; and in 1879 the thanas of Sonāmukhi, Kotālpur and Indās were retransferred to Bānkurā, while the Jehānabād subdivision was transferred to Midnapore.

Archæology. The most interesting remains in the district are the fine stone temples at Barākar and the shrine of Kalyaneswari under the Hadla hill, some four miles north of Barākar in the Asansol subdivision. There are some interesting tombs in Burdwān, among which may be mentioned those of Sher Afgan, Kutb-ud-dīn and Pīr Bāhrām. There are also some fine temples of comparatively recent date at Kālna, in the grounds of the Mahārājā's palace, including one particularly fine one of carved brick. The remains of the old Muhammadan royal or *bādshāhi* road from Rājmahāl to Midnapore with the mosques attached still exist, and ruins of old forts are found at Dihi Shergarh, Dighi, Rajgārh, Churulia, and Kāksa, in the Asansol subivision, and at Mānkur, Burdwān, Kātwa, and Kālna.

CHAPTER III.

THE PEOPLE.

GROWTH OF POPULATION.

BEFORE 1872 no regular census of the district had ever been taken though several rough attempts were made from time to time to estimate the number of inhabitants. Of these the first having any pretensions to accuracy was made in 1813-14 by Mr. W. B. Bayley, who at the time was Judge and Magistrate of the district. He succeeded in obtaining returns of the population of 98 towns and villages situated in different parts of the districts of Burdwān, Hooghly, Midnapore, Bīrbhūm and the Jungle Mahāls. Having satisfied himself of the accuracy of the returns, he deduced from them an average of eleven inhabitants to every two houses, and then proceeded to ascertain the number of houses in the district. As a result of his calculations he estimated the population of the district as then constituted at 1,444,487. The average density was approximately 602 to the square mile as compared with 610 in 1872, and the figures would seem to show that the population of the district, whatever it may have been before the outbreak of the fever epidemic of 1862, was in 1872 not much in excess of what it had been in 1814. In 1838 Mr. Adam collected certain statistics of the population to illustrate his report on the state of vernacular education, and the Kālna thāna of Burdwān was one of the areas selected for the purpose. A comparison of his figures with those obtained at the census of 1872 show that the resident population was no larger in 1872 than it had been in 1838. The number of houses had increased, but the average number of persons to a house had fallen from 5 to 3·7.

Census of 1872.

The first general census which in any way approximated to the truth was that of 1872. The census coincided with the climax of the terrible epidemic of fever which ravaged the district between 1862 and 1874, and any increase that might have been expected since Mr. Bayley's time had been completely wiped out. The result of this census was to show for the district as now constituted a population of 1,486,400 persons. No figures or estimates exist showing the population of the district in 1860, immediately before the outbreak of the fever epidemic, but there can be no doubt that the mortality from the disease between 1862, when it first appeared in the Kālna subdivision, and 1872 was enormous. Dr. French in his special report on the outbreak estimated the total mortality at about one-third of the whole population, and the specific instances which he quotes show that the estimate was not extravagant. In 1869 the population of the town of Burdwān was estimated at 46,121, whereas the census of 1872 gives a population of 32,687, a decrease in three years of over 30 per cent. In seventeen villages of the Kātwa subdivision containing an estimated population of 14,982 before the appearance of the disease no less than 6,243 persons, or 41·7 per cent. of the population, were reported to have died of fever between the period of the outbreak and 1872. The figures for fifty villages in the Kālna subdivision showed a similar mortality.

Census of 1881. In 1881 it was found that the population had decreased still further to 1,394,220. This decrease was entirely due to the mortality from the fever which after 1873 made no further westerly progress in Burdwān, and although still severe in the Kālna and Ausgrām thānas was gradually dying out in those parts of the district where it had been first observed. In the census report of 1881 it was estimated that during the twelve years from 1862—1874 the epidemic had carried off not less than three-quarters of a million of persons.

Census of 1891. During the next decade the population remained practically stationary, the total number of persons recorded in 1891 being 1,391,880. The thānas of Kāksa, Ausgrām and Bud-Bud in the west still showed a large decrease, which was undoubtedly due to the after effects of the epidemic. On the other hand, the increase in the Asansol thāna, 28·9 per cent., was phenomenal, the development of the Railway works at Asansol consequent on the opening of the Bengal-Nagpur Railway and the increasing activity in the coal and iron fields having attracted a large immigrant population from Mānbhūm, Bānkurā and Behār.

Census of 1901. During the next decade conditions were generally favourable: crops were as a rule good and the district in consequence made a rapid recovery, the population recorded exceeding by more than 30,000, the number returned in 1872. The results of the census of 1901 are summarized as follows in the Bengal Census Report of that year: "The growth of the population in the Asansol thāna is phenomenal: it has increased by more than 30 per cent. since 1891 and by 130 per cent. since 1872. Nearly one-third of the present inhabitants were born in other districts, and of the district-born many have doubtless migrated from other thānas.

Rāniganj shows an increase of 12 per cent. since 1891, which is somewhat surprising in view of the fact that its coal-mines are nearly worked out, and that the people find more remunerative employment in the new mines further west. The town of Rāniganj, however, is a great trading centre, and is probably one of the busiest places in Bengal. The increase is also considerable in the Burdwān and Kātwa subdivisions where there has been comparatively little immigration. It is most noticeable in the Ausgrām and Galsi thānas which were mentioned in the last census report as then forming with Kāksa the focus of the fever. Apart from the fever these thānas are naturally healthy, and the disappearance of the epidemic has been followed, as is usual in such circumstances, by a rapid recovery in the population. That the improvement is not equally marked in Kāksa is due to the poverty of the soil in that thāna and to its proximity to the coal-mines where good wages are obtainable. The only part of the district that has failed to share in the general revival are two of the three thānas of the Kālna subdivision, Kālna and Purbasthāli, where the Burdwān fever first appeared forty years ago. These thānas lie along the bank of the Bhāgīrathi; the soil is water-logged, and they are full of *jhils* and jungle; they are thus more unhealthy than any other part of the district." The principal results of this census are shown in the table below:—

Subdivision.	Area in square miles.	Number of		Population.	Population per square mile.	Percentage of variation in population between 1891 and 1901.
		Towns.	Villages.			
Burdwān ...	1,268	1	1,688	679,412	536	+ 9·6
Asansol ...	618	2	811	370,988	600	+19·6
Kātwa	404	2	465	248,806	616	+ 8·1
Kālna	399	1	698	233,269	585	+ 0·8
District Total ...	2,689	6	3,662	1,532,475	570	+10·1

GENERAL CHARACTERISTICS.

Density of population.

The density of the population in Burdwān has increased since 1872 by only 17 per cent. From 1872 to 1881 the years during which the fever epidemic reached its climax, there was an actual fall of 35 per cent., and in the succeeding decade there was no advance at all: the recovery in 1891—1901 is very marked, and the district now supports a population of 570 persons to the square mile. Speaking generally, the eastern part of the district where the soil is alluvial is much more thickly populated than the western which rests on the laterite, but the development of the coal-mines in the Asansol subdivision has led to a rapid growth of the population there, and Asansol itself, with 839 persons to the square mile, is now the most densely peopled thāna in the district. On the other hand, the density is least in the Kāksa and Ausgrām thānas where the laterite gradually merges into the alluvial silt. Large tracts here are covered with *sāl* jungle. There are no mines, and the soil is too poor to support a large population.

The steadily increasing demand for labour in the mines and factories of Asansol and Rānīganj has led to a continued flow of immigration into Burdwān. In 1901 the total number of immigrants was returned as 158,347, a larger number than was found in any district in the province with the exception of the 24-Parganas and the metropolis itself. There is a good deal of periodic and permanent immigration from the neighbouring districts of Bānkurā, Mānbhūm and the Santāl Parganas, and more than two-thirds of the immigrants enumerated at the last census were found to be inhabitants of the contiguous districts; at the same time labourers for the coal-mines, iron works, paper mills, and potteries are collected in large numbers from Patna, Gaya, Shāhābād, and Monghyr in Behār and from the Chotā Nāgpur plateau. In the eastern portion of the district there is a continual demand for Beharis and west countrymen who are employed as durwāns and peons by the local land-holders, and the increasing trade of Asansol and Rānīganj has drawn a considerable number of Mārwāri merchants and traders to those towns. Migration.

The volume of emigration is also considerable, and the statistics of the census of 1901 show that 6·16 of the population of the district were enumerated outside it. The district sends out numerous clerks to Calcutta and labourers to Assam, and loses more than it gains by the casual migration across the boundary line, dividing it from Bīrbhūm and Hooghly. The loss in both cases is due mainly to the demand in these districts for wives born in Burdwān.

There are six towns—Burdwān, Kālna, Kātwa, Dāinhāt, Rānīganj and Asansol. These are all municipalities, and the total number of their inhabitants is 72,270, or 5 per cent. of the population. The district outside the coal-mine area is almost entirely agricultural, and the towns here are unprogressive, of little commercial importance and, on the whole, distinctly rural in character. Burdwān itself, which was formerly the principal Towns and villages.

seat of trade in Western Bengal, has few special industries, and owes its position to the fact that it is the headquarters of the district and the principal seat of the Mahārājā. The town really consists of 93 small villages, and the greater part of the population are engaged in agriculture. It is growing in importance as a railway centre, and is fairly prosperous; but in spite of this, the population has grown but little of late years. The fine strategical position of Kātwa at the confluence of the Ajay and the Bhāgīrathi was soon recognized by the Muhammadan invaders, and in the time of the Nawābs this town was one of the most important places in Bengal, and was regarded as the key of Murshidābād. In recent years, however, the channel of the Bhāgīrathi has silted up, and with the advent of the railway the trade of the place has greatly declined. Kālna, which is also situated on the Bhāgīrathi, was formerly an important trading centre, and was considered one of the principal ports of the district. The railway has, however, drawn most of the traffic away from it, and its prosperity has long been decreasing. Of late, the town has been extremely unhealthy, and many of the brick-built houses in the bazar are now in ruins. A considerable river-borne trade was also formerly carried on from Dāinhāt, but the Bhāgīrathi has now receded more than a mile from it, and its trade has suffered considerably in consequence.

The western portion of the district is one of the busiest industrial tracts in Bengal, and its coal and iron fields have attracted a large immigrant population. Both Rānīganj and Asansol are progressive towns and are growing rapidly. Their prosperity is almost entirely due to the development of the coal-mines. Rānīganj possesses large potteries and paper mills which employ a very considerable number of operatives, and the town is also a busy trading centre for coal and rice. The mines in the vicinity have been practically worked out, and the centre of the coal industry has moved further west, but the town still continues to increase in prosperity. The head-quarters of the subdivision have recently been transferred to Asansol which is situated in the centre of the coal-field and is now one of the most important railway centres in Bengal. In 1881 this town was a rural tract. In 1891 its population was returned at 11,000, and in 1901 at 14,906. There is a large European community connected with the railway, and the bazar is growing rapidly. The town is situated in the middle of the Rānīganj coal-field, and since coal of a better quality is obtainable here than further east, it has practically taken the place of Rānīganj as the centre of the coal industry.

The rest of the population is contained in 3,662 villages of no great size, 52 per cent. of the people living in villages containing less than 500 inhabitants. In the alluvial portion where practically the only occupation of the people is cultivation, the villages are usually situated on the higher ground between the rice swamps, and are buried in the dense foliage characteristic of Lower Bengal. The large immigrant population of Asansol and Rānīganj are mainly housed in small groups of huts clustering round the various mines and factories.

The language current in the district is the dialect known as *Rārhi boli* or Western Bengali which is also spoken in Bānkurā, Bīrbhūm, Mānbhūm, Singhbhūm, and the Santāl Parganas. The name means the language spoken in Rārh, the old name for the Western Division of Bengal, the country lying to the west of the Bhāgīrathi and south of the Ganges. Languages.

Bengali, or Banga Bhāsha, was formerly thought to be a very modern language, but Dr. Grierson has shown that this is not the case, and that the language of the fifteenth, differs very little from that of the eighteenth, century. The present literary form of the language has developed since the occupation of the country by the English, and its most marked characteristic is the wholesale adoption of Sanskrit words in the place of words descended through the Prakrit, due at first, it is thought, to the great poverty of the original material in a country where the vast majority of the inhabitants were of non-Aryan descent. The Bengalis are unable to pronounce many of the words that have been borrowed from the Sanskrit, but they have nevertheless retained the Sanskrit spelling. "The result of this state of affairs," says Dr. Grierson, "is that, to foreigners, the great difficulty of Bengali is its pronunciation. The vocabulary of the modern literary language is almost entirely Sanskrit, and few of these words are pronounced as they are written." The book language is quite unintelligible to the uneducated masses, and as, apart from it, there is no generally recognized standard, the variations in the spoken language are very great. The well-known adage that the dialect changes every twelve *kos* applies probably with greater force to Bengali than to any other language in India.

"Bengali," Dr. Grierson writes, "has a fairly voluminous literature dating from pre-historic times. According to the latest authority its oldest literary record is the song of Manikchandra, which belongs to the days of the Buddhists, though it has no doubt been altered in the course of centuries through transmission by word of mouth. Of the well-known authors, one of the oldest and most admired is Chandi Das, who flourished about the 14th century and wrote songs of considerable merit in praise of Krishna. Since his time to the commencement of the present century, there has been a succession of writers, many of whom are directly connected with the religious revival instituted by Chaitanya."

This dialect was returned in 1901 as the language of 91·9 per cent. of the population. The number of persons returned as speaking Hindi rose from 46,000 in 1891 to 73,000 in 1901, or 4·7 per cent., and this is obviously due to the large influx of labourers from Behār and Western India which followed on the development of the coal industry. Santāli is spoken by 39,428 persons and some 5,000 persons were returned as speaking Korā.*

Religions. Altogether 1,221,027 persons, or 79·6 per cent. of the population, are Hindus: 287,403, or 18·7 per cent., are Muhammadans; and 21,048, or 1·3 per cent., are Animists. There are 2,960 Christians, of whom 1,061 are Europeans, 872 Eurasians and 1,072 natives of the country. Other religions are practically unrepresented, numbering only 37.

Christian Missions. The Church Missionary Society early fixed on Burdwān as a centre from which to carry on its missionary work. A most interesting account of the foundation of the mission is to be found in the memoir of the Revd. J. J. Weitbrecht, with whose name missionary work in this district must always be most closely associated. "The mission was commenced in 1816 by Captain Stewart, a pious and devoted servant of the East India Company, and he continued to take a deep interest in it till his death in 1833. In the first year he established two vernacular schools, and in two years the number had increased to ten, containing a thousand children, and costing 240 rupees a month. In the beginning he encountered considerable opposition; the Brāhmans circulated reports among the people that it was his design to ship all the children to England, and an instance occurred in which a parent exposed his little son to the jackals to be devoured during the night to prevent the possibility of his being educated by Captain Stewart. The introduction of printed books into the schools at first caused some alarm, the people conceiving it to be a plan for depriving them of their caste as all instruction had been previously conveyed through manuscripts: and it was remarked of the village school-masters—'If you put a printed book into their hands, they are unable to read it without great difficulty, and are still less able to understand its contents.' Besides the outlines of Geography, Astronomy and History, Captain Stewart

* Bengal Census Report, 1901.

caused instruction to be given in some few of the preambles of the East India Company's regulations, which are particularly calculated to convince the Hindus that Government anxiously desires to promote their comfort and advantage. In these seminaries the children knew of no precedency but that which was derived from merit. The Brāhman boy and his ignoble neighbour sat side by side, and if the latter excelled the former in learning, as was often the case, he stood above him." These schools became so celebrated that the Calcutta School Society sent its Superintendent for five months to Burdwān in 1819 to learn the system of Captain Stewart's schools, as he educated a greater number of children with fewer teachers and at half the expense of the old system. When Mr. W. Adam, who had been directed by Government to enquire into the state of education, visited Burdwān in 1837, he reported that Burdwān was the best educated district in Bengal. In 1819 Captain Stewart purchased a plot of ground on the Grand Trunk Road two miles north-west of Burdwān on behalf of the Church Missionary Society, and there a mission centre was gradually established with a church, orphanage, school and mission houses. The mission continued to prosper, and, under the Revd. John James Weitbrecht, who worked in Burdwān from 1830 to 1852, became one of the best organized mission churches in Bengal.

We read of 14 schools scattered over an area of 40 miles with an attendance of 1,000 boys, of a girls' school, of one of the first high schools in Bengal with a hostel for Hindu students attached to it, of an orphanage, of out-stations at Kālna since taken over by the Free Church of Scotland, and Bānkurā, now a flourishing mission under the Wesleyan Society, and Nadiā, which has greatly outgrown the mother church with its eight churches and 6,000 Protestant Christians. Then come the dark days of the mission. Burdwān fever decimated the town, the Christian congregation was scattered, the orphanage was removed to Agarpārā, the schools were gradually closed and the European staff reduced. The Church Missionary Society has never re-occupied the district as it once hoped to do, Nadiā taking the place of the Burdwān district as the Society's principal field of effort. The out-stations were left undermanned and were eventually occupied by other societies. The town of Burdwān was retained, but the institutions were transferred elsewhere. At the present time the mission is a purely evangelistic one with a small congregation consisting mainly of mission workers, whose work is to itinerate in the cold weather in the villages round Burdwān. There is one European Missionary in charge who also acts as

Honorary Chaplain to the European residents. Some twenty miles north of Burdwān is a church medical mission with a hospital and dispensary with three European ladies in charge, and an efficient staff of workers under the Church of England Zenana Society. This mission is the survival of a flourishing Zenana Mission in Burdwān which had to be closed for want of funds in 1900. The ladies of Mānkur superintend also an elementary Hindu girls' school in Burdwān, which, with another Church school of a similar nature supported by voluntary local subscriptions, is all that is now left of English Church educational work in the district.

At Rānīganj there is a Wesleyan Methodist Mission which was established in 1878. In addition to a European Superintendent and two native ordained ministers there are women workers, who visit zenānās, and evangelists in village stations. The adult congregation is about 350. An English church and three native chapels are attached to the mission, and it also manages an orphanage with an industrial class attached, a refuge for the sick and destitute, day schools and a shop for the sale of Christian literature. In addition the Superintendent of the mission is entrusted with the management of the Leper Asylum maintained at Rānīganj by the Mission to Lepers of which an account will be found in the following chapter.

In Asansol town there is a Roman Catholic Mission. A church was built in 1872-73, and the following year the building of a convent and schools was commenced. The building of the scholastiate for the clerical students of the Society of Jesus was finished in 1883, having been constructed by the late Archbishop Goethals. In 1889, the students were moved to Kurseong, and the building was made over by the Archbishop to the mission. It was enlarged and became St. Patrick's school which numbers at present about 140 boarders and 50 day-scholars.

A mission has also recently been established by the Methodist Episcopal Church at Asansol. The mission had its origin in services held by itinerant preachers, but a site was eventually granted by Government in 1883, and a church was erected in the following year. The mission now consists of a boys' middle English boarding school with an attendance of about 50, and a girls' boarding school with an average attendance of 85. Many of the children are orphans, and the greater number come from the poorest classes of the population. Preaching, the distribution of literature and visiting are carried on at Asansol and the outlying villages, and the mission also manages a Leper Asylum which is supported by the Mission to Lepers in India and the

East. There are out-stations at Bolpur and Sainthia where a girls' primary school has been established. The United Free Church of Scotland Medical Mission maintains a charitable hospital at Kālna.*

Muhammadans are distributed fairly evenly over the eastern portion of the district, and are found in greatest strength in the thānas lying along the Bhāgīrathi. The Muhammadan invaders who followed Bakhtyār Khilji soon spread over Burdwān and possessed themselves of the principal places of importance in the district. Pandua in Hooghly, Māhmadpur near Manteswar police-station, Kālna and Kātwa all became Muhammadan settlements. It is probable therefore that a considerable proportion of the Muhammadan population are the descendants of the numerous soldiers of fortune and their followers who formerly found a livelihood in Bengal. The numerous *aimmā* estates which are found in the district and the traditional history of the Muhammadan settlements at Kāksa and at Churulia under Rājā Narottam's fort show that grants of land to such followers were very common. At the same time there can be little doubt that local converts bulk largely in the total, and the general opinion seems to be that the lower classes of Muhammadans have been mainly recruited from such converts. According to the census report for 1901, "almost the whole of the functional groups such as Jolaha and Dhunia throughout the province, and the great majority, probably nine-tenths, of the Sheikhs in Bengal Proper are of Indian origin." Muhammadans

The conversion of the Hindus to Islam was in most cases voluntary. The Mughals were, as a rule, tolerant in religious matters, and the Afghan rulers who preceded them did not often use force to propagate their faith. The only organized persecution of the Hindus of which there is any record in history is that of Jalal-ud-dīn mentioned by Dr. Wise, who is said to have offered the Koran or death, and who must have effected wholesale conversions. But although there was no general attack on the Hindu religion, there are numerous traditions of conversions on a large scale by enthusiastic freelances, such as the renowned Shāh Jalal of Sylhet. In Mandaran thānā in the Arāmbāgh subdivision of Hooghly, where the Muhammadan population preponderates over the Hindu, there is a tradition that Muhammad Ismail Shāh Ghazi defeated the local Rājā and forcibly converted the people to Islam. These traditions are not confirmed by history, but history tells us very little of what went on in Bengal during the

* For this account of the missions at Burdwān, Rānīganj and Asansol, I am indebted to the Revd. Mr. Clarke, the Revd. Mr. Bleby, and the Revd. Mr. Koele.

reigns of the independent kings, and, when even the names of some of them are known to us only from the inscriptions on their coins, while there is no record whatever of many of the local satraps, it is not to be expected that, even if forcible conversions were common, there would be any written account of them. There must doubtless, here and there, have been ruthless fanatics like the notorious Tippu Sahib of more recent times, who forcibly circumcised many of his Hindu subjects and perpetrated many acts of the grossest oppression, and the fact that many of the Muhammadan mosques, especially in this district, were often constructed of stones taken from Hindu temples, clearly shows that, at some times in some places, the Hindus were subjected to persecution at the hands of their Musalman conquerors. In the accounts of Chaitanya's life, for instance, we read that two of his leading disciples were Brāhmans who had been compelled to embrace the faith of Islam.

In spite, however, of the fact that cases of forcible conversion were by no means rare, it seems probable that very many of the ancestors of the Bengal Muhammadans voluntarily gave in their adhesion to Islam. The advantages which that religion offered to persons held in low esteem by the Hindus are sufficiently obvious, and under Muslim rule there was no lack of pious Pirs and Fakirs such as Pir Bahrām, of Burdwān, and Majlis and Bādr Saheb of Kālna who devoted their lives to gaining converts to the faith. There were special reasons which, during the early years of the Muhammadan supremacy, made conversion comparatively easy. Although the days when Buddhism was a glowing faith had long since passed, the people of Bengal were still to a great extent Buddhistic, and when Bakhtyār Khiliji conquered Behār and massacred the Buddhist monks assembled at Odontapuri, the common people, who were already lukewarm, deprived of their priests and teachers, were easily attracted from their old form of belief, some to Hinduism and others to the creed of Muhammad. The higher castes probably found their way back to Hinduism, while the non-Aryan tribes who had, in all probability, never been Hindus, preferred the greater attractions of Islam.

At present but few conversions to Islam occur, and as a rule the persons who come over from the one religion to the other do so for material and not for religious reasons, as for instance when a Muhammadan takes a Hindu widow as his second wife, or a Hindu falls in love with a Muhammadan girl and must embrace her religion before he can marry her.*

* Census Report, 1901.

By far the greater majority of the Muhammadans in Burdwān are Sunnis of the Hanifa sect, but in some parts of the district, more particularly in Kātwa, the Wahabis have gained a large number of adherents, and the higher class Muhammadans are often Shiahs. The unreformed Muhammadans of the lower and uneducated classes are deeply infected with Hindu superstitions, and their knowledge of the faith they profess seldom extends beyond the three cardinal doctrines of the unity of God, the mission of Muhammad and the truth of the Korān. The veneration of Pīrs and Saints is common among them, and many pilgrims frequent the more famous shrines and make offerings of sweetmeats, etc., in order that the Pīr may look with favour upon them and grant them the fulfilment of their desires. One of the most famous of such shrines is that of Pīr Bahrām whose tomb is shown in Burdwān. He is mentioned in the Memorandum Book of Khusgo in the following note, "Hajrat Haji Bahram Sekka was a native of Turkestan. He belonged to the Bayet sect of Musalmans"; he is also noticed in the Memorandum Book of Nudrat. Tradition relates that he was at one time a water-carrier in the streets of Mecca and Najaf. The date of his death as engraved on the tombstone is 970 Hizri. Two other famous Pīrs are Badr Sāheb and Majlis Sāheb who are regarded by Muhammadans and Hindus alike as the patron Saints of Kālna. Their tombs stand onlthe river bank, and are worshipped equally by the followers of both religions, the commonest offerings being small clay horses which are supposed to signify the horse sacrifice which is so common in ancient Indian history.

The animists are almost entirely represented by the Santāls, the side drift of the great immigration northwards, who are found almost entirely in the Asansol subdivision. The following brief account of their religious beliefs is condensed from that given in the Bānkurā Gazetteer. The religion of the Santāls is of a primitive nature, its main feature being sacrifices made to a number of village and household deities. The village deities are usually supposed to reside in trees. The household deities reside in a little apartment reserved for them in every house, however small. Grain and other articles are stored here, but it is a sacred spot; all the household sacrifices being made at the entrance to it, and no female from any other house may even enter it. The names of the household deities are kept secret and are known only to the head of the family. Generally among the village deities the spirit of the founder of the village, and, among the family deities, those of departed ancestors, are worshipped. Chickens, goats and sometimes even cows are sacrificed: the flesh of Animists.

the animals is consumed by the sacrificers and the friends, and the feast is almost invariably accompanied by drinking and dancing.

A strong belief in witchcraft is firmly established, and the Jān, or witch doctor, whose aid in cases of misfortune is always invoked, is a person of great importance and power. The Jān also has the power of divining from *sāl* leaves, but the secret of his greatness lies in the fact that he is a spirit medium and that his pronouncements are made when he is under intense spiritual influence. He is often resorted to not only by Santāls, but also by low-caste Hindus, many of whom firmly believe in his power of casting out the demon of cholera from any village that may be attacked.

Hinduism. Burdwān, with its large contingent of high caste Brāhmans, has from pre-historic times been a stronghold of Hinduism. But the pure and lofty faith of the Aryan invaders here, as elsewhere in the lower valley, has been corrupted by the superstitions of the animistic races whom they conquered, and the popular religion exhibits in consequence a marked mixture of the Animism of the aboriginals and the Monotheism of the higher race. Much of the demon worship and of that propitiation of malignant power which is now so marked a feature of the worship of Siva and Kāli was undoubtedly borrowed from the aboriginals, and, as Hunter has pointed out, whatever mythology Siva or Rudra may originally have belonged to, there can be no doubt that Siva worship as performed by the lower classes in Lower Bengal is the reverse of the Aryan spirit of devotion, and represents the superstition of the black races. Yet this is the only form of religion which has now any hold on the lower classes, and it is Siva and his more terrible wife Kāli who are invoked by the people in all times of trouble or necessity.

Saktism. Siva-worship or Saktism (Sanskrit Saktī), the worship of power or energy, is based on the worship of the active-producing principle (Prakriti) as manifested in one or other of the goddess wives of Siva (Durgā, Kāli, Pārvatī), the female energy or Saktī of the primordial male, Purusha or Siva. The object of the worship is the acquisition of magical and supernatural powers through the help of the goddess, or the destruction of enemies through her co-operation. In this cult the various forces of nature are deified under separate personalities, which are known as the divine mothers or Mātrigān. The ritual to be observed, the sacrifices to be offered, and the *mantras*, or magic texts, to be uttered, in order to secure the efficacy of the worship and to procure the fulfilment of the worshipper's desire, are laid down in a series of religious writings known as Tāntras. The central idea of these books is to identify all force with the female principle in nature, and to inculcate the exclusive admiration of Siva's wife as the source of every kind of supernatural faculty and mystery. The cult is supposed to have originated in East Bengal or Assam about the fifth century. Kāli is said to be the same as Durgā, but she can assume any number of forms at the same time. The characteristic of Durgā is beneficence, while Kāli is terrific and blood-thirsty, as the following translation from one of the sacred books of this cult will show. "A Kaulika (*i.e.*, a Sakta) should worship Kāli who lives amongst dead bodies: who is terrible and has fearful jaws: who has uncombed hair and a glowing tongue: who constantly drinks blood: who stands over her husband Mahā-Kāla and wears a garland of skulls on her blood-besmeared throat: who has prominent breasts: who is waited on by all the Siddhas as well as by the Siddhis." *

In the Kālika Purān the immolation of human beings is recommended, and numerous animals are enumerated as suitable for sacrifice. At the present time pigeons, goats and more rarely, buffaloes, are the usual victims at the shrine of the goddess. The ceremony commences with the adoration of the sacrificial axe; various *mantras* are recited, and the animal is then decapitated at one stroke. As soon as the head falls to the ground, the votaries rush forward and smear their foreheads with the blood of the victim. The great occasion for these sacrifices is during the three days of the Durgā Pujā. The opposition between Saktism and Vedic Hinduism is expressly stated in the Mahānirvāna Tāntra where it is said that the *mantras* contained in the Vedas are now devoid of all energy and resemble snakes deprived of their venom. In the Satya and other ages they were effective, but in the Kāli Yuga they are, as it were, dead.†

Modern Vaishnavism, as preached by Chaitanya, represents a revulsion against the gross and debasing religion of the Tāntras. Vaishnavism.
Chaitanya was a Baidik Brāhman and was born in Nabadvip (Nadiā) in 1484 or 1485, some two years before Luther. His father was an orthodox Brāhman named Jagannāth Misra. Various legends have grown up about his birth and childhood. He was thirteen months in the womb. Soon after his birth a number of holy men, including Advaita, his future disciple, arrived at the house of his parents to do homage to the child, and to present him with offerings. In his childhood,

* Monier Williams' Religious Life and Thought in India.

† Bengal Census Report, 1901.

like the young Krishna, he took part in all boyish sports and yet rapidly acquired a complete knowledge of Sanskrit purānas and literature. His favourite study was the Bhāgavata-purāna and the Bhāgavad-gitā. He married twice, his first wife having died from snake-bite, and at the age of twenty-five resolved to abandon all worldly connections and give himself up to a religious life. Accordingly he commenced a series of pilgrimages. His travels occupied six years and he is known to have visited the most celebrated shrines of India, including Benares, Gaya, Mathura, Srirangam, and ultimately the temple of Jagannāth at Puri. Having thus prepared himself for his mission he addressed himself to the work of preaching and propagating his own idea of the Vaishnāva creed and, after making many converts, appointed his two disciples Advaita and Nityānanda to preside over his disciples, living for the rest of his life at Puri. He preached mainly in Central Bengal and Orissa, the towns of Kātwa and Kālna in this district being particularly favoured by him. His doctrines found ready acceptance amongst large numbers of the people, especially amongst those who were still, or had only recently been, Buddhists. This was due mainly to the fact that he ignored caste and drew his followers from all sources, so much so that even Muhammadans followed him. The first principle he inculcated was that all the faithful worshippers were to be treated as equals. "The mercy of God," said Chaitanya, "regards neither tribe nor family." He preached vehemently against the immolation of animals in sacrifice and the use of animal food and stimulants, and taught that the true road to salvation lay in Bhakti, or fervent devotion to God. "He recommended Rādha worship and taught that the love felt by her for Krishna was the best form of devotion. 'Thou art dear to my heart, thou art part of my soul,' said a young man to his loved one, 'I love thee, but why I know not.' So ought the worshipper to love Krishna and worship him for his sake only. Let him offer all to God and expect no remuneration. He acts like a trader who asks for a return." Such are the words of a modern exponent of Chaitanya's teaching. The acceptable offerings are flowers, money and the like, but the great form of worship is that of the *sankirtan* or procession of worshippers playing and singing. A peculiarity of Chaitanya's cult is that the post of spiritual guide or Gosain is not confined to Brāhmans, and several of the best known belong to the Baidya caste. They are all of them descended from the leading men of Chaitanya's immediate entourage. The holy places of the cult are Nabadvip, Chaitanya's birth-place, and, in a still greater degree, Brindaban, the scene of Krishna's sports with the milk-maids, which Chaitanya and his disciples reclaimed from jungle, and where he personally identified the various sacred spots, on which great shrines have now been erected. At Nabadvip the most important shrines are in the keeping of Brâhmans who are themselves staunch Saktas.

In course of time the followers of Chaitanya split into two bodies, those who retained, and those who rejected, caste. The latter, who are also known as Jât Baishtams or Bairâgis, consist of recruits from all castes, who profess to intermarry freely amongst themselves. Except for the fact that outsiders are still admitted, they form a community very similar to the ordinary Hindu caste. Its reputation at the present day is tarnished by the fact that most of its new recruits have joined owing to love intrigues, or because they have been turned out of their own caste, or for some other sordid motive. Those who have retained their caste and are merely Vaishnâvâs by sect are, of course, in no way connected with the Jât Baishtams just described, and their religion is, on the whole, a far purer one than that of the Saktas. The stricter Vaishnâvâs will have nothing to do with Saktism and are vegetarians, but amongst the Bâgdis and other low classes, many of the professed followers of the sect will freely eat animal food and follow in the Durgâ procession, though they will not on any account be present when the sacrifices are offered up.*

The largest aboriginal substratum of the population consists of the Bâgdis and Bauris, of whom the former have been admitted within the pale of Hinduism, while the latter are still outside it and are regarded by all orthodox Hindus as unmitigated *chuars*. The Bâgdis worship Siva, Vishnu, Dharmarâj, Durgâ, the Saktis and the myriad names of the modern Hindu Pantheon in a more or less intelligent fashion under the guidance of degraded (patit) Brâhmans. But together with these greater gods we find the Santâl goddess, Gosain Era and Barapahâri, "the great mountain" (Marang Buru) of the same tribe. According to the Bâgdis themselves their favourite and characteristic deity is Manasâ, the sister of the snake king Vâsuki, the wife of Jarat Karu and mother of Astika, whose intervention saved the human race from destruction by Janmejaya.

Religious beliefs of the lower castes.

The Bauris profess to be Hindus of the Sakta sect, but in Western Bengal, at any rate, their connection with Hinduism is of the slenderest kind, and their favourite objects of worship are Manasâ, Bhâdu, Mânsingh, Barapahâri, Dharmarâj and

---

* Monier Williams' Religious Life and Thought in India.
Bengal Census Report, 1901.

Kudrāsinī. Goats are sacrificed to Mānsingh, and fowls to Barapahāri. Pigs, fowls, rice, sugar and *ghi* are offered to Kudrāsinī on Saturdays at the *ākhrā*, or dancing place, of the village through the medium of a Bauri priest, who abstains from flesh or fish on the day preceding the sacrifice. The priest gets as his fee the fowls that are offered and the head or leg of the pig; the worshippers eat the rest. In Western Bengal Bauris have not yet attained to the dignity of having Brāhmans of their own. Their priests are men of their own caste, termed Lāyā or Degharīā, some of whom hold land rent-free, or at a nominal rent, as remuneration for their services. The headman of the village (parāmānik) may also officiate as priest.

Manasā. Of all the snake godlings, Manasā, the snake goddess, in Bengal Proper at least, holds the foremost place, and her worship is conducted with great pomp and circumstance by both Bāgdis and Bauris who claim that it secures immunity from snake-bite. Popular tradition makes her the mother of Astika Muni, the sister of the snake king Vāsuki and the wife of Jarat Karu Muni, but she is also known as Bishahari and is worshipped by Hindus of all castes in order to secure immunity from snake-bite. It is said that if her worship is neglected some one in the family is certain to die of snake-bite. She is worshipped in various forms. Sometimes a simple earthen pot is marked with vermilion and placed under a tree, where clay snakes are arranged round it and a trident is driven into the ground; sometimes the plant called after her is taken as her emblem, and sometimes an image of a small four-armed female of yellow colour, her feet resting on a goose, a cobra in each hand and a tiara of snakes upon her head. Rams and he-goats are sacrificed in her honour, and rice, sweetmeats, fruit and flowers are also offered. Most families have a shrine dedicated to her in their homes, and sometimes a separate room is set apart for her. On the Dasahāra day a twig of the Manasā plant (Euphorbia ligularia) is planted in the courtyard and worshipped on the fifth day of the moon, the Nāgpanchamī day. It is thrown into the water when the image of Durgā is immersed at the Durgā Pujā. Manasā is also worshipped on the last day of the solar month of Srāban and Bhādra. Songs about the goddess are sung, especially those recounting her dealings with Chānd Sadāgar, a merchant of Gandhabanik caste, which are said to be based on a legend found in the Padma Purān. Amongst the higher castes the worship is performed by Brāhmans, but the Hāris, Bauris and Dōms perform the ceremony themselves.

The following account of the origin of this worship is given by Mr. R. C. Dutt:—"The semi-Hinduized aborigines may take to themselves the credit of having added some godheads to the Hindu Pantheon, and the goddess of Manasā is perhaps the most remarkable instance. Hindu gods are rather revered and venerated even by the advanced semi-aboriginals than actually worshipped; but Manasā is universally worshipped by the most backward as well as the advanced semi-aborigines of Western Bengal, and the worship is continued for days together, and is attended with much pomp and rejoicing, and singing in the streets. The fact of the introduction of this aboriginal worship among Hindus is crystallized in the story of Chānd Saudāgar, and is handed down from generation to generation. It is said that the Saudāgar refused to worship that goddess till his trade was ruined and his dearest child was killed by snake-bite on his marriage day; then, and then only was the merchant compelled to recognize the power of the snake goddess. It is significant, too, that the place which is pointed out as the site of this occurrence is near the Dāmodar river, which may be considered as the boundary line between the first Hindu settlers of Bengal and the aborigines. At what period the worship of Manasā crossed their boundary line and spread among the Hindus cannot be ascertained; but up to the present day the worship of this goddess among Hindus is tame, compared to the universal rejoicing and enthusiasm with which she is worshipped by her ancient followers, the present semi-Hinduized aborigines."*

Dharmarāj.

Both Bāgdis and Bauris worship Dharmarāj, but the cult is not confined to them and his shrines are common all over West Bengal. By some Dharmarāj is regarded as Yāma and by others as the Sun. Some again consider him to be the god of snakes, and some a form of Siva or Vishnu. He is usually worshipped by a low caste priest, often a Dōm or a Bāgdi. As a rule, he is represented by a shapeless stone daubed with vermilion and placed under a tree, but he is sometimes worshipped in the form of a tortoise. He is frequently believed to possess certain curative powers and his priests administer medicines as specifics for various diseases. Hogs, fowls and ducks are sacrificed before him, and offerings are made of rice, flowers, milk and *pachwai*. The worship takes place in the months of Baisākh, Jaishta and Āsārh, on the day of the full moon, and in some places on the last day of Bhādra. All castes, even Brāhmans, make offerings through the medium of the officiating priest.

The worship of Dharma is believed by Mahāmahopādhyāya Hara Prasād Sāstri to be a corrupt form of Buddhism. The writers of Tāntrik compilations among the Hindus, he says,

* The Aboriginal Element in the Population of Bengal, *Calcutta Review*, 1882.

incorporated as many of the Tāntrik Buddhist divinities as they could possibly do without jeopardizing their reputation for orthodoxy. But there were still divinities, to whom even with their wonderful power of adaptation, they could not venture to give a place in the Pantheon, and one of these is Dharma. Originally Dharma was the second person in the Buddhist Trinity, but the term came to be applied to the worship of stūpas, the visible emblem of Buddhism to the ignorant multitude. "Dharma worship remained confined to the lowest classes of the people—the dirtiest, meanest and most illiterate classes. All the lowest forms of worship rejected by the Brāhmans gradually rallied round Dharma, and his priests throughout Bengal enjoy a certain consideration which often excites the envy of their highly-placed rivals the Brāhmans, who, though hating them with a genuine hatred, yet covet their earnings wherever these are considerable; and there are instances in which the worship of Dharma has passed into Brāhman hands, and has been, by them, transformed into a manifestation either of Siva or of Vishnu."

After recapitulating the arguments by which he identifies Dharma worship as a survival of Buddhism, the Paṇdit goes on to say:—"The Dharma worshippers are fully aware that Dharma is not an inferior deity, he is higher than Vishnu, higher than Siva, higher than Brāhmā and even higher than Pārvatī. His position is, indeed, as exalted as that of Brāhmā in Hindu philosophy. In fact, one of the books in honour of Dharma gives an obscure hint that the work has been written with the object of establishing the Brahmāhood of Dharma. The representation of Dharma in many places is a tortoise. Now a tortoise is a miniature representation of a stūpa with five niches for five Dhyāni Buddhas. At Saldā in Bānkurā an image of Buddha in meditative posture is still actually worshipped as Dharma. The worshippers of Dharma are unconscious of the fact that they are the survivors of a mighty race of men, and that they have inherited their religion from a glorious past."* To this it may be added that at the present day the image of Dharma is generally found in the houses of low-caste people, and that a popular saying is *Dharma nichagāmi, i.e.,* Dharma favours the low. At the same time Dharma is offered cooked food even by a Brāhman.

The Grāmya Devatā. The worship of the village and household gods is very prevalent among the lower classes. These are called the Grāmya Devata and are worshipped on the occasion of every religious ceremony, and also on special occasions, for instance when disease breaks out or a newly-built house is occupied for the first time.

* Bengal Census Report, 1901.

The landlord of the village celebrates *pujā* usually under a pipal or banyan tree, while each ryot performs his own ceremony at home. Sometimes a Brāhman officiates, but frequently the people conduct the worship themselves.

"On the plains, the village god has ever been an object of veneration with the low castes of mixed descent, rather than of the Brāhmans, and in many places the worship has altogether died out among the higher ranks. At the beginning of this century, however, Buchanan found it existing everywhere throughout the north-western districts of Lower Bengal. 'The vulgar,' he says, 'have never been entirely able to abandon the worship of the village deities, and imitate their ancestors either by making such offerings as before mentioned (betel, red-lead, rice, water) to an anonymous deity, under whose protection they suppose their village to be, or call by that name various ghosts that have become objects of worship, or various of the Hindu Devatās. The ghosts, in fact, and the others called village deities, seem to be the gods most usually applied to in cases of danger by all ranks, and their favour is courted with bloody sacrifices and other offerings. They are not in general represented by images, nor have they temples; but the deity is represented by a lump of clay, sometimes placed under a tree, and provided with a priest of some low tribe.' Several of these village gods are older than the Aryan settlement, being deified personages sprung from the aboriginal tribes, whose distinctive nationality has been forgotten for ages in the districts where their representative men are still worshipped. Everywhere the ceremonies bear the stamp of the old superstitious terrors, and the carnivorous, gluttonous habits of the black races. Indeed, Buchanan well describes them as 'sacrifices made partly from fear, and partly to gratify the appetite for flesh'. The fierce aboriginal instincts, even in the mixed castes, who approach nearest to the Aryans, and accept in a greater degree than their neighbours the restraints of Hinduism, break loose on such festivals: and cowherds have been seen to feed voraciously on swine-flesh, which at all other times they regard with abhorrence." *

CASTES AND TRIBES.

Bāgdi	...	197,000
Bauri	...	113,000
Brāhman	...	109,000
Sadgop	...	106,000
Goālā	...	70,000
Aguri	...	66,000

The marginal table shows the strength of the different tribes and castes, numbering over 50,000. Ethnically there is a wide difference between the Asansol subdivision and the rest of the district. In Asansol the lowest stratum of the population to be found are the Bauris, but even within the last

* Hunter's "Annals of Rural Bengal."

century this tract was an unpeopled wilderness, the haunt of thieves and banditti, and it is only since the discoveries of coal that it has become settled country. The deltaic portion of the district was perhaps the seat of the oldest civilization in Bengal; the aboriginal element here is represented by the Bāgdis who, according to Mr. Oldham, are descended from the Mālli and were once the ruling race. Of the various castes noted above it is unnecessary to give any further special description of the Goālās. The Brāhmans of Burdwān, however, and the Sadgop and Aguri castes, which are peculiar to the district, deserve further mention, while the Bāgdis and Bauris as representing the aboriginal element in the population are also interesting.

Brāhmans. The Rārhi Brāhmans derive their name from Rārh, the high-lying alluvial tract on the west bank of the river Bhāgirathi. Their claim to be of comparatively pure Aryan descent is to some extent borne out by the results of anthropometric enquiries. According to current tradition Adisura, or Adisvara, king of Bengal, early in the eleventh century A.D., finding the Brāhmans then settled in Bengal too ignorant to perform for him certain Vedic ceremonies, applied to the Rājā of Kanauj for priests thoroughly conversant with the sacred ritual of the Aryans. In answer to this request five Brāhmans of Kanauj were sent to him: Bhatta Nārāyana of the Sāndilya section or *gotra*; Daksha of the Kasyapa *gotra*; Vedagarva or Vidagarbha of the Vatsa *gotra*, or as other accounts say, from the family of Bhrigu; Chandra or Chhāndara of the Sāvarna *gotra*, and Sriharsa of the Bharadwāja *gotra*. They brought with them their wives, their sacred fire and their sacrificial implements. It is said that Adisura was at first disposed to treat them with scanty respect, but he was soon compelled to acknowledge his mistake and to beg the Brāhmans to forgive him. He then made over to them five populous villages, where they lived for a year. Although the immigrant Brāhmans brought their wives with them, tradition says that they contracted second marriages with the women of Bengal, and that their children by the latter were the ancestors of the Barendra Brāhmans.

By the middle of the eleventh century, when Ballal Sen, the second of the Sen kings of Bengal, instituted his famous enquiry into the personal endowments of the Rārhi Brāhmans, their numbers seem to have increased greatly. They are represented as divided into 56 *gains*, or headships of villages, which were reserved for them, and might not be encroached upon by Brāhmans of other orders. Tradition is silent concerning the precise method in which Ballal Sen carried out his somewhat inquisitorial measures. It seems, however, to be certain that some kind of inquiry into the nine characteristic qualities was held under his orders, and that the *kul* or social and ceremonial standing of each family was determined accordingly. Some say that twenty-two *gains* were raised to the highest distinction. Lakshmana Sen discarded fourteen *gains* on account of their misconduct, and they become *gauna Kulins*, an order which has now disappeared. Nineteen families belonging to the other eight *gains* were made Kulins. The other families of these eight *gains* were lost sight of. Thus two classes of grades of sacerdotal virtue were formed:—(1) the *kulin*, being those who had observed the entire nine counsels of perfection; (2) the *srotriya*, who, though regular students of the Vedas, had lost *avritti* by intermarrying with families of inferior birth. The Srotriya were again subdivided into Siddha or perfect, Sādhya or capable of attaining purity, and Kashta or difficult. The last named group was also called Ari, or enemy, because a Kulin marrying a daughter of that group was disgraced. The relations of these three classes in respect of marriage were regulated by the principle laid down in the Institutes of Manu for members of the three twice-born castes, a principle now generally known as *hypergamy*. This singular and artificial organization deranged the natural balance of the sexes, and set up a vigorous competition for husbands among the women of the higher groups.

The invasion of Bengal by the Muhammadans and the instant collapse of the Hindu kingdom was not without its effect upon the matrimonial organisation of the Rārhi Brāhmans. Ballal Sen's reforms had been imposed upon the caste by the order of a Hindu ruler, and their observance depended upon the maintenance of his supervising authority. When this check was removed, the system could no longer hold together, and soon showed signs of breaking up completely. Artificial restrictions had been introduced; the natural balance of the sexes had been disturbed, and a disastrous competition for husbands had set in among the three original groups. New and inferior groups had sprung up, and their natural ambitions still further swelled the demand for Kulin husbands. The pressure of necessity soon showed itself too strong for the rules. Poor Kulins sold their family rank and honour for the bridegroom-price, which had taken the place of the bride-price of earlier times; they added to the number of their wives without regard to the respectability of the families from which they came; and they raised their prices as the supply of suitable husbands diminished, and competition ran higher for a Kulin bridegroom.

The reforms undertaken in the fourteenth century by Devi Vara, a *ghatak* or genealogist of Jessore, extended only to the Kulins. These were divided into three grades—(*i*) Swabhāva or original Kulins, (*ii*) Bhanga, (*iii*) Bansaja. The Swabhāva grade was further subdivided into 36 *mels*, or endogamous groups, each bearing the name of the original ancestor of the clan or of his village. This restriction of the marriages of Kulins to their own *mel* was the leading feature of Devi Vara's reform. Its principle was adopted and extended, it is believed, by the Kulins themselves, in the singular arrangement known as Pālti-Prakriti, or preservation of the type, by which families of equal rank were formed into triple groups, as it were, for matrimonial purposes, and bound to observe a sort of reciprocity.

Meantime the rush of competition for Kulin husbands on the part of Bhanga, Bansaja and Srotriya classes was as strong as before, while the proportionate number of pure Kulins had been reduced by the loss of those who had become Bhangas and Bansajas. In order to dispose of the surplus of women in the higher groups, polygamy was introduced, and was resorted to on a very large scale. It was popular with the Kulins because it enabled them to make a handsome income by the accident of their birth; and it was accepted by the parents of the girls concerned as offering the only means of complying with the requirements of the Hindu religion. Tempted by a *pan*, or premium, which often reached the sum of two thousand rupees, Swabhava Kulins made light of their *kul* and its obligations, and married Bansaja girls, whom they left after the ceremony to be taken care of by their parents. Matrimony became a sort of profession, and the honour of marrying a daughter to a Bhanga Kulin is said to have been so highly valued in Eastern Bengal that as soon as a boy was ten years old his friends began to discuss his matrimonial prospects, and before he was twenty he had become the husband of many wives of ages varying from five to fifty.*

With the spread of education among the upper classes of Bengal an advance in social morality has been made and the grosser forms of polygamy have fallen into disrepute. But the artificial organization of the caste still presses hard on a Kulin father who is unlucky enough to have a large family of daughters. These must be married before they attain puberty, or disgrace will fall on the family, and three generations of ancestors will be dishonoured. But a Kulin bridegroom can only be obtained

* Risley's Tribes and Castes of Bengal.

by paying a heavy premium, many of the *mels* instituted by Devi Vara have died out, and in such cases, reciprocal marriage being no longer possible, the son of a family left without a corresponding *mel* must marry the only daughter of a widow; while the daughter of a Kulin widow, for whom no husband of equal birth can be procured, may be married to a Srotriya, and a premium accepted without endangering the family prestige.*

Sadgops. As has already been noticed in Chapter II, Gopbhūm, the furthest headland of the promontory from Central India which juts into the district, was formerly the seat of a Sadgop dynasty of which some traces are still extant. According to Mr. John Boxwell, "Sadgop" is nearly pure Sanskrit, a *tatsama*, and probably a modern name: it means "good cowherd". The Sadgops are supposed to have separated from the *goālās* by abandoning pastoral pursuits and taking exclusively to agriculture, and their separation into two sub-castes—Paschim Kuliga and Purba Kuliga living to the west and east of the Bhāgīrathi—is referred by tradition to the time of Ballal Sen. It is doubtful, however, whether this theory of their origin is correct. The Sadgops are undoubtedly a modern caste, and their realm Gopbhūm could not have been ancient. They have no counterpart in Hindustan; they are not widely diffused and all the scattered members of the caste refer back to Gopbhūm. They now utterly repudiate connection with the *goālā*, and with the profession of cow-herding or milking. Though they must have been Gops before they were Sadgop, and though Gopbhūm is more pastoral than agricultural, they assert that they were the lords, not the attendants, of cattle, and the only profession they acknowledge for themselves is agriculture. They actually stand at the head of the Bengal agricultural castes, but their pretension to head the Nabasakh, or nine chief Sudra castes, who interchange the *hukah*, is contested by the Telis. The Sadgop, nevertheless, pretend to rank with the Kayastha, and, like them, take the surname Ghosh, which is borne, too, by some *goālās*. They have not yet, however, like some of the Bengal Kayasthas, claimed Kshatriyahood in the sense that it is now being claimed, as merely the next rank to the Brāhmans. Nor can they be thought quite analogous to the Kayasthas in view of the infinitely wider diffusion, purer Aryan blood, and known antiquity of the latter. The closest actual analogy that can be found to them are the Aguri, whose formation and recentness are known. But the conclusion that the Brāhmans have had much to do with the

* Risley's Tribes and Castes of Bengal.

Sadgop is irresistible. In no other way can the large mixture of Aryan blood as shown by the occurrence among the Sadgop of so many individuals with the large bones, fine frames, acquiline features and carriage of the Brāhmans, be accounted for. The only Aryans in the small locality concerned must have been the Brāhmans or the Kayastha. If the latter, we can know from other instances that the status of the Sadgop could not be so high as it is. In a country like Gopbhūm, the largest class of servants and attendants on the conquering Brāhmans must have been cowherds and milkmen. The conjecture that the Sadgop have sprung from the Brāhmans and the earlier *goālās* would account for all the peculiarities to be noticed among them—their Aryan blood and their high social position, their position in Gopbhum as a dynasty, and their name. Their repudiation of all connection with the modern *goālā* would be further accounted for by the very humble or degraded position of the latter. The Sadgop do not claim to represent even the legendary Gops and Gopis. Whether their genesis was actually in Gopbhūm or Gopbhūm took its name from them, is immaterial.

One curious custom of the caste may be noticed. Sadgops will not eat pumpkin (*lau*) and *dal* in the month of Asārh, and by way of accounting for this prohibition tell the absurd story that they are descended from one Kalu Ghosh, who, being appointed by one of the gods to look after his cattle, killed and ate the sacred animals. Oddly enough, instead of being punished for his sacrilege, his descendants, who thenceforth applied themselves to cultivation, were permitted to rank above the children of the other brother, Mūrāri Ghosh, who faithfully discharged his trust.

Aguris. The Aguri caste is peculiar to this district, and its chief settlement is the old deltaic soil between the great line of marshes to the west of the Bhāgīrathi and the present boundary of Gopbhūm, in which the Sadgops are still the most prominent caste. The tract is now the pargana Asmatashāhi, a name which indicates that it was formed by the Mughals, and the prevalence of the Aguris in it points to its having formed part of the kingdom to Gopbhūm. As usual, the unmixed section of the race is found clinging to the wild and uncultivated portion of its country. For the Aguris, by their own admission, are the product of unions between the Khetris of the house of Burdwan and the Sadgops of the Gopbhūm dynasty, and the caste arose within the last two hundred years, if not within a still shorter period. Two hundred years ago was the era of the Burdwān Khetris first assuming prominence. True to the policy of the old Aryan invaders, or mere acquirers of the soldier caste, they began to form alliances with the members of the royal race (it matters not whether purely aboriginal or semi or wholly Aryan, provided it was royal) with which they came in contact. The Khetris, however, had scarcely risen to the state of Rājās themselves when a combination of circumstances, which at this moment are influencing them, induced them to assert their exclusive character as an immigrant people from either Oudh or the Punjab, and not as settled inhabitants of Bengal. They have, throughout the last two hundred years, shown this anxiety to keep up by this means their connection with the other Khetris who are scattered throughout India. The consequence was that the Aguri caste, though esteemed highly respectable, has never attained the full status of the Kshatriya, as it would have done, to judge from other examples, had its origin been less recent. Though its name Aguri is contracted from Ugraha-Khetri, or "the fierce Khetris" (probably in allusion to its semi-barbarous ancestors, the Sadgops of wild Gopbhūm), it is a distinctly cultivating caste. Its members, at least those of one section of the caste, wear the sacred thread, and assert their superiority over the Sadgops from whom they have in part sprung, a pretension which, though scorned by the Sadgops, is practically admitted by other Hindus.*

The Aguris are popularly believed to be the modern representatives of the Ugra or Ugra Kshatriyas mentioned in Manu: "from a Kshatriya by a Sudra girl is born a creature called an Ugra (cruel) which has a nature partaking both of Kshatriya and of Sudra and finds its pleasure in savage conduct." According to the same authority, their occupation is "catching and killing animals that live in holes." They are distinctly, however, a cultivating class: many of them hold estates and tenures of various grades, and the bulk of the caste are fairly prosperous cultivators. In 1872 they were almost peculiar to the territories of the Burdwān Rāj, and it is clear that the Burdwān Khetri could have been the only Kshatriya concerned in a development which appeared in a single estate in Bengal, though the text which accounts for it is over 1,800 years old, and refers to the Punjāb. The Burdwān Brāhmans readily found the text when it was necessary to assign a particular status to these new families. If popular rumour is to be credited, the Aguris still "find their pleasure in savage conduct," for they are said to be extraordinarily short-tempered, and the criminal records of the district seem to show

* Oldham. Some Historical and Ethnical Aspects of the Burdwān district.

that in proportion to the number of the caste an unusual number of crimes of violence are laid to their charge.

Bauris. The Bauris are a low aboriginal caste who work as cultivators, agricultural labourers and *pálki*-bearers. Traces of totemism still survive in their reverence for the red-backed heron and the dog, and perhaps in their strong objection to touching horse-dung. The heron is looked upon as the emblem of the tribe, and may not be killed or molested on pain of expulsion from the caste. Dogs also are sacred, so much so that a Bauri will on no account kill a dog or touch a dead dog's body, and the water of a tank in which a dead dog has been drowned cannot be used until an entire rainy season has washed the impurity away. They themselves account for this custom by the ridiculous story that they thought it necessary that their caste should have some animal which should be as sacred to them as the cow is to the Brāhman, and they selected the dog as it was a useful animal when alive and not very nice to eat when dead!

Bauris admit into their caste members of any caste higher than themselves in social standing. No regular ceremony is appointed for such occasions: the new member merely pays to the caste *panchāyat* a sum of money, varying from Rs. 10 to Rs. 15 to be spent on a feast, at which, for the first time, he openly eats with his adopted caste brethren. The origin of this singular practice is perhaps to be sought in the lax views of the Bauris on the subject of sexual morality. In other castes a woman who has an intrigue with an outsider is punished by expulsion from the caste; but Bauris not only allow their women to live openly with men of other castes, but receive those men in their own community when, as frequently happens, they are outcasted by their own people for eating rice cooked by their mistresses. Divorce is easily obtained, and divorced wives may always marry again.

The Bauris are addicted to strong drink, and, with few exceptions, are indifferent to the nice scruples regarding food which have so important a bearing on the status of the average Hindus; for they eat beef, pork, fowls, all kinds of fish, and rats. Nevertheless they pride themselves on not eating snakes and lizards; and it may be that this is connected in some way with the worship of the snake-goddess Manasā, who is supposed to preserve her worshippers from snake-bite.

Bāgdis. The Bāgdis are a caste of non-Aryan origin, who account for their genesis by a number of legends. One of these is to the effect that they originally came from Cooch Behar and were the offspring of Siva and Pārvatī. Bāgdis practise both infant and adult marriage indifferently. In the case of girls who are not married in infancy, sexual license before marriage is virtually tolerated, it being understood that if a girl becomes pregnant, she will find some one to marry her. Like the Bauris, the Bāgdis admit members of any higher caste into their circle, and the process of initiation is like that already described in the case of the Bauris, except that a man admitted into the Dulia sub-caste has to take the palanquin or *duli* on his shoulder as a sign of his acceptance of their hereditary occupation. Most of the Bāgdis are to some extent engaged in agriculture, usually as *korfā* or under-raiyats, and comparatively few have attained the more respectable position of occupancy tenants. Large numbers work as landless day labourers, paid in cash or kind, or as nomadic cultivators, tilling other men's lands on the *bhāg-jot* system, under which they are remunerated by a share of the produce. Their social rank is very low, and they are usually classed with Bauris and Bhuiyas as dwellers on the outskirts of Hinduism. Some Bāgdis eat beef and pork, and most indulge freely in flesh of other kinds, and are greatly addicted to drink. Tentulia Bāgdis, however, will not eat beef, and many members of this sub-caste have become Vaishnāvas and abstain from all sorts of flesh. A very full account of both Bāgdis and Bauris may be found in the Gazetteer of the Bānkurā district.

SOCIAL CONDITIONS.

A hundred years ago the undulating rocky country to the west was a vast wilderness, sparsely inhabited by savage and aboriginal tribes, whose constant inroads upon the settled country to the east were with difficulty kept in check by lines of forts along the Ajay and Dāmodar rivers. This country is now one of the busiest industrial tracts in India. The discovery of coal and iron, and the consequent rapid development of the factories at Rānīganj, Barakar, Andāl and Durgapur, and of the great railway centre at Asansol have called into existence an entirely new set of conditions, and the interdependence between capital and labour is here as fully established as in any of the manufacturing or mining centres of Europe. The largest land-owner in the Asansol subdivision at present is the Bengal Coal Company, and the great mass of the population depend for their livelihood on the collieries and factories which are dotted over the country.

In the eastern or deltaic portion of the district social conditions have altered little of recent years. The railway has replaced the rivers as the great thoroughfare for trade, and the prosperity of such towns as Kātwa and Kālna, which were formerly regarded as the ports of the district, has declined greatly in consequence. The population is still almost entirely agricultural. The district has always been regarded as one of the most fertile and prosperous in Bengal, and, although it suffered severely from the terrible epidemic of fever between 1863 and 1873 and the famine of 1866, the recovery has been rapid and complete. The wealth of the district centres in the Mahārājā of Burdwān, who is the proprietor of the greater portion of the land and who also owns extensive estates in other parts of Bengal. There are no other great land-owners, and the under-tenure-holders such as *patnīdārs* and *darpatnīdārs*, who hold their lands under a perpetual lease and without liability to enhancement of rent, are as a rule far wealthier than the superior landlords.

Village life.

An excellent description of a typical Burdwān village may be found in "Bengal Peasant Life"* by the Revd. Lal Behari Day.

"Kanchanpur is a large and prosperous village. There is a considerable Brāhman population, the great majority of whom are of the Srotriya order. The Kayasthas, or the writer caste, are comparatively few in number. Ugra-Kshatriyas, or Aguris, as they are called in common parlance, who are all engaged in agricultural pursuits, though less numerous than the Sadgopas, are an influential class in the village; while there is the usual complement of the medical caste, of blacksmiths, barbers, weavers, spice-sellers, oilmen, bāgdis, domes, hādis and the rest.

"Kanchanpur, like most villages in Bengal, has four divisions agreeably to the four cardinal points of the compass—the northern, the southern, the eastern and the western. The village lies north and south, and the northern and southern divisions are much larger than the eastern and western. A large street runs north and south, straight as the crow flies, on which abut smaller streets and lanes from the eastern and western divisions. The bulk of the houses are mud cottages thatched with the straw of paddy, though there is a considerable number of brick houses, owned, for the most part, by the Kayasthas and the banker caste. The principal street is lined on both sides by ranges of houses, either of brick or of mud, each having a compound, with at least a tree or two, such as the plum, mango, guava, lime or papaya, and the invariable plantain. Outside the village, the main street is extended nearly a quarter of a mile at each end, with rows on either side of the magnificent *asvatha*, the *ficus religiosa* of botanists. In the centre of the village are two temples of Siva, facing each other; one of them has a large colonnade, or rather polystyle, as there are no less than four rows of columns; and the intervening space between the two temples is planted with the *asvatha*. There are other temples of Siva in other parts of the

* Macmillan & Co., London, 1902.

village, but there is nothing about them worthy of remark. In the central part of each of the four divisions of the village there is a *vakula* tree, the foot of which is built round with solid masonry, raised three or four feet above the ground, in the form of a circle, in the centre of which stands the graceful trunk. As the diameter of this circle is seldom less than twelve feet, a good number of people can easily sit on it, and you meet there, of an afternoon, the gentry of the village, squatting on mats or carpets, engaged in discussing village politics, or in playing at cards, dice or the royal game of chess.

There are not more than half-a-dozen shops in the village in these are sold rice, salt, mustard-oil, tobacco and other necessaries of Bengali life. The villagers, however, are supplied with vegetables, clothes, cutlery, spices and a thousand knick knacks, twice a week, from a *hât*, or fair, which is held on Tuesdays and Saturdays, on a plain on the south-western side."

From the same authority is taken the following description of the ordinary well-to-do peasant's house:—

"You enter Badan's house with your face to the east, through a small door of mango wood on the street, and you go at once to the *uthân*, or open yard, which is indispensable to the house of every peasant in the country. On the west side of the yard stands the *bara ghar*, or the big hut. Its walls, which are of mud, are of great thickness and the thatch, which is of the straw of paddy, is more than a cubit deep. The hut is about sixteen cubits long and twelve cubits broad, including the verandah, which faces the yard, and which is supported by props of palmyra. It is divided into two compartments of unequal size, the bigger one being Badan's sleeping-room, and the smaller one being the store-room of the family, containing a number of *handis*, or earthen vessels, filled with provisions. The verandah is the parlour or the drawing-room of the family. Their friends and acquaintances sit on mats. In Badan's sleeping-room are kept the brass vessels of the house and other valuables. There is no *khat* or bedstead in it, for Badan sleeps on the mud floor, a mat and a quilt stuffed with cotton interposing between his body and mother earth. There is not much light in the room, for the thatch of the verandah prevents its admission, while there is but one small window high up on the wall towards the street. I need scarcely add that there is no furniture in the room—no table, no chairs, no stools, no almirah, no wardrobe, no benches; there is only in one corner a solitary wooden box.

"On the south side of the yard is a smaller hut which is used as a lumber-room, or rather as a tool-room, for keeping the implements of husbandry. In the verandah of this little hut is placed the *dhenki*, or the rice-husking pedal. From this circumstance the little hut is called *dhenkisālā* (pedal-house), or more familiarly *dhenskal*.

"In the south-east corner of the yard is another living hut the verandah of which serves the purpose of a kitchen. From this latter circumstance it is called *pāksālā* (cooking-house), but Badan and his family always called it by the more familiar name of *rannaghar*. The only other hut on the premises is the cow-house, called *gosālā*, or more familiarly *goāl*. Several large earthen tubs, called *nānds*, which serve the purposes of troughs, are put on the floor, half buried in small mounds of earth, near which are stuck in the ground tether-posts of bamboo. In one corner is a sort of fire-place, where every night a fire, or rather smoke, of cow-dung cakes is made, chiefly for the purpose of saving the bovine inmates from the bite of mosquitoes and fleas. The eastern side of the premises opens on a tank which supplies the family of Badan, as it does other families in the neighbourhood, with water, not, indeed, for drinking, but for every other purpose; the drinking water being obtained from one of the big tanks which are situated on the outskirts of the village.

"About the middle of the *uthan*, or yard, and near the cow-house, is the granary of paddy, called *gola* in other parts of the country, but in the Burdwān district invariably called *marai*. It is cylindrical in shape, made entirely of ropes of twisted straw, with a circular thatch on the top. It contains a quantity of paddy sufficient for the consumption of the family from one harvest to another. Not far from the granary is the *palui*, or straw stack, which is an immense pile of paddy-straw kept in the open air, to serve as fodder for cows and oxen for a whole year.

"Behind the kitchen, and near the tank, is the *sarkuda*, or the dust-heap of the family, which is a large hole, not very deep, into which the sweepings of the yard, the ashes of the kitchen, the refuse of the cow-house, and all sorts of vegetable matter, are thrown. This dust-heap, though somewhat hurtful in a sanitary point of view, is essentially necessary to our raiyat, as it supplies him with manure for his fields."

Village officials. The principal village official met with in the district is the *māl gumāshta*, a revenue officer appointed by the zamīndār to collect rents and grant receipts. He is usually paid by a money salary and is sometimes assisted by a *faujdāri gumāshta* whose duty it is to look after any case in which the landlord's interests are involved. The *mandal*, sometimes called *mukhya*, is the hereditary headman of the village. Formerly the *mandal* was a person of great importance, and in old Sanskrit writings he is spoken of as the village king, but the respect now shown to him is a mere shadow of what it formerly was. His authority, however, is still recognized by offerings of betel and sweetmeats at pujās, and by the present of a piece of cloth from the zamīndār at the *punya*, or first rent-day of the year. Petty local disputes are decided by the *mandal*, and intercourse with the police is carried on through him. He may belong to any caste; and he is often a very illiterate man. In some large villages there exist *chaudhries* whose business is to decide questions of price-currents, fix rates for cart-hire, etc., in return for which they receive an allowance from the shopkeepers; formerly both *mandals* and *chaudhries* received fees from the zamīndār.

Under the old municipal system of the Hindus a large number of watchmen were employed by each village for the protection of the persons and property of the community. Village *simāndārs* and *halshands* were charged with the protection of the village crops and boundaries; *phāridārs* and *piyādās*, with the watch and guard of roads; *ghātwāls*, with the care of roads and passes in the hills. All these officials were remunerated by grants of rent-free lands. These lands have now been resumed and the village watch has been transformed into a subordinate rural police.

The other conspicuous personages in village life are: The *purohit*, or priest, who is usually paid by gifts of money, called *dakshina*, for each ceremony performed by him, and also by a portion of the offerings made to the idols; the *acharjya*, or fortune-teller, who prepares horoscopes, and predicts the destiny of infants according to the planets under whose influence they were born; the *napit*, or barber, who also performs certain ceremonies at births, marriages, etc., and the *mahājan*, or village usurer and grain merchant. The *kamār*, or blacksmith; the *chhutār*, or carpenter; and the *māli*, or gardener, who prepares garlands for festivals, are all generally paid in money by the job, according to the services rendered by them. The *dhobi*, or village washerman, is remunerated either in money or in kind. All these persons, however, who in the old Hindu village had lands assigned for their maintenance by the community, ceased to exist as village officials long ago, and are now merely artisans or servants, carrying on their caste occupations and remunerated by those who employ them.

The ordinary food of all classes of the people consists principally of rice, pulses (*dāl*), fish, milk and vegetables, and the general practice is to take two meals—one in the day between Food.

10 A.M. and 12 noon and the other at night between 8 and 9 P.M. Sweetmeats are very largely consumed by the higher and middle classes, and the confectioners of Burdwān and Mānkur are famous for their '*olā*', '*khājā*' and '*kadmā*.' Among the peasantry, however, the only sweetmeat consumed, besides treacle in its raw unmanufactured state, is '*mudki*,' *i.e.*, parched and husked paddy dipped in treacle and on high days and holidays '*pātāli*'.

Clothing.

The ordinary clothing of a gentleman appearing at a social gathering in the cold weather consists of a *dhuti*, or waistcloth of cotton, a shirt and coat, a shawl and a pair of stockings and shoes. In other seasons of the year a *dhuti*, shirt or coat, a *chādar* and shoes are worn. When appearing at office, the clothing consists of pantaloons, a shirt, a *chapkān*, a *chādar*, and a pair of stockings and shoes; persons of somewhat higher position use *chogās*, or loose overcoats, instead of *chādars*. The ordinary clothing of a man of the middle classes consists of a *dhuti*, *chādar* and a pair of shoes or slippers; shirts and coats are also occasionally used. A cultivator wears merely a coarse *dhuti* and a scarf (*gāmchā*) thrown over the shoulders or wrapped around the waist. Men of the lower classes have a coarse *dhuti* only. In the cold weather shawls and various wrappers are used, such as the *banāts* made of serge or broadcloth, the *dhusa* and *bālāposh* made of cotton and cloth, the *garbhasuti* woven with *tasar* and cotton thread, and the *gilāp* or *pāchkuri*, which is a double *chādar* made of coarse cloth. The dress of the women generally consists of a *sāri* only, but in rich families the use of bodices and wrappers in the winter has been introduced. As a rule, females, with the exception of prostitutes, do not use shoes, shawls, or other garments used by the males.

Amusements.

The amusements of the people consist chiefly of the *jātra*, a theatrical entertainment given in the open air, *baithaki* songs, *i.e.*, songs in the *baithak* or general sitting room, and dancing. In all of these both vocal and instrumental music is employed. Men of all classes attend *jātras*, but the mass of the people amuse themselves with *Harisankīrtan*, in which they sing and dance in the name of *Hari* (God). Sometimes *Harisankīrtan* continues without intermission for several days and nights, and is called, according to its duration, *ahorātra* (one day and night), *chabbisprahar* (three days and nights), *pancharātra* (five days and nights) and *nabarātra* (nine days and nights). The people of the *Rārh desh* are famous *jātra* performers, and almost every village has its theatrical society.

The population is a mixed one, including pure Hindu castes of Aryan descent, semi-aboriginals recently admitted in the pale of Hinduism, and pure aboriginal tribes. The following account of the general conditions prevailing is quoted from an article by Mr. R. C. Dutt "The Aboriginal Element in the Population of Bengal" (*Calcutta Review*, 1882) which is especially applicable to Burdwān :—" Living in the same district, and often in the same village, the Hindu and the semi-Hinduized aboriginal nevertheless present differences in their habits and ways of living which cannot but strike even the most careless observer. Belief in a highly developed religion and an elaborate superstition has made the Hindu even of the lower castes timid and contemplative; a higher civilization has made him calculating, thoughtful and frugal, and a long training in the arts of peace has made him regular in his habits, industrious in his toil, peaceful in his disposition. The semi-aboriginal, on the other hand, presents us with a striking contrast in character in all these respects. He is of an excitable disposition and seeks for strong excitement and pleasures; he is incapable of forethought, and consumes his earnings without a thought for the future; he is incapable of sustained toil, and, therefore, oftener works as a field labourer than as a cultivator. Simple, merry in his disposition, excitable by nature, without forethought or frugality, and given to drunkenness, the semi-aboriginal of Bengal brings to his civilised home many of the virtues and vices of the savage aboriginal life which his forefathers lived. In every village where semi-aboriginals live, a separate portion of the village is reserved for them, and the most careless observer will be struck with the difference between neatness and tidiness, the well-swept, well-washed and well-thatched huts of the Hindu neighbourhood, and the miserable, dirty, ill-thatched huts of the Bauri *Pārā* or the Hāri *Pārā*. If a cow or a pig dies in the village, it is flayed, and the meat carried home by the Muchis or Bauris, while the Hindus turn aside their face and stop their nose in disgust when passing near such scenes. If there is an outstill in the village, it is in the Bāgdi *Pārā* or in the Bauri *Pārā*; it is thronged by people of these castes, who spend their miserable earnings here, regardless of their ill-thatched huts and their ill-fed children.

General Conditions.

" The mass of the Hindu population are dead against drink and drunkenness; their thrift and habitual forethought, their naturally sober and contemplative turn of mind, as well as their religious feelings, keep them quite safe from contracting intemperate habits. A few educated young men and a larger number of the upper classes may be addicted to drink, but the mass of working classes, the frugal and calculating shop-keeper, the patient and hard-working Sadgop or Goālā, the humble and laborious Kaibartta, all keep away from drink. The boisterous merriment that is caused by drunkenness is foreign to their quiet, sober nature, and if a very few of them drink, they drink quietly at home before they retire at night. Far different is the case with the semi-Hinduized aborigines. Barbarians hanker after strong excitements and boisterous joys, and nowhere is drunkenness so universal as among barbarians. The Bauris, the Bāgdis, the Muchis have enough of their old nature in them to feel a craving for drink, and the outstill system with the cheapening of spirits has been a boon to them. When spirit was dear, they made themselves merry over their *pachwāi*; and now that spirit is cheaper, they take to it naturally in preference to *pachwāi*. Of the numerous outstills and *pachwāi* shops in Burdwān and Bānkurā that we have visited, we have not seen one which did not mainly depend for its revenue on semi-aboriginal consumers. We never saw one single Hindu among the crowds of people assembled in liquor or *pachwāi* shops; when the Hindu does drink, he sends for the drink and consumes it at home.

"The distinction between the Hindus and the semi-Hinduized aborigines is no less marked in the position of their women, nowhere, except in towns, are Hindu women kept in that absolute seclusion which Musalmān women delight in. In villages the wives and daughters of the most respectable and high caste Hindus walk with perfect freedom from house to house, or to the tank or river-side for their ablutions. Respectable women go veiled, while those of the lower classes go without veil, or only half veiled. No respectable woman will speak to, or can be accosted by a stanger, while even among the lower class Hindu women, except when verging on old age, few will often speak to strangers. Those restrictions entirely disappear in the case of the semi-Hinduized aborigines. Their women have the perfect freedom of women in Europe. Young wives, as well as elderly widows walk without the apology of a veil through the streets or the village bāzār: they will talk to any one when necessary; and being naturally of merry, lively dispositions, they chat and laugh gaily as they pass through the most crowded streets. The young Tānti or Chhutār woman, the Kumhār or the Kāmār's wife, will often stand aside when a stranger is passing by the same road, but custom imposes no such rule of modesty on the women of the Bauris. But, if the semi-aboriginal women enjoy the perfect freedom of European women, they have often to pay dear for their liberty. Household work is the lot of Hindu women, but the semi-aboriginal women must do out-door work also. Wives as well as widows, mothers and daughters, are all expected to work in the field, or at the village tank or road, and so eke out the miserable incomes of their husbands, sons or fathers. When a road is constructed by Government, or a tank excavated by a village *zamindar*, Bauri men and women work together, the men using the spades and the women carrying the earth in baskets. Wives often carry things for sale to the village market, while husbands work in the fields. For the rest, the lot of these semi-aboriginal women is not a hard one, to judge from their healthy appearance and their merry faces, but when the husbands get drunk, as they do as often as they can, the wives, we fancy, have a bad time of it, and wife-beating is very much worse among the semi-aboriginal castes than among Hindus.

"In their social and religious ceremonies the semi-Hinduized aborigines are every day being drawn closer to Hinduism. The more respectable and advanced among them may indeed be said to have adopted Hinduism in all its main features, while even the most backward castes have adopted some Hindu customs."

CHAPTER IV.

PUBLIC HEALTH.

CLIMATE. THE conditions which prevail in the eastern and western halves of the district differ completely. The western half beyond Galsi where the land begins to rise is very dry, and the soil which is here composed of laterite is dry and porous. This half of the district therefore suffers little from malarial fever. But in the eastern half, which is a part of the great Gangetic delta, and which lies only a few feet above sea-level, malarial fever is very prevalent especially on the banks of the great rivers such as the Dāmodar, the Ajay, the Kharī and the Bhāgīrathi. Floods are common in these rivers during the rainy season, and the flood water backing up the numerous creeks and drainage channels overflows the surrounding country and renders large tracts water-logged and unhealthy. The thānas most liable to flood are Manteswar, Satgāchia, Purbashthāli, and Raina, which lies to the south of the Dāmodar. The land here is low-lying and badly drained, and such drainage as there is, is much obstructed by the dams or weirs constructed across the rivers and drainage channels in the interior for purposes of irrigation.

Any excess of rainfall is sufficient to flood the smaller rivers whose channels are too small and have too slight a slope to carry off much water. But such floods are sometimes beneficial. In August 1909, when 13 inches of rain fell in 36 hours, the Bānkā overflowed its banks and flooded the surrounding country. The flood water, which was held up by the Grand Trunk Road on the west and the Kātwa Road on the east, took several days to flow off, and a great part of the town of Burdwān itself was under water for several days. The vital statistics, however, show that this flood, serious and extensive as it was, had no injurious effect on the health of the city, and 1909 was one of the most healthy years Burdwān has ever experienced. The explanation is that the excessive rainfall scoured out the insanitary tanks, which abound in the town, and drowned the mosquito larvæ. The following meteorological statistics for Burdwān town will give a fair idea of the climate in the eastern portion of the district.

The average rainfall (1861–1909) is 59·31 inches, but in 1909 the rainfall was 79·85 inches which was distributed as follows:—

	Inches.
January	0·06
February	0·09
March	Nil
April	9·92
May	6·60
June	10·63
July	6·20
August	33·98
September	9·89
October	1·73
November	0·07
December	0·68
Total	79·85

The mean annual temperature is 79·9. And in 1909 the following temperatures were recorded in Burdwān :—

	Mean of Maximum.	Mean of Minimum.	Mean daily range.	Mean.
January ...	82·1	57·4	24·7	69·8
February ..	85·5	59·3	26·2	72·4
March ...	99·0	67·8	31·2	83·4
April ..	93·7	73·0	20·7	83·4
May ...	97·7	79·9	19·8	87·8
June ...	90·6	79·0	11·6	84·8
July ...	89·6	79·0	10·6	84·3
August ...	88·5	79·9	10·6	83·2
September ...	89 8	78·9	10·9	84·4
October ...	88·8	74·7	14·1	81·8
November ...	85 8	65·7	20·1	75·8
December ...	78·5	57·7	20·8	68·1
Mean of year ...	89·1	70·7	18·4	79·9

A maximum temperature of 106·4 was recorded on the 11th May 1909, and a minimum temperature of 49·8 on the 3rd February of that year.

VITAL STATISTICS.

The duty of reporting deaths was imposed on the village chaukidars in 1869, and in 1876 they were ordered to report births as well. The system proved a failure as the returns obtained were so incomplete and inaccurate as to be practically useless, and, except in towns, deaths alone were reported until 1892, when the present system of collecting vital statistics was introduced. Under the present orders deaths and births are reported by the chaukidars to the police on chaukidari parade days, and the police submit monthly returns to the Civil Surgeon who consolidates the statistics for the whole district. As in every other district where this system is in vogue, little or no reliance can be put on the statistics as regards the cause of death. The chaukidars are mostly illiterate and uneducated, and they can hardly be expected to possess the amount of medical knowledge required to distinguish one disease from another. To them fever is a comprehensive term, and is made to include practically everything with febrile symptoms, from malaria or typhoid to pneumonia. Experiments were recently made in selected circles in the Burdwān district under the supervision of the Sanitary Commissioner to the Government of India in order to check the accuracy of the chaukidars' reports. In the Galsi thāna 618 births and 919 deaths during six months as reported by chaukidars were inquired into by Assistant Surgeons, who visited the houses where these were reported to have taken place immediately on the reports being received at the thānas. Out of these 919 deaths it was found that 508 cases were wrongly diagnosed, *i.e.*, 55·3 per cent. In another experiment 2,616 deaths were recorded in the thāna registers out of which 1,056 cases were wrongly reported. In spite of this defect, however, the vital statistics may be regarded as sufficiently accurate for the purpose of calculating the growth of the population.

"BURDWAN" FEVER.

Before 1862 the district was noted for its healthiness, and the town of Burdwān particularly was regarded as a sanitarium. In fact it was customary for persons suffering from chronic malarial fever to come to Burdwān where cures from the disease were common. But in 1862 the terrible epidemic fever, which for several years had ravaged the neighbouring districts of Jessore, Nadiā and Hooghly, crossed the border of Burdwān appearing first in the Kālna subdivision. Thence it spread gradually but steadily over the district, following the main lines of communication, until it was fairly established in all the eastern thānas. The towns of Burdwān, Kātwa and Kālna suffered severely, and throughout the district the mortality was enormous. Dr. French, who made a special enquiry into the outbreak, estimated the total mortality at about one-third of the population in the tracts attacked by the epidemic. The instances given by him show that this was no exaggeration. In 1869 the population of the town of Burdwān was estimated at 46,000. Three years afterwards the population had fallen to 32,687, a decrease of over 30 per cent. In seventeen villages of the Kātwa subdivision, containing an estimated population of 14,982 upon the appearance of the epidemic, no less than 6,243 persons, or 41·7 per cent. of the population, died of fever in these disastrous years, while the figures for fifty villages in the Kātwa subdivision showed a similar mortality. Still more significant proof of the enormous mortality is to be found in the fact that the population was in 1872 not much in excess of the estimate formed by Mr. Bayley, nearly sixty years before. In the census report for 1881 it was estimated that during the twelve years from 1862-1874 the epidemic had carried off not less than three-quarters of a million of persons. The fever was either intermittent or remittent and of a very malignant type, relapses being the almost invariable rule when the patient survived the attacks. It recurred every autumn and lasted throughout the winter up to the close of the year 1875. It is reported that since that date no fever exactly similar to this fatal type has been known to occur. No special cause for the outbreak has ever been discovered. By some it was supposed to result from the interference of the natural drainage of the country by river and railway embankments, by changes in the course of the large rivers, and by the silting and drying up of the channels of the smaller streams. Others regarded the drinking water as the cause of the disease. Neither theory has ever been proved. But as a rule it was the overcrowded, low-lying, badly drained, filthy village that suffered most severely, while the villages situated on higher ground with good natural drainage and scanty population escaped. Relief was given by Government on a large scale and no expense was spared in order to check the ravages of the epidemic as far as possible. In spite of all efforts, however, it spread slowly across the district, travelling always westwards, until on reaching the laterite soil of the Asansol uplands it was finally checked and eventually died out altogether. On the 31st March 1876 Government operations for the relief of the fever were brought to a close, as the improved health of the district no longer required such measures. Between August 1871 and that date nearly four million persons were treated in the local dispensaries: the expenditure of quinine alone amounted to 3,212 lbs. valued at Rs. 16,245; and the total cost of European medicines during the four and a half years was Rs. 2,45,071. The expenditure on account of the extra establishment of medical officers during the same period was Rs. 2,82,559. Thus the total public expenditure on fever relief amounted to nearly 5½ lakhs of rupees. The after-effects of the epidemic continued to be felt for two decades after the real Burdwān fever had disappeared. The census of 1881 showed that the population was decreasing, and during the next ten years it remained practically stationary. The district has since made a rapid recovery, and in 1901 the population exceeded by some 30,000 persons the number returned in 1872. If, however, the vital statistics for the past ten years are to be trusted, they seem to show that at present the population is not increasing, the average birth-rate for the last ten years being only 32·15 as compared with a death-rate of 34·15. During these years the highest birth-rate recorded was 37·63 in 1904, and the highest death-rate 44·62 in 1908. In 1909 the birth- and death-rates were 31·89 and 25·94, respectively.

PRINCIPAL DISEASES.

The following account of the diseases prevalent in the district has been contributed by Captain N. W. Mackworth, I.M.S., the Civil Surgeon. There are so many varieties of fever prevalent in the district, and the knowledge of their nature is often so partial that the classification attempted below cannot pretend to be either complete or altogether scientific:—

Fevers.

1. Intermittent fever—
   (a) quotidian; (c) quartan;
   (b) tertian; (d) double quotidian.
2. Remittent fever—
   (a) bilious remittent; (b) typho-malarial.
3. Pernicious malarial fever.
4. Unclassified fever.
5. Pernicious cachectic fever.
6. Typhoid fever.
7. Kala azar.

Intermittent fever is the prevailing disease. It is very generally associated with the enlargement of the spleen, and not infrequently with that of the liver also. The tertian variety is many times less common than the quotidian, while the double quotidian and quartān types are rare. The double quotidian variety may occur where quinine has failed to eradicate the poison in a patient who has suffered from remittent fever which afterwards becomes intermittent.

Bilious remittent fever is a true malarial fever, and is associated with gastro-hepatic complications, with slight jaundice, and enlargement of the spleen. If unchecked before the close of the second week, typhoid symptoms appear, and death may result. Typho-malarial fever is due to the combined action of malaria and some septic poison. There is tenderness in the right iliac fossa, but no eruption; both liver and spleen undergo enlargement, and jaundice is of frequent occurrence; the motions are dark and offensive. During the second week typhoid symptoms may appear, with dry furred tongue frequent, fluttering pulse, and delirium. Improvement may set in after the fourteenth day, or death from coma may take place. This fever as a rule yields to quinine. Pernicious malarial fever is a malignant and destructive fever characterized by dangerous local mischief in important organs. It may be intermittent or remittent. It may assume a comatose, delirious, or algid form, and terminate fatally in from one to three days. Quinine is less efficacious here. In addition to the above types of malarial fever may be added a *choleraic variety* of the disease which may very readily be mistaken for Asiatic cholera, since the fever is accompanied by watery stools, but these are not altogether devoid of bile. Several of these cases occurred in Burdwan in September of 1909 when there was no cholera about. The infection was confirmed microscopically. Unclassified fever is a fever attended with slight evening rise of temperature, general uneasiness and a burning sensation in the eyes, palms of the hands and soles of the feet. It does not yield to quinine. Pernicious cachectic fever generally assumes an intermittent type, but attacks of a remittent type may supervene. It generally terminates fatally after a prolonged course, the immediate cause of death being anæmia with dropsy and diarrhœa, dysentery or cancrum oris. Both liver and spleen are enlarged, but towards the close of the disease the enlargements often tend to disappear. A case of this type has been known to last for over a year in which quinine had no specific action, even in very large doses.

Typhoid fever is not at all an uncommon disease in Burdwān much more common than was hitherto supposed. Several cases were observed throughout their course during 1909 and the diagnosis confirmed bacteriologically. The disease would seem to manifest itself in a more severe form than that seen in England. Lysis is much delayed. There is more ulceration of the bowel, and hæmorrhage from the bowel is common. A large proportion of the cases prove fatal. Typhoid is most often confused with malaria and dysentery, but very often there is a mixed infection of typhoid and malaria present. The municipal water-supply of the town is free from typhoid contamination, but it is not difficult to trace Typhoid Fever.

the source of infection. Many of the inhabitants of the city make use of the tank water for drinking purposes, and great numbers use the water for washing their teeth and mouths whilst bathing.

Kala Azar.

Two cases of Kala Azar were identified in the Sadar hospital recently, but it was thought inadvisable to continue as spleen puncture is not a popular operation. These cases however are not common.

Seasonal incidence of fevers

The season in which fevers are most prevalent begins after the close of the rains and ends about the middle of December. Quotidian fever occurs in every season; the tertian variety is most generally met with in the spring. Remittent fever is most prevalent during and immediately after the rains. The marginal statement shows the number of deaths, and the death-rate per mille, from fevers in the towns and rural areas of Burdwān for the past ten years.

YEAR.	Number of deaths.	Deaths per 1,000 of total population.
1900 ...	32,072	23·04
1901 ...	33,662	21·96
1902 ...	28,718	18·74
1903 ...	36,953	24·11
1904 ...	30,425	19·85
1905 ...	38,847	25·35
1906 ...	39,496	25·77
1907 ...	45,815	29·89
1908 ...	42,816	27·93
1909 ...	28,210	18·41

Cholera.

Cholera did not prevail in epidemic form in the district till the year 1900. At present when it occurs, it almost invariably does so in epidemic form. Drinking of polluted tank water is the primary cause of cholera. In the coal-fields in the Asansol district the coolies are rarely provided with latrines. Excrementaceous matter becomes dessicated and gets blown into the adjacent tanks, and thus many bowel-complaints are given origin to. The native doctors, who were during 1909 appointed on special cholera duty, advanced the following opinions as to the causes regulating the outbreaks of the disease: "Scarcity of food, unsuitability of food such as raw Indian corn cobs, scarcity of water. The water-supplies of the villages visited were nearly all contaminated. From want of water the people used to wash their clothes saturated with urine and stools of cholera patients in the last remaining drop of tank water."

The total mortality in the district from this cause from 1904 to 1909 was—

1904	2,560
1905	4,301
1906	2,814
1907	5,933
1908	14,268
1909	1,399

A severe epidemic of cholera broke out in 1907 and continued till June 1908. From July 1907 to June 1908 it carried away 16,446 people, or 10·73 per thousand of population. The following thānas suffered most:—Manteswar, Rāniganj Purbasthali, Kātwa, Asansol, Mangalkot, Ketugrām, and Sāhebganj. The high death-rate of 20 per thousand from cholera alone took place in Manteswar in 1908. This was said to be due to the contamination of the river water by the cholera corpses which were thrown into it. The epidemic ceased at the end of June 1908.

Prior to the year 1900 small-pox did not show itself in epidemic form in this district. Since that date, however, it has become much more prevalent, and generally begins in the month of February and continues till July. The average annual mortality from small-pox for the past five years is 982 or 0·64 per thousand of the population. Small-pox.

Only one or two cases of plague have occurred in this district recently. These cases were for the most part imported from Calcutta. A small epidemic, however, broke out in Kātwa in 1906 and some 90 deaths occurred, but there was no recrudescence in the following year. Plague.

On an average 165 deaths are reported annually as due to the wounds caused by animals. No case of snake-bite was treated in the dispensaries of the district during 1909 and although a number of Brunton's permanganate of potash lancets have been distributed, no case in which one of those instruments has been used has as yet been reported. Snake-bite cases are for the most part treated by *sadhus* and quacks who allege that they can cure their patients by certain nostrums; amongst other remedies they use small pebbles which look like polished pieces of larva, which have a certain amount of power of absorption. Snake-bite.

Amongst the other common diseases which are prevalent may be noted the following:—Dysentery and diarrhœa, syphilis, gonorrhœa, leprosy and cataract.

In the year 1892 the Vaccination department came under the control of the Civil Surgeon. Prior to this it was controlled by the Superintendent of Vaccination, Metropolitan Circle. Vaccination is now carried out by means of the licensed agency system, 32 licensed vaccinators being generally engaged for the rural areas, who work during the vaccination season from the 1st October to the 31st March, and are paid two annas per head for successful operations. In municipal areas paid vaccinators are entertained, two being employed in the VACCINATION.

Burdwān Municipality, one in each of the Asansol, Rānīganj and Kālna Municipalities, and one for the Kātwa and Dāinhāt Municipalities. In the municipalities there are fixed stations where vaccination is performed free. In Burdwān town there are six such stations, which the two vaccinators attend twice weekly, and in Asansol there are two stations at which the vaccinator is present on alternate days. Vaccination is compulsory in towns, but not in rural areas. The people in general appreciate vaccination, but it is not very popular amongst the lower class Muhammadans and Aguris, who strongly object to having themselves and their children vaccinated. Only the lanoline lymph, which is supplied by the Central Animal Vaccination Depôt, Calcutta, is used in this district; 54,395 vaccinations are performed annually, of which 50,713 are primary and 3,698 revaccinations. Each licensed vaccinator performs on an average 1,575 operations, while 711 are performed by each paid agent entertained by the municipalities. The ratio of successful operations is 97·48 per cent., and the rate of successful vaccinations per thousand of the population is 7·26, the average cost of each successful case being 11½ pies. The degree of protection afforded to infants in the rural areas of this district is 527·12. The above figures are the averages of five years from 1904-05 to 1908-09.

MEDICAL INSTITUTIONS. In the towns of Burdwān, Kātwa, Rānīganj and Dāinhāt there are municipal charitable dispensaries. Besides these the District Board maintains ten dispensaries. All these are under Government supervision but there are also dispensaries at Kanchannagar and Chakdighi which are maintained by private individuals. Other private dispensaries are the Burdwān Rāj hospital, the Kālna Rāj hospital the hospital maintained by the United Free Church of Scotland Medical Mission at Kālna, and the Brahmomoye Debi Charitable dispensary at Bokra in Raina thāna. The East Indian Railway Company have their own dispensaries at Burdwān, Asansol, Ondal and Sītārāmpur. The Dinanath Das Charitable dispensary at Kanchannagar was established by Babu Dinanath Das, a medical practitioner and contractor who, by a deed of trust, made over to a Managing Committee Government securities of the nominal value of Rs. 50,000, bearing interest at 3½ per cent., for the maintenance of the institution and a free Middle English school. The dispensary and the school are situated in a fine building at Kanchannagar. In the Burdwān, Kātwa, Rānīganj and Chakdighi dispensaries both indoor and outdoor patients are treated. In these four dispensaries there are 32 beds for females and 77 for males. The figures in the following table are the averages of three years 1907, 1908 and 1909 :—

No.	Name of the dispensary.	Date of establishment.	Total treated.	Daily average.	Number of operations.
1	Burdwan ...	1837 ...	22,014	180·51	2,047
2	Kātwa ...	1st February 1860	5,481	59·71	190
3	Rānīganj ...	1st January 1867	4,321	47·37	461
4	Dāinhāt ...	1st June 1802 ..	5,502	43·77	268
5	Purbasthali ...	1st August 1896	6,552	51·23	286
6	Kulingrām ...	1st December 1805	4,895	31·62	93
7	Mahta ...	1st June 1802 ...	7,344	92·28	549
8	Meral ...	1st June 1802 ...	7,413	38·38	242
9	Jamna ...	1st April 1806 ...	8,736	61·66	154
10	Adra ...	15th May 1804 ...	10,729	133·26	394
11	Khandaghosh ...	9th September 1804	7,170	64·59	135
12	Mangalkot ...	11th November 1804	6,502	64·66	228
13	Ketugrām ...	1st September 1805	7,034	45·88	291
14	Ausgrām ...	18th September 1805	6,854	47·65	126
15	Chakdighi ...	15th April 1859 ...	8,335	57·01	354
16	Kanchannagar ...	8th July 1906 ...	4,334	46·64	9

A new hospital is at present under construction in Burdwān, the foundation stone of which was laid by Sir Andrew Fraser, Lieutenant-Governor of Bengal, in July 1908. The entire scheme is estimated to cost 2 lakhs, of which the Māhārāj Adhirāj has contributed Rs. 80,000 besides giving a site for the building, while Government has contributed Rs. 80,000. During recent years it has been the custom of the District Board to open temporary fever dispensaries for a few months in the most fever-stricken parts of the district. During the last two years five such dispensaries were opened at Boro Baloon, Bongopalpur, Nādanghāt, Okarsha and Satgāchia. For the relief of the inhabitants of the eastern border of the district a temporary floating dispensary was opened last year. It remained open from the 13th September to the 10th December 1909. The boat touched at thirteen stations—eleven on the Bhāgīrathi and two on the Kharī. The total distance it had to traverse was 78 miles of the Bhāgīrathi and 18 miles of the Kharī river.

There are two Leper Asylums in the district at Rānīganj and Asansol. The Leper Asylum at Rānīganj was founded by Mr. Smith in 1893, and has gradually grown into a large, well-filled and well-organized establishment. There are at present 206 lepers in the Asylum and 19 untainted children of leper parents are in the orphanage. The financial responsibility is borne by the Mission to Lepers in India and the East, the Wesleyan Mission being responsible only for the management and pastoral

Leper Asylums.

care. A native doctor is employed and there is a well-equipped dispensary. Government gives a yearly subsidy, and the Asylum is under the Act and is the Government Asylum for Burdwān. The Mahārājā of Burdwān and Babu Bhagaba Das Marwari have each presented a ward to the Asylum. The accommodation is still deficient and more wards are required. No pressure is brought to bear upon the inmates, all of whom were Hindus on admission, but most have become Christians, and there is a large church for their use. There is also a small Leper Asylum at Asansol which is supported by the Mission to Lepers and which is under the management of the Methodist Episcopal Mission in that town.

CHAPTER V.

AGRICULTURE.

THE following account of the agriculture of the district is condensed from a very complete report by Mr. A. C. Sen.*

RAINFALL.

For successful cultivation, the most important point is the distribution of rainfall and in Burdwān, as in other districts of Bengal, the total amount is a secondary consideration. The distribution suitable for paddy—by far the most important crop of Bengal—may be gathered from the following rural doggerels:—

1.	Yadi barshe āghane, Rājā nāmen māgane.	If it rains in Agrahayan, kings have to beg.
2.	Yadi barshe poushe, tākā hay tushe.	If it rains in Pous, even husk brings money.
3.	Yadi barshe māgher sesh, dhanya rājār punya desh.	If it rains at the end of Magh, blessed is the king's virtuous land.
4.	Yadi barshe fāgune, chinā kāon dwigune.	If it rains in Falgun, the yield of china and kangu is doubled.
5.	Chaitre māthamāthar,	Slight rains in Chaitra.
	Baisākhe jhar pāthar;	Storms and hail in Baishakh are good,
	Jaistye re nā uthe,	In Jaistya the grass should never be allowed to grow;
	Ashāre barshā ba the;	Ashar should be a month of endless rain,
	Karkata chharkata,	Frequent showers of rain are required in Sraban;
	Sinha sukānā,	Bhadra should be a dry month,
	Kanyā kāne kān;	The fields should be brimful of water in Aswin;
	Binābāy tulā barshe,	If there be rain without wind in Kartik,
	Kothā rakhho dhān.	Where shall I keep the paddy?

*Calcutta, 1884, (reprinted 1897).

These verses were probably composed at a time when some of the crops now under cultivation had not been introduced and as regards those crops they require recasting. Rain at the end of Magh for instance would not be welcomed by the potato grower.

IRRIGATION. The great want of the Burdwān district, especially of its western and central parts, is a proper supply of water for irrigation purposes. The rainfall being often deficient in total amount or irregular in distribution, artificial irrigation is necessary for almost all the important crops except pulses and barley. In fact the cultivation of sugarcane, potatoes, onions and other important crops can only be undertaken in places where water is available.

The importance of irrigation was fully understood in ancient times. In no other part of Bengal are so many tanks to be found, but almost without perhaps exception they have been long neglected, and are now overgrown with weeds and filled up with silt. Wells are not numerous and the cultivators have a superstitious dread of irrigating lands with water raised from them.

In the hill tracts of the west the practice of storing up rain-water is well understood, and the whole system of cultivation there may be said to be dependent upon it. Terrace cultivation, wrongly supposed by many to be peculiar to China, is the outcome of attempts to store rain-water. The hillsides are converted into tiers of rice fields, often of the smallest size conceivable, which are embanked along their lower edges. The rain-water in its downward course is thus arrested and, instead of being allowed to pass down the hillside in a torrent, is made to irrigate the fields one after another, each retaining its just share and no more. The cultivators along the banks of the smaller streams have also discovered that at the season when they are apparently quite dry all that is necessary is to make holes in the coarse red sands of which their beds are formed in order to obtain a good supply of pure sweet water.

Water lifts. The implements used in irrigation are simple and inexpensive, but fairly efficient. Water is raised from wells by means of buckets or earthen pots with a rope which is occasionally put round a pulley on a wooden bar fixed on supports. For irrigating from fields, tanks or shallow depressions a *donga* is used to raise the water. This is a canoe-shaped trough of which the free end is attached by a rope to a long lever fixed in an upright above the irrigation channel with a counterpoise. The lever is depressed by the labourer and the free end of the trough dipped into the water. On its release the lever rises pulling up the trough, the contents of which are poured into the irrigation channel. *Dongas* are now generally made of iron. Water can be raised in this way two or three feet, and if a further lift is required, either the basket (*sini*) which is worked by two men is used, or more than one stage is constructed. This adds considerably to the cost of irrigation.

The question of improving the canal system of the district was fully discussed by the Irrigation Commission. There is only one protective irrigation work, the Eden Canal, an irrigation channel 22 miles in length from Kānchannagar to Jamālpur, which was constructed in 1881 with the object of flushing the old river beds, whose stagnant and insanitary condition was believed to be largely responsible for the epidemic of malarial fever. Though the canal was constructed primarily for sanitary purposes it has been largely used for irrigation, and in 1904 the Collector reported that some 20,000 acres of land were irrigated from it. At present about 33 square miles in the Burdwān and Jamālpur thānas and the Memāri outpost are irrigated from this canal and its distributaries. The finding of the Irrigation Commission on the subject of the Eden canal is as follows:— Canals.

"That although they were assured in evidence that there was a great demand for irrigation on the Eden Canal, there was no evidence to show that the irrigators would be willing to pay more for the use of the water than they now do, that is, about a rupee per acre. We are of opinion that the irrigation system of the Eden Canal can never be satisfactory until there is a weir across the river at its head sluices. But this canal is not required for protection against famine, and until the irrigators are ready to pay for the water rate sufficient to ensure a fair return on the capital cost we cannot recommend Government to incur this outlay." The conclusion thus reached is that the district does not require irrigation works as a protection against famine. The cost of the weir across the Damodar, to which the Commission referred, is estimated at 8 lakhs of rupees, and as the canal works at an average annual loss of Rs. 10,572 there is no inducement to incur this heavy capital outlay.

Burdwān is separated from the Gangetic delta by an important branch of the Ganges, and it is probable that at no very ancient date the main stream of that river used to pass along its eastern boundary. The soil of most parts of the district differs considerably from that of central Bengal, both chemically and physically, as might be expected from the difference in their geological origin. The whole of the western and a very large area in the eastern portions of the district are formed from the debris of the hills of Manbhūm, Singhbhūm and the Santāl Parganas. In the west in many places the soil is formed Soils.

directly from the subjacent rock more or less altered by the action of rain-water, atmosphere and other disintegrating agencies. The greater portion of the eastern tract consists of materials transported by mountain streams having their origin in the hills mentioned above and pouring their waters into the Hooghly. Soils showing very evident marks of glacial action are also to be met with. The soil is partly a laterite clay, more or less altered, and partly a red-coloured coarse-grained sand, characteristic of the eastern ranges of the Vindhya formation, large surfaces composed of which are to be found in the beds of the Dwārkeswar, Dāmodar and Ajay rivers.

Paddy and sugarcane are the two characteristic crops of the Burdwān district. These crops grow both in the laterite clay and the red sand, though a soil formed of a mixture of the two is considered the best for sugarcane. The clay is very difficult to work, turning into a mass of most tenacious mud in the rainy season, and being as hard as stone in the summer. On account of this difficulty in many places nothing but paddy is grown, to which crop this clay is well-suited. After the rains have set in and the clay has been softened by deep ploughing, the rice seedlings are planted. Sugarcane also grows well on this red clay which contains the hydrated sesquioxide of iron and is rich in phosphorus, the latter mineral being, as agricultural chemistry tells us, the predominant element in sugarcane. This crop, however, requires irrigation in April when water is very scarce, and lowlying land is unsuited on account of the danger of inundation during the rainy season. It is therefore only within limited areas that this important crop can be successfully grown.

The most practical classification of soils is into high land, low land and *diārā*, or alluvial river land. From the nature of their formation, the elevated tracts lie along the river banks and slope towards the interior. Generally speaking they consist of either sand or sandy loam, whilst the low grounds are more or less of clay. As might be expected, the high grounds are mainly occupied by human habitations and form village sites. The high land remaining for agricultural purposes is that lying around villages, and is more or less sandy, and above the ordinary flood level. In the rainy season the washings of the villages manure this land which fetches the highest rents. It grows a variety of crops. In the rainy season it is sown with *aus* rice or jute, or if it is safe from inundation it may be planted with sugarcane. Vegetables may also be grown on it, and it will pay to manure it heavily and to cultivate potatoes, sugarcane, onions, plantains and other valuable crops. Unfortunately such land forms a very small portion of the area under cultivation.

Greatly the larger part of the cultivated land consists of the lowlying tracts separating the village sites from one another. This land is mostly clay, is submerged during the rains and remains dry only during the few hot months of the year. The sole crop this land grows is rice except in very rare cases, when near the homesteads a little summer sesamum is sometimes grown. The diārā lands are formed by the deposition of river silt in the beds and on the banks of rivers and are most sought after by the cultivators. They are renovated every year during the rains by a deposition of silt, and require no manures. They are the most suitable for winter and spring crops, pulses, wheat, barley, oilseeds and vegetables. These also grow the most luxuriant indigo, and if any fodder and fuel reserves are to be made these are the lands to which attention should be directed. The cultivation of *diārā* lands is the simplest in existence. Tillage operations are confined to one or two ploughings, and often the seed is sown broadcast on the soft mud left by the receding inundation without any previous preparation of the land.

The following table shows the normal acreage of the crops of the district and their percentage on the normal net cropped area:— PRINCIPAL CROPS.

Name of crop.	Normal acreage.	Percentage on normal net cropped area.	Name of crop.	Normal acreage.	Percentage on normal net cropped area.
Winter rice	874,800	81	Summer rice	300	...
Sugarcane	25,800	2	Wheat	1,800	...
			Barley	7,000	½
			Gram	9,100	1
Total *aghani* crops (*a*) ...	900,600	83	Other *rabi* cereals and pulses.	51,200	5
			Other *rabi* food crops ...	40,000	4
Autumn rice	140,000	13	Linseed	22,500	2
Maize	3,000	¼	Rape and mustard ...	21,100	2
Other *bhādoi* cereals and pulses.	6,700	½	*Til* (*rabi*)	500	...
Other *bhādoi* food crops	2,200	½	Other oilseeds	1,500	...
Other *bhādoi* non-food crops.	19,000	1	Tobacco	400	...
Jute	16,500	1½	Other *rabi* non-food crops	1,200	...
Til (*bhādoi*)	3,300	3/10	Total *rabi* crops (*c*) ...	156,600	14½
Total *bhādoi* crops (*b*) ...	181,700	17	Orchards and garden produce (*d*).	5,000	½
Total of (*a*), (*b*), (*c*) and (*d*)				1,243,900	115
Deduct area cropped more than once				162,200	5
Net area (normal) cropped				1,081,70	100

Rice. Rice is by far the most important crop of the district: in fact in the alluvial plains to the east little else is grown. All the different varieties cultivated may be grouped under three primary classes distinguished from one another by marked characteristics—the *āus* or autumn, the *āman* or winter and the *boro* or marsh rice. The first is a coarse grain difficult to digest and eaten by the poorer classes alone. It is grown on high lands, and requires much less water than the other two. When sown broadcast, as is the general practice, it is a good deal more troublesome to grow than the *āman*. It also yields a smaller outturn and fetches a lower price. But it supplies the cultivator with food and his cattle with fodder at a time of year when both are very scarce. It is reaped early enough to permit of the preparation of the land for the spring cereals, pulses, vegetables, potatoes and sugarcane. The *āman* rice includes much the greater number of varieties and is grown over a larger area than any other crop. It is cultivated on low lands with a clay soil, and requires much more water than the *āus*. The finest descriptions of rice belong to this class. The *boro* is a coarse rice, some of the varieties being the coarsest known, and is less nutritious than the other kinds. It is grown on soft mud on the sides of rivers, canals or lakes. Edges of rivers subjected to strong tides are of all places the most suited to growing this class of paddy.

Almost every considerable village has a variety of its own, and every year sees the extinction of some of the old varieties and the appearance of some not known before. Rice is perhaps the best instance known of the variations which plants have undergone under cultivation. Originally an aquatic grass, the one characteristic which it has most persistently retained amidst all the changes brought about by differences of climate, soil and mode of cultivation is the need of abundant moisture for its proper growth. According to the popular saying "*dhān pān nitya snān*"—rice and betel should have a bath every day. It is the well justified belief of the cultivators that give rice but this one thing needful, and it will grow in any soil and under any climate. Indeed, the facility with which it adapts itself to different classes of soil from the stiffest clay to the lightest of sands, and from the peaty to the saline, is wonderful. Compared with the advantages of a proper water-supply all other questions regarding its cultivation are matters of very minor importance.

Āus rice. The high lands on which *āus* rice is grown generally produce two crops in the year; but where irrigation is available three are sometimes grown, viz., *āus* rice, potatoes and onions. As soon as it has been gathered the field is prepared for one of the spring crops, generally in this part of the country one of the pulses or oilseeds. In *diārā* lands it is sometimes followed by wheat, barley or potatoes.

Āus lands are almost always manured excepting those near large rivers, which receive a yearly deposit of silt. As the same field generally gives two crops in the year the practice is to apply as much of the manure as possible before rice is put in, and to let the crop following benefit by what is left after the rice has taken its share. This plan is adopted because the direct application of manure is not beneficial to such crops as the pulses, potatoes, etc., and in some cases it is positively injurious. As soon as the previous crop is off the field the land is ploughed twice, once lengthwise and once across the field. Ploughing does not begin usually till the 15th February, unless the rice is to be followed by one of the spring crops or potatoes. In some places the first ploughing is delayed till the 15th April, but good cultivators are well aware of the advantages of early and frequent ploughing in the case of upland. The fields are ploughed seven or eight times and by the end of April are well dried, and the roots of the weeds and grasses are destroyed by the burning heat of summer.

Implements to drill in the seed are seldom used, and it is generally broadcasted. In the case of rice, however, the general tendency now is to sow in nurseries, and to transplant the seedlings when favourable weather occurs. The plants come out in four or five days, and when they have grown to a height of about nine inches it is well to take advantage of a shower of rain and harrow the field. The greater part of the weeds are thus removed, but sometimes as many as three weedings are needed: and weeding is a most tedious and expensive operation. The harvest time for *āus* rice extends over the last three weeks of September. It is reaped while yet slightly green, for if allowed to ripen fully it would shed some of the grain, and the straw being brittle would break. It is cut close to the ground with a sickle and laid in the field in parallel lines for nearly a week. It is afterwards made into sheaves and taken to the threshing-floor, or put in heaps of some 100 to 150 sheaves each, the tops and sides of which are carefully smoothed to let rain water run off easily wihtout penetrating into them. The outturn per bigha varies from 4 to 8 maunds of grain and 6 to 8 *pons* of straw.

Aman rice is grown on lowlying clayey lands, and it requires such a large quantity of water that high lands, unless situated very close to tanks, canals or any other reservoirs of water, are not suited for its production. Some of the best varieties *Aman rice.*

require a clay soil and about one and a half feet of water almost from the time of planting to harvest time. The method of cultivation differs according to the comparative height of the land to be sown, that is, according as it is situated below the *aus* land or much lower down, remaining under water for the greater part of the year. In the first case the land is generally loam and the rice is either sown broadcast or transplanted. In the other case the soil is almost invariably clay, and transplanting is the general rule.

The lowlying clay lands suitable for transplanted *āman* rice receive very little tillage. Some cultivators are of opinion that these lands ought not to be ploughed in summer, for this operation destroys the grasses on the growth of which the success of the crop depends. In April or May, after a heavy shower of rain, the land may be once ploughed, while the soil still contains a large amount of water. This ploughing of the wet land instead of destroying the grasses encourages their growth. At the end of June, when the land has been quite saturated by the monsoon rains, the low embankments round the field should be repaired and water allowed to collect within them. The grasses are then ploughed into the soil and the seedlings planted. There is no doubt some truth in the statement that grasses serve the purpose of green manuring; but this practice can be carried too far, as is evident from the fact that rice grown on lands which have not been early ploughed frequently suffer from the disease known to the cultivators as *kādamārā.*

For the nursery a plot of ground is chosen either in a corner of the field itself or in a place where water is easily available. It is heavily manured with well-rotted dung and ashes after careful ploughing. For sowing advantage is taken of a slight rain, or the moisture necessary for the purpose is obtained by artificial irrigation. A maund of seed is sown broadcast on a bigha of nursery land. Sometimes a little more. The field must not be watered after sowing, for this causes the soil to sink and cake, which greatly interferes with the proper germination of the seed. The seedlings are ready for transplantation when they are about a foot high. After they have been taken out their roots are well washed. They are then made into bundles, each bundle containing as many plants as can be grasped with both hands and kept floating in water. They may be transplanted either on the day they have been removed from the nursery or the day after, further delay being, according to general opinion, injurious. But on this point opinions differ. Some think that the seedlings should never be planted fresh, and that they can be kept for three or four days without being any the worse for it. One bigha of land will require 60 to 70 bundles of seedlings, and this is the produce of about two kāthās of nursery.

The usual time for transplanting is the end of June and the beginning of July, but very much depends in this respect on the period and amount of rainfall. The seedlings are planted in the soft earth at a distance of nine to fifteen inches apart, four to five being placed together. Being a crop of the rainy season *āman* rice does not generally require artificial irrigation, but in October and November, just when the plants begin to blossom, it is sometimes necessary. Manuring is not much practised in its cultivation, but in some places the more intelligent cultivators use 20 baskets of cowdung or a maund of oil-cake per bigha just before transplanting the seedlings.

Potatoes. This valuable crop is largely cultivated in the Burdwān district, and the cultivation is yearly increasing. The localities generally selected for its cultivation are the old beds of rivers, and the crop is grown with great success in the neighbourhood of Chakdighi, Saktigarh, Sātgachiā and Bohār. It is also grown largely in the portion of the district which lies to the south of the Dāmodar river. The best potato soil is a sandy loam having as fine a texture as possible. It must not be saline, nor contain too much iron. Soils containing *kankar* or nodules of carbonate of lime are also considered unsuited for potatoes. As artificial irrigation is indispensable canals, tanks, marshes or some other form of reservoir must be close by. Irrigation from wells is not resorted to, but the practice of potato-growers in the Patna and Shāhābād districts shows that where labour is cheap and the water is within a reasonable depth this mode of irrigation can be profitably adopted. Potatoes are often grown on the same field year after year, a newly broken field not giving a good outturn. They are generally grown after autumn rice as a second crop; but a field which grows only potatoes gives a better and much earlier crop which brings greater profit to the cultivator, although early sowing is attended with risk of serious injury from late rain. Of the other crops sugarcane, oilseeds and pulses are grown everywhere and a small quantity of jute is grown in the thānās of Kālna and Jamālpur. Indian-corn is raised on the western border.

EXTENSION OF CULTIVATION. No statistics showing the extension of cultivation are available, but it is known that large areas have been brought under cultivation within the last half century, especially in the western part of the district, which a hundred years ago was an unpeopled wilderness of *sāl* forest and jungle. There is now little land in the district of any agricultural value which is not used for crop.

IMPROVEMENT OF METHODS.

Little has been done to improve the methods of cultivation and, until recent years, to introduce new crops or to improve the fertility of the crops grown. The implements used by the ordinary cultivator are simple and inexpensive and yet efficient; and it would be hard to find any substitutes that would so well suit the conditions of the people and the climate. Perhaps the most important mechanical advance has been the introduction of the Behia sugar mill which has in most places superseded the old wooden screw. Iron pans have replaced earthen vessels for boiling the sugarcane juice and, as has already been noted, irrigation vessels are now often made of iron instead of wood. Attempts have from time to time been made to introduce iron ploughs, but without much success.

Manures.

Manures are largely used and their use is well understood. In most villages few fields, excepting those grown in rice, can be found which receive none, while no farmer would dream of growing without manure such crops as sugarcane, potatoes, onions, etc.

Those generally used are—

Cowdung,
Cowdung ashes,
Oil-cakes, including both castor and mustard cake,
Hide salt, and
Tank mud.

Cowdung is to some extent wasted by being used as fuel, but generally no good cultivator would think of doing so. Cowdung is considered *the* manure, and the Bengali term for manure is synonymous with it. An idea may be formed of the high appreciation in which it is held by the popular rural saying "*sār satya Lakshmi*"—Cowdung is the real Lakshmi (goddess of fortune). Every farmer has his dung-heap. For this a piece of low ground is selected close to the cowshed, or a hole is made in which is collected the daily supply of dung, dung ashes, wood ashes, waste straw, refuse of vegetables, and in fact everything that has the least manurial value. Both castor and mustard cakes are now very largely used especially in potato, sugarcane, ginger and cabbage fields. The other manure most commonly used is the black mud which is scraped off the bottom of tanks. To obtain the best results it is necessary to apply it in large quantities.

The rotation of crops is practised, but it cannot be said that any regular system of rotation is followed. The condition of the field at the time, the state of the weather, the demand in the market and the individual means of the particular farmer are the considerations that usually determine the particular crop. The general custom is to grow rice after rice on the lowlying lands, and on the higher grounds surrounding the village sites to grow autumn rice in the rainy season and one of the pulses as a winter crop. Potatoes, onions, etc., sometimes take the place of the pulses. Sugarcane is a special crop requiring a full year to ripen, and is grown at intervals of three or four years.

CATTLE

The plough cattle of the district, like those of the rest of Bengal, seem to belong to a special breed, perhaps indigenous to the Gangetic delta. Generally speaking only as many animals are kept as are needed for the cultivation of the land and the supply of a few ounces of milk for family use. All the live-stock that an average farmer possesses consist of a pair of bullocks and a milking cow and calf. Sometimes one spare bullock is kept, but as often as not the cow and the calf are wanting. The area of land that can be worked with a pair of bullocks depends very much on the nature of the soil. Where rice is the only crop grown a pair of good animals is considered sufficient for 20 to 25 bighas of land. Cattle suffer much from want of pasturage. In the west the country is hilly and undulating and mostly devoid of natural vegetation; the wild grasses on the laterite soil are few in number and yield a very small amount of fodder. In the eastern portion of the district the pressure of the population is such that no land which is in any way fit for cultivation can be spared for pasture or for raising any crop specially meant for fodder. The grazing grounds which were formerly common to the village have been absorbed, and the rice straw which is by far the most important, if not the only fodder for the cattle, is required for thatching. Hay-making is practically unknown, and the system of grazing followed is most wasteful. The grazing grounds, where such exist, and the fields are never protected by fences, and the cattle are at liberty to run over them at all times without restriction. Grasses thus get no chance to grow as the cattle crop them down as soon as they appear above ground.

Fairs.

Annual fairs are held at Agradwīp in the Kātwa subdivision, at Bāgnāpārā and Uddhanpur in Kālnā, and at Dādia and Kānchannagar in Burdwān. These gatherings, particularly those at Bāgnāpārā, which is a Vaishnavite place of pilgrimage, and Agradwīp where there is a religious festival in April every year at which some 10,000 people assemble, are mainly of a religious character, but are also used for trade purposes.

Burdwan Agricultural Farm. The Pālla farm was started by the Burdwān Rāj in 1885 and is situated at Pālla on the bank of the Eden Canal, about three miles south of the Burdwān Railway Station. The area is 31 acres of which 25 are cropped, the remainder being under roads, buildings, etc. The station is maintained by the Burdwān Rāj under the supervision of the Agricultural Department. The annual expenditure amounts to Rs. 4,500 and the annual income now is about Rs. 2,000. Under a recent agreement the Rāj deposits annually in the Burdwān Treasury Rs. 2,500 to the credit of the Deputy Director of Agriculture. If in any year the profit on the station exceeds Rs. 2,000 or the total expenditure is less than Rs. 4,500 the proportionate sale-proceeds will be credited to the Rāj. The chief crops grown are paddy, jute, potatoes and sugarcane.

Agricultural Association. An Agricultural Association has recently been started, the members are landholders and pleaders and the proceedings are usually conducted in English. The cultivators' holdings are generally very small, but it is hoped to reach the actual cultivator of the soil through the landlord by means of the Association. It has already done much in the way of seed distribution to cultivators, and there is an annual agricultural show in connection with it.

CHAPTER VI.

NATURAL CALAMITIES.

THE earthquake of 1897 was felt all over the district, its effects being particularly severe at Rānīganj and Asansol where many of the masonry buildings were damaged. Four lives were lost in the district, but otherwise little serious damage was done. Slight earthquake shocks are experienced fairly often, the most recent having occurred in August 1909. EARTH-QUAKES.

The great cyclone of 1874 caused widespread damage in the district, the vortex passing right over the town of Burdwān itself. The following account is condensed from the Collector's reports. The storm burst upon Burdwān at 8 P. M. on the 15th of October 1874 from the north-east, and towards the morning of the 16th the wind shifted to the east attaining its utmost fury. The vortex passed over the town at 5 A. M. on the morning of the 16th, and towards 12 o'clock the storm gradually abated. The storm was throughout accompanied by heavy rain, and the Bānkā and Bhāgīrathi overflowed flooding the surrounding country. The area of the greatest destruction was from Pānāgarh to Memāri. Many large trees were uprooted and others broken. According to the police reports 99 lives were lost mostly by the fall of houses, and in one thānā (Bud-bud) 57 cattle and 393 goats and sheep were killed. Five per cent. of the houses in Burdwān town were completely destroyed and fifteen per cent. unroofed or partially damaged, and the Collector estimated the total number of houses destroyed in the district at 21,677. The force of the wind was so great that a train on the East Indian Railway near Khāna junction was blown completely over. The lowest barometric reading recorded at Burdwān was 28·44, or reduced to sea-level 28·54 at 5-51 A. M., showing a depression of 1·36 inches below the normal atmospheric pressure, and the velocity of the wind was estimated to be at least 92·5 miles per hour. CYCLONES.

On the whole Burdwān is less liable to famine than most other districts of the Province. The Asansol subdivision depends on industry for its prosperity rather than on agriculture, and it is improbable that the failure of the crops here would ever cause serious distress. The deltaic portion of the district is more liable LIABILITY TO FAMINE.

to famine, as the people depend almost entirely upon the winter rice crop for their means of subsistence; and a failure of this crop could not be compensated for by the autumn rice crop which is only cultivated on a comparatively small scale. The means of communication, however, are good and amply sufficient to avert the extremity of famine from the greater part of the district, though certain tracts in the south and north-east, such as thānās Khandaghosh and Raina, and portions of Manteswar are more or less isolated. Burdwān suffered seriously in the great famine of 1770 an account of which has been given in Chapter II. During the past half century the district has experienced two famines—in 1866 and 1874.

Famine of 1866. Burdwān was one of the districts of Lower Bengal in which the famine of 1866 was severely felt, although not to anything like the same degree as in the adjoining district of Midnapore. The early or autumn rice crop of 1865 was a full one, and the winter rice crop, taken over the whole district, probably did not average less than two-thirds of a full outturn. By March 1866, however, distress began to make itself felt, and coarse rice, which formerly sold at from Re. 1-4 to Rs. 2 per maund at that time of the year was then selling at Rs. 4-8. In June the price rose to Rs. 5 a maund against Rs. 2-2, the usual rate in that month. In the beginning of July there was a sudden influx of paupers into the town of Burdwān, principally from the weaving towns of Chandrakonā in Midnapore (then in Hooghly), and Bishnupur in Bānkūrā, and from the Bīrbhūm district. The attraction to the town was caused by the customary distributions of rice made by the Mahārājā, and by the trustees of various religious endowments. The Mahārājā increased his daily charitable distributions of rice, but the increasing number of applicants made it impossible for all to gain access to the existing relief-houses, and it was soon found that charitable subscriptions were unable to cope with the increasing distress. Government aid was invoked and in August the Board of Revenue granted a sum of Rs. 3,000 for the relief of the distress, which was soon after followed by a further grant of Rs. 2,000. Upon receipt of these funds, the Commissioner of the Division formed a committee, consisting partly of official and partly of private gentlemen. At the first meeting of the committee a letter was read from the Mahārājā of Burdwān, offering to provide for all the destitute paupers in Burdwān town entirely at his own expense, the arrangements being subject to the supervision and approval of the Commissioner. This munificent offer was at once accepted, and from the 6th September the work of gratuitous relief in the town was made over o the Mahārājā. The Mahārājā's representative at first appeared to be unwilling to make labour a condition of relief. He eventually found, however, that the number of applicants could never be expected to decrease as long as all who asked were fed gratuitously. Clothes were distributed gratuitously to 2,183 persons in all; and money was given to enable the paupers to return to their homes, as the distress began to subside. In October the number of applicants fell gradually, and on the 31st of that month the returns showed only 1,206 as being fed daily. The total expenditure of the Mahārājā up to the 4th November amounted to Rs. 14,550. It was reported officially that the people in the town at the end of the year did not show any signs of emaciation or starvation. Men and women were stout and in good case. There appeared to be no limit to their rations. Several of them had been for months subsisting on this charity, and, though probably stronger and haler than they ever were in their lives before, had not done a day's work. Not a man was being employed in the labour yard. In fact, it seemed that labour had been almost optional and not compulsory.

Outside the town the distress was not very serious; but the country on the opposite side of the Dāmodar, which is unprotected by embankments, was flooded and 3,065 houses were destroyed the inhabitants of which left their homes for the towns in search of food. The Rānīganj subdivision probably suffered most severely in the famine. At that time this part of the district was included within the magisterial jurisdiction of the Bānkurā district, only the revenue jurisdiction being attached to Burdwān. The town of Rānīganj contained several emigration dépôts, and in the first four months of 1866 no fewer than seventeen thousand emigrant coolies left Rānīganj by rail. In the middle of June, emigration was stopped, as small-pox had broken out among the coolies and was being imported into the town. Severe distress was manifested in June, when it was reported that, in consequence of the drain on the male population due to emigration, Rānīganj was full of women and children, who followed carts laden with rice, picking up the grains which fell. Soon afterwards, numbers of destitute people began to flock in from Mānbhūm and on the 30th June a sum of Rs. 500 out of the Rs. 5,000 which had been assigned to the Bankurā district was allotted to Rānīganj. The means at the disposal of the Committee were still inadequate, and a further grant of Rs. 2,000 was made by the Board of Revenue; a sum of Rs. 1,000 was also received from a fund subscribed by the servants of the East Indian Railway Company and Rs. 500 more from the Bānkurā Central Committee

Centres of relief were thereupon opened at four places in the interior of the subdivision, where gratuitous distributions as well as cheap sales of rice were made. The mortality in the town from diseases induced by privation of food was very considerable, and a pauper hospital and, afterwards, a small-pox hospital were established. The number of deaths in the streets and hospital was estimated at an average of fifteen a day during the months of July, August and September, and numbers of children were deserted. Employment on the roads was found for 1,500 paupers in September. The mortality, however, still continued very great, the paupers flocking in from Bānkurā, Mānbhūm and Deogarh in a state of utter prostration, and dying soon after they arrived from the effects of starvation, dysentery and diarrhœa. The total amount expended on relief in the Rānīganj subdivision was Rs. 7,568, and the aggregate of the daily total of persons who received relief was returned by the Committee at 348,296 a daily average of 2,902 for the four months, from the middle of July to the middle of November, during which the operations were in progress.

In Burdwān generally (excluding the Rānīganj subdivision which did not then belong to the district), the total amount expended on relief by the Burdwān, Kātwa and Kālna Relief Committees was as follows:—From the Board of Revenue, Rs. 3,000; from the Calcutta Central Relief Committee, Rs. 2,000; private subscriptions Rs. 9,558; total Rs. 14,558. The Kātwa and Kālna relief centres were maintained solely by private subscriptions. This sum, however, does not include the expenditure incurred by the Mahārājā and other private individuals in giving relief, besides Rs. 4,830 granted and Rs. 4,210 advanced for special works.

In concluding the district narrative of the famine in Burdwān the Famine Commissioners remarked that "speaking comparatively, the people of this district did not suffer severely. The generally prosperous condition of the cultivating classes, caused by their proximity to the Calcutta markets, enabled them to oppose a greater power of resistance to famine than that which could be offered by the cultivators of the less advanced districts to the west and south-west, and they also received much support from their landlords. The day-labourers were driven into the towns to seek for subsistence, and there swelled the crowds of paupers who had come in from districts which had suffered more severely. In these centres disease and death were unavoidable. Although the external relief granted to this district was small we think that it probably did not fall short of the requirements.

It would, however, have been well if the organised relief at the different points in the interior of the district had been begun earlier in the season."

The following account of the famine of 1874 is condensed from Mr. A. P. Macdonnell's "Food Grain Supply and Famine Relief in Bihar and Bengal." Relief operations in Burdwān during 1874 were for a lengthened period very widespread, but the distress which called for them cannot be wholly attributed to the failure in the harvests of 1873. The year 1874 found the district suffering from the effects of two years of markedly adverse harvests and nearly ten successive years of virulent epidemic fever. Not only were the material resources of the people reduced, but their physical capacity was also seriously impaired. In 1872 the rains commenced very late and they were not equally distributed. There was a very short outturn of the winter rice crop, the principal food supply of the people. Several plots of land, even entire villages, remained uncultivated. Only in the Katwā subdivision—less than one-eighth of the district—was the rainfall seasonable or the harvest good. The rains in 1873 were not so greatly deficient in quantity as unseasonable in distribution, and in September and October there was great deficiency. FAMINE OF 1874.

Distress which had gradually been making way, first attracted serious attention in the north-west of the district about the beginning of April. The Collector on proceeding to the spot found "the condition of some of the people very wretched, the labourers complained very loudly of want of work, and it appeared that many of the men had emigrated to Kachar and elsewhere leaving their women and children. The so-called respectable classes were nearly as loud in their complaints as the poor; goldsmiths complained that their trade was at a standstill; barbers, that the people had given up shaving; cultivators that the grain-lenders had refused the usual advances; Brāhmans, that their sources of income had failed; village watchmen that their service lands yielded next to no crops, and that their money dues were not paid; mendicants, cripples and lepers, that charity was no more; weavers, that advances were no more to be had. Allowing of course for some exaggeration in all these complaints, still the looks of many of the complainants were enough to prove that they were in the main founded on truth." On the 1st of June the Collector after a tour of inspection wrote:—"The eye is at once caught by the anæmic, clammy faces of the sufferers from chronic fever." The circle of distress as the year wore on widened still more. In July around Kātwa in almost every village visited by him and the Civil Surgeon more or less distress was found; some of the poorest people were even found to be eating grass seeds.

Charitable relief began in the first week of April, when nearly seven thousand persons were gratuitously fed. The number rose to eleven thousand in the end of May and twenty-six thousand in the end of June, whilst during the three following months of July, August and September, the recipients of charitable relief never fell below fifty-five thousand and rose in the middle of August to seventy thousand. In all 6,812 tons of rice were gratuitously distributed, 3,002 tons advanced on loan and 1,495 tons paid as wages. At the same time Rs. 5,46,723 were expended in charitable relief, Rs. 62,277 in wages and Rs 70,559 advanced on loan. Labourers employed on relief works numbered on a daily average 1,168 in January, 3,513 in February, 3,359 in March, 6,430 in April, 9,613 in May, 11,574 in June, 7,571 in July, 5,252 in August, and 2,206 in September, after which this form of relief ceased; but on the last day of November 3,475 persons were still being fed at the cost of Government. All relief was brought to a close with the end of the year.

Since this famine the district has been singularly immune from serious scarcity. In 1884-85 there was some considerable distress due to failure of the crops in two successive years. Local relief works were opened, gratuitous relief was distributed and loans were advanced. The supply of food was, however, always plentiful in the markets and prices never reached famine rates. In 1896-97, when the adjacent district of Bānkura was seriously affected with scarcity, Burdwān escaped scatheless; not a single relief work was opened and not a single person publicly received gratuitous relief. During 1904 some portions of the Burdwān and Kātwa subdivisions suffered from scarcity as a result of the failure of the *āus* rice crop, but the distress was local and short-lived. The total cost of the relief operations which were closed in July was Rs. 26,600; Rs. 3,000 was expended in gratuitous relief and loans amounting to Rs. 35,000 were made.

FLOODS. From the earliest times the district has been protected from flood by embankments along the Dāmodar and Ajay. At first individual effort rather than public contribution provided for their construction. A farmer or landowner whose field was threatened would construct a *bāndh* to save it with the result that the flood water would attack some other point further down. The process would be repeated again and again until the banks of the rivers were protected by a series of regular embankments Before the last half of the 19th century, however, these wer neither so extensive nor so strong as to effectually check the fury of the great floods to which hill-fed streams, such as the Dāmodar and Ajay, are liable, and the early history of the district is full of accounts of disastrous floods which breached the embankments and caused widespread damage. The earliest recorded occurred in 1770 and the injury which it caused to the winter rice crop, following on a previous season of scarcity owing to drought, intensified the famine of that year. The inundation was first observed on the 29th September, when the waters of the Dāmodar rose to a level with the top of the embankment, and near the western extremity of the town of Burdwān the embankment gradually gave way. The damage was repaired, but four or five days afterwards a second rising of the river resulted in the entire destruction of the embankment. Every effort to check the violence of the torrent proved in vain and the town of Burdwān was almost totally destroyed: not an earth-built house remained, and even those constructed with bricks suffered considerably. The Ajay had also flooded its banks, and the whole tract between that river and the Dāmodar was under three or four feet of water. Sugarcane and cotton, both which crops appear to have been cultivated to a much larger extent than at present, suffered severely and the whole of the embankment was in a state of ruin. A sum of Rs. 80,000 was remitted from the land revenue payable by the Mahārājā, in consideration of his undertaking the necessary repairs, the cost of which, however, is said to have far exceeded the sum remitted. It was not till a period of two years had elapsed that the cultivators began to recover from the disaster. The Mahārājā and other zamīndārs, in spite of the destruction of their crops, cattle and homesteads insisted on the payment of rent, and it does not appear that any further abatement in the Government demand for land revenue was granted on account of the calamity.

Another flood which seems to have been equally disastrous occurred in 1787. Describing the damage caused by it the Collector, Mr. Kinloch, wrote: "The town is totally destroyed, not a vestige of a mud house remaining, and even those built of brick are many of them fallen or so entirely damaged that a longer residence in them becomes dangerous. Many people have lost their lives and a great number of cattle are drowned." And again: "Every house in Burdwān and every village contiguous to it fell down—nothing but the banks of tanks remained for the reception of every living animal."

The inundation of 1823, which commenced on the night of the 26th September, was caused by the bursting of the embankments FLOOD OF 1823.

of the Dāmodar, the Bhāgīrathi and minor streams. A correspondent of the "Calcutta Monthly Journal" has described the inundation :— "Picture to yourself a flat country completely under water, running with a force apparently irresistible, and carrying with it dead bodies, roofs of houses, palanquins and wreck of every description. It lasted for three days; communication was cut off, and the owners of masonry houses took refuge on the roofs. For many miles the thatched and mud houses, as well as thousands of trees, were prostrated. Such trees as had withstood the ravages of the flood formed the resting places of men." The area embraced by the flood commenced from Bali, and extended for twenty-five miles. The villages on both banks of the Bhāgīrathi, especially on the west bank, were submerged. The height of the water in these villages was at first about three feet. The inundation rose, and at its height, on the 2nd October, the water was about seven feet deep. On the 29th September a boat sailed across country from Calcutta to Burdwān. The loss of life was immense. The crops were destroyed; the houses were submerged and ultimately carried away; the people were destitute of food, so that parents sold their offspring for a mouthful of rice. The landmarks distinguishing the holding of the cultivators were swept away, and great confusion and endless litigation naturally ensued. The owners of properties were converted into claimants for land which had been in their possession and that of their forefathers for generations.

FLOOD OF 1855. The inundation of 1855 resulted in the destruction of the embankment on the right side of the Dāmodar. Previous to this time the embankments had been in charge of the zamindārs or landholders within whose estates they lay; but as their neglect caused the periodical breaching of the embankments Government took the matter into its own hands and maintained the embankment itself, debiting each landlord with a portion of the cost. After the destruction of the embankments on the right side of the Dāmodar in 1855 it was resolved to abandon them, and to keep up only those on the left bank. New embankments have accordingly been constructed along the whole of the left bank of the Dāmodar, a measure which has resulted in the comparative immunity of the country north of it from flood. Floods still do occur as in August 1909 when, owing to heavy rains, the Bānkā and other rivers overflowed and flooded large tracts of country. The water took several days to run off and the crops were damaged by their continued immersion. Many houses were damaged and five lives were lost.

CHAPTER VII.

RENT, WAGES AND PRICES.

IN the early days of our rule the relation between landlord and tenant in the district seems to have been anything but satisfactory. The zamīndār generally let out his estates in small parcels to farmers and, while these were under engagement for the revenue to their landlord, they had themselves no similar agreements with the tenants. In a letter to the Board of Revenue, dated June 1788, the Collector (Mr. Kinloch) remarks: "But I must observe that in this extensive district not more than one-fourth of the ryots are in possession of *pattahs* and these have been granted by the farmers or their *gumashtas*." He goes on to particularise the several classes of tenants. "The first, he says, are the *Khoad Kasht*, or aborigines, being ryots of inferior caste, who pay house rent and a greater revenue for the lands they cultivate than the *Pykhast* who are *ryots* of a superior rank, that neither pay rent for their dwelling house, nor do they pay so high a revenue for their lands, these last are again distinguished by the application of the *Nis Gong Pykasht*, who cultivate the lands of their own village, and the *Basa Gong Pykasht*, who pay a still lower rate of rent. Besides these are the *Muttariffa* ryots who do not cultivate lands but have shops and carry on a profession, and pay a high house rent, to all the above ryots." The permanent settlement does not seem to have improved matters much and in a letter from the Judge and Magistrate, dated the 9th of March 1802, the confusion and fraud which permeated the relations of landlords, farmers, and tenants is very vividly described. RENTS.

"The interchange of engagements between the parties, with few exceptions, extends no farther than to the zamīndār's farmer who is here termed the *Sudder* farmer and to those amongst whom he subdivides his farm, in portions. An engagement between the latter and the cultivators or heads of a village, is scarcely known, except the general one, mutually understood to receive and pay, agreeably to past and preceding years; and for ascertaining this the accounts of the farm are no guide.

"The zamīndār himself seeing that no confidence is to be placed in the accounts rendered him of the rent-roll of the farm from the practice, which has so long prevailed, of fabrication and false accounts, never attempts to call for them at the expiration of the lease; and instead of applying a correction of the evil, increases it, by farming out the lands literally by auction; and the same mode is adopted in almost every subdivision of the farm. The consequence of such a system must be obvious; needy rapacious farmers and fraudulent tenants become friends, and collusively agree, at the expiration of the lease, to defraud the succeeding farmer. A trifling douceur for the ryot, or the ryots of a whole village, is sufficient to procure a fabrication of the accounts, and a receipt to correspond with them for a sum much below that actually paid in the revenue demand for the year; and these are the valid and incontrovertible vouchers, held out to the successor in farm for his guide.

"The practice is, however, too universal and too well-known to deceive him; but he is without an alternative, and acts his predecessor's part, in the repetition of it, for if honestly disposed (which is rarely the case) he has not time to have recourse to a measurement for ascertaining the quantity and quality of lands in the occupancy of the cultivators, with a view to a fair and equitable assessment: and the ryots finding their benefit in the confusion, and despairing of honest dealing towards them while the present system exists, would oppose it, so as to make him a sufferer for the attempt."

The creation of patnī tenures did much to remove these abuses by securing some permanence of tenure to the farmer; written leases between tenure holder and tenant are now practically universal, and most of the tenants possess occupancy rights; but in a great many cases they are not the actual cultivators, the holdings being let out to sub-tenants for produce rents. No settlement of rents has yet been carried out in the district, but it is reported that the average rent per acre paid by the actual cultivator to his immediate landlord is approximately Rs. 6. For the inferior class of rice land in the neighbourhood of Rānīganj and Asansol the rent is considerably less but on the other hand rice lands which are favourably situated, *diārā* lands, and lands growing cane, potatoes or similar special crops demand a much higher rate. The latest survey and settlement in the district of any size was that of the Khas Mahals of the Burdwān Rāj. The statistics collected from this show that the assessment per acre for the low land varied from Rs. 15 to Rs. 3 with an average assessment of Rs. 9, while the assessment for high land varied from Rs. 6 to annas 12 per acre with an average assessment of Rs. 3-6. The average area of the tenant's holding as ascertained from the records of this settlement was 4 acres. As has already been noticed, a tenant usually pays rent in cash, but in many cases he does not actually cultivate the whole of his holding himself but sub-lets portions of it to under-tenants who pay rent in kind. Under this system the actual cultivator tills the land at his own cost, reaps the crop in the presence of the superior tenant or his agent, and carries it to the threshing floor where the grain and straw are divided in equal shares.

Wages both for skilled and unskilled labour are fairly high. The monthly wages paid in the factories during 1908 were as follows, the variations depending on the class of work required, *e.g.*, whether for brick-works, potteries, iron works or paper mills. Blacksmiths Rs. 12 to Rs. 17; potters Rs. 13-12-6 to Rs. 20; carpenters Rs. 14 to Rs. 20; brick-layers Rs. 11; engine drivers Rs. 11 to Rs. 16; potters Rs. 15; moulders Rs. 14-6 to Rs. 16-6; boiler-men Rs. 10 to Rs. 23; fire-men Rs. 8 to Rs. 10. For unskilled labour the wages were Rs. 6 to Rs. 9 and for a woman Rs. 4 to Rs. 5; durwans and messengers Rs. 8; jamadar durwan Rs. 13. The Chinese carpenters employed in the Bengal Paper Mills, however, are paid as much as Rs. 60 a month. In the town of Burdwān itself wages are considerably higher; an ordinary carpenter or mason gets Rs. 22-8 a month while a skilled carpenter or mason gets Rs. 30; an ordinary labourer is paid Rs. 11-4 and a woman Rs. 8-14 a month; a *ghorāmi* gets Rs. 15-8. Miners are usually paid from five annas six pies to seven annas a tub. Of late there has been a considerable rise in the price of both skilled and unskilled labour—a result doubtless of the general rise in prices which has been so marked a feature of recent years. In 1900 the average monthly wage of an able-bodied agricultural labourer was Rs. 7. It is now over Rs. 9, and in the years 1903-1905 rose so high as Rs. 11-4. During the same period the wages of a common mason, carpenter or blacksmith rose from Rs. 15 to Rs. 16-8.

Wages.

Landlords and large farmers with holdings of more than 5 or 6 acres usually engage farm servants to assist them in the cultivation of their lands. Those employed temporarily, at seasons when extra assistance is required, are usually paid and engaged by the day, and are known as *majurs* (*i.e.*, labourers, from *majuri* a wage). Generally, however, one or more permanent servants are also kept. These are known as *krishāns* (*i.e.*, cultivators, from *krisha* to cultivate) and are paid and engaged by the month. Their wages are usually Rs. 4 to Rs. 5 a month

Village labourers.

besides food and clothing or a little over Rs. 10 a month altogether. The monthly labourer is generally secured by the advance of a loan which is not paid off and for the recovery of which a suit would be filed if the labourer worked for any one else. A similar custom exists in Patna where such a labourer is known as a *kamia* but in that district the failure of the employer to maintain his *kamia* involves the breaking up of the contract, and no further action is taken to recover the original debt. In Burdwān the debtor, though his service ceases for the time, returns to his master when required for fear of being sued for his debt. A daily labourer gets annas four to annas five a day during the cultivating season, and annas three to annas four during the harvest besides food for two meals daily and tiffin (*jalpān*). When not engaged in actual agricultural operations such labourers find occupation in excavating tanks and embankments, in repairing the ridges of earth between the rice fields (*ails*), levelling and manuring fields, thatching, brick making, etc. The women who get much the same wages if paid in cash, are chiefly employed in husking rice and catching fish.

Prices. The steady rise in prices, which has been so marked a feature of the recent economic history of India, is reflected in the figures reported for the district. Common rice, the staple crop of the district, sold at Burdwān on the 30th of June 1890 for Rs. 2-9 per maund. The average price for the five years ending 1894 was Rs. 2-15. In 1899 this had risen to Rs. 3-1-5, in 1904 to Rs. 3-5-8, and the average price for the five years ending with 1899 was Rs. 4-11-7. It is interesting to note that on the 18th of April 1788 the Collector reported that rice sold at Burdwān at 25—28 pucca *seers* a rupee, at Mandalkote (*sic*) at 20—24 pucca *seers*, and at Sheogarh at 25 pucca *seers*. Similarly the price of gram and *arhar*, the cheapest of the pulses, rose from Rs. 2-1-6 and Rs. 2-0-9 per maund on the 30th of June 1890 to Rs. 3-6 and Rs. 4-12-6, respectively. The price of other articles has also risen in much the same proportion. The price of rice and other food stuffs reached its highest point in 1907-08, when the price of ordinary common rice rose to over Rs. 5. Prices remained almost stationery till the end of 1908-09. They have fallen considerably since, but it is improbable that they will ever again fall to the level at which they stood before the recent rise.

MATERIAL CONDITION OF THE PEOPLE. Sir William Hunter in his statistical account gives a somewhat gloomy account of the material condition of the people of Burdwān. But in 1874, when this account was written, the district had only recently experienced two famines, and was still suffering from the epidemic fever which in 1867-69 had almost entirely depopulated many of the smaller villages. The recovery from the effects of these disastrous years was surprisingly rapid. Fourteen years later the Collector reports that even the poorest cultivators and field labourers were much more prosperous than was generally supposed; they were able to procure and did procure a sufficiency of wholesome food for themselves, and their wives, children and dependents; and besides this they had a surplus to bestow in charity, to expend on festivals and celebrations and to enable them to meet at least the approaches of a time of scarcity.

"Twenty years ago as said, though probably thirty years were meant (and whatever the period, it was one within the memory of the people), the rate used to be for a reaper or ordinary field labourer his food and four *seers* of *dhān* each day. The rates are now his food and five *seers* of *dhān* per diem. The price of *dhān* has nearly doubled in the period. Moreover, in the height of the field season, from August to December, labour is at a premium and special rates have to be given. The disappearance of indebtedness, which was general in 1872, is a remarkable circumstance. The rural *mahājans*, to whom the poor cultivators and labourers were practically bound as serfs, have also disappeared. The present class of *mahājans* only deal with the middle class on the security of landed property, which is nearly always rent-free. Most of the people whom I questioned owed nothing at all; others owed a rupee or two to a fellow labourer, or a rupee or two to their permanent employer. These employers still retain their field labourers by lending grain to them in the slack season without interest. These transactions are not regarded as loans, still less as *mahājani*. The only women and children whom I found employed on out-door labour for hire belonged to the poor relation and semi-dependant class, widows and orphans. The poorest Bauri labourer did not let his wife work for any one but himself."

Nor was this increase in prosperity confined to these classes. "The average income of the ordinary village artisans, such as the carpenters, blacksmiths or potters is higher far than those of the labourers, and if sometimes they are not really so well-off, it is solely because their standard and status are higher. The labour of the coal mine coolies is always at a premium and though their circumstances and surroundings look squalid and wretched in the extreme, their bodies are invariably well nourished, and they get quite enough to eat and far more than enough to drink. The other special labourers engaged at molasses manufacture, at railway yards and grain stores, in driving carts, as boatmen, and in piece work of all kinds are all men of exceptional physique'; their average earnings are not less than Rs. 8 a month and for some months are much higher.

"The material surroundings of the poorer classes, their houses, clothes, utensils and ornaments often indicate a very different position from that in which an examination into their incomes shows them to be. The plainest case is that of the colliery coolies whose earnings are the highest of any ordinary labourers, and whose huts, clothes, and surroundings are sordid in the extreme. The state of these externals much depends on the race to which the people belong, and the social position which they hold and feel themselves bound to maintain. The Bauris and Sântals care for brass ornaments only. Brass utensils are everywhere now in use, and the adoption of the umbrella even by coolies is as universal."*

General Conditions. The improvement has gone on steadily in the past twenty years and is now noticeable in every class of the community. The peasant, the artizan, and the labourer are infinitely better off than their predecessors of two or three generations back. Evidence of this meets the eye on every side in the shape of better houses, richer food and dress, and a more liberal expenditure on ornaments, brass eating vessels and luxuries. The rise in the price of rice and other crops has made the cultivating classes practically independent of the money-lenders, and has put them in possession of an amount of ready money which they never possessed before. The discovery of coal and iron and the consequent development of industry has filled the Asansol subdivision with a throng of busy and prosperous artizans and miners, whose wages are high and whose labour is in constant demand. The standard of comfort is gradually rising, and the people are no longer content with the bare necessaries of life. All classes are well fed and indulge in a display of clothing and jewellery which their fathers never dreamed of. Articles of food which were formerly considered luxuries are now in common use, and better houses, better appliances, and better clothing are becoming general. The following is a brief sketch of the material condition of the different classes of the community.

Landlords. During the last century almost the whole of the vast estates of the Mahārājā of Burdwān were parcelled out into tenures known as "*patnī tāluks*" the grantees of which not only gave him a high premium, but covenanted to pay an annual rental

* Report on the condition of the lower classes of population in Bengal, Calcutta, 1888.

in perpetuity, which, in every case, largely exceeded the Government revenue. The system was recognized by law in 1819 and a power of sale precisely similar to that possessed by Government was given to the landlord. The system has developed on the same lines; the *patnīdārs* and tenure holders under them have again and again sublet on the same terms, until estates are continually found with three or four or even more families introduced as middlemen between the landlord and the actual cultivator. The results of such a system of subinfeudation are obvious. The landlords and intermediate tenure-holders have become mere annuitants upon the land, taking but little interest in their nominal estates beyond ensuring the payment of their rent, and practically indifferent to their improvement, or the condition of the cultivators from whom their income is drawn. Embankments, drainage channels, tanks for irrigation or water-supply and other works of public utility constructed by the generosity of former landlords, are allowed to fall into disrepair; it is no one's business to repair them. And the landlords have no incitement to undertake any fresh work of improvement as they can hope for no pecuniary benefit from it. Generally speaking the *patnīdārs* and *dar-patnīdārs* are as a body far wealthier than the landlords from whom they hold their leases. The district is also sprinkled with numerous *aimmā* tenures, relics of the Muhammadan occupation, but the *aimmādārs* are for the most part in needy circumstances.

Professional classes. The professional classes are few in number and cannot with the exception of those in the legal profession be said to be prosperous. Even at the bar success is the exception, and although large fortunes have been made by pleaders and barristers, and the Burdwān bar is famous as one of the strongest in the province, the lawyer who is undistinguished by influence finds it hard enough to make a living. Properly qualified medical men are scarce and these in Asansol, Rānīganj and Burdwān do fairly well, but among the professional classes and those who work as clerks in Government or private employ, the struggle for existence has grown harder. Their incomes or salaries have not increased with the increase in prices, and they are prevented by custom and tradition from engaging in other labour.

Trading classes. The commercial and industrial classes, who form but a very small proportion of the population, have shared largely in the general increase in prosperity. The rise of prices, the increased demand for imported articles and luxuries, and the development of communications have given a great stimulus to trade. Silk and cotton weaving has again become a profitable industry as the result of the

Swadeshi movement, and a brisk trade is now carried on, the goods being exported to Calcutta and even to Madras and Bombay. Brass and bellmetal ware and cutlery are manufactured on a fairly large scale and find a ready market. Sweetmeat makers are numerous and the district is famed for its sweetmeats of which the best known are the *khāja* and *olā* Grocers and small shop-keepers are to be found in every village, and in Rāniganj and Burdwān there are a large number of very wealthy Mārwāri merchants engaged in banking and money-lending, the sale of cloth, and the manufacture of oil and oil-cake, and flour.

Cultivators. The average cultivator in Burdwān is on the whole fairly prosperous. The increase in prosperity of late years is due partly to the introduction of more profitable crops such as jute and potatoes, but mainly to the steady rise in the price of rice which alone represents nearly four-fifths of the total agricultural produce of the district. The annual budget of the ordinary cultivator as estimated in 1892 was as follows* :—

"The average area held is five acres, and the total annual value of the produce Rs. 252-8. The females husk rice for their wealthier neighbours, thus earning Rs. 12 per annum. They never work in the fields, but assist in such operations as threshing and winnowing if carried on in the dwelling-house yard. The total income of a cultivator of this class will therefore be Rs. 264-8. His outgoings are food, including fuel, pulse, oil, and salt, Rs. 120. The ordinary scale of diet is 2 lbs. of rice per adult male, 1½ lb. per female, and 1 lb. per child. This is boiled and eaten with two ounces of boiled pulse and condiments, in two meals taken at midday and sunset. Breakfast consists of a little parched rice only. Clothing Rs. 15. This, in the case of males, consists of a *dhuti* or waist-cloth, generally of European make, a *gamcha* or scarf, which also serves as turban, costing 12 annas and 4 annas respectively; so much is obligatory in all classes. But a cultivator of the upper rank will also indulge in a *pirān* or shirt costing Re. 1-6, and a Manchester *chādar* (sheet) worn toga-wise, eight annas, a pair of leather shoes worth Re. 1-2, and an English umbrella Re. 1-4. The total equipment on the former scale stands a ryot in only Re. 1, and he need have but two 'suits' a year. The latter, which is also the garb of the lower middle class, will cost less than Rs. 4 annually. A female of this class wears a long strip of Manchester or mill-made cloth, named a *sari*, wrapped round her person from head to foot. Its price is Re. 1 to Re. 1-8. Rent of land Rs. 17-8. Rents are

* (Memorandum on the Material Condition of the Lower Orders in Bengal, by F. H. B. Skrine, 1892.)

very high is this district, a fact due in some measure to the extensive sub-infeudation that prevails. Land which in the northern districts would not be charged more than Rs. 3-12 per acre here fetches Rs. 4-8. Wages of labourers employed in emergent seasons such as reaping time, Rs. 5. The present rates are 10 lbs. of paddy, equivalent to rather more than 6 lbs. of cleaned rice, and worth four annas per diem, *plus* food Repairs of implements, purchase of bullocks (four are kept, price Rs. 10 each), social and religious ceremonies, Rs. 25. Total outgoings, Rs. 182-8. A ryot of this class should therefore have a surplus of Rs. 82 at the year's end, but unfavourable seasons, litigation, and extravagant expenditure on ceremonies leave him very little. At the same time it must be observed that the cultivators of this division are not serfs of the money-lenders, as too many are in the central districts. Money-lenders exist, but their clients are people of a higher stratum, the large middle-class with interests on land to dispose of. The disappearance of the money-lender was noticed by Sir W. Hunter in his monumental Gazetteer published 20 years ago: and it is still more complete at the present day."

Since that estimate was made the price of rice, the main source of income, has nearly doubled, while the expenditure has not increased to anything like the same extent, and there is little doubt that the cultivators are now much better off than they were thirty years ago.

The artizans may be divided into the ordinary artizans, such as carpenters, blacksmiths and potters who are necessary for every community, and the artizans engaged in special industries, such as the weavers and braziers, or workers at other hardware in the district. The ordinary village artizans were formerly paid in kind, but this system is dying out and money wages are becoming the rule. These have risen, but it is doubtful whether they have risen proportionately to the increase in prices, and although the average income of this class is considerably higher than that of the ordinary labourer; their standard and status are also higher, and they are frequently not so well off. As to the special handicraftsmen it is difficult to obtain definite information. When their trade is brisk they flourish, when it is slack they suffer, and suffer the more because they cling to it notwithstanding its decay, and refuse to seek the more remunerative occupations open to them. At present the Swadeshi movement has led to a considerable increase in the demand for country-made cloth and other articles, and the silk and cotton weaving which was formerly such an important industry is reviving. The skilled artizans Artizans.

employed in the mines and factories receive much higher wages.

Labourers. In this district it is impossible to draw a sharp distinction between the poorer cultivators and the agricultural labourers. There are very few cultivators holding less than 4 acres who do not supplement their income by working as labourers, and there are scarcely any agricultural labourers who do not hold some land from a garden patch of ten *kāthās* to a share in rice fields. Even the non-agricultural labourers very often hold patches of cultivation. Agricultural labourers are usually paid in grain, and the increase in the price of food-stuffs has practically doubled the money value of their wage. The increase, however, is more apparent than real as the labourer requires much of the grain which he receives for his own consumption. It is doubtful therefore whether this class has increased much in material prosperity of recent years, though their circumstances are often much better off than might be supposed. In the factories and mines most of the hands earn much higher wages than they could get at home. At Rānīganj the labourers are mostly Bauris who will not as a rule work more than half the month. Though they could easily cut two tubs a day, they are usually content with cutting one, and they take frequent holidays. In Barākar Santāls form the majority of the miners. The rate of payment has risen of recent years and in 1906 varied between 5 annas and 6 pies and 7 annas a tub as compared with 3 annas in 1891 and 4 annas in 1895. The miners are usually a strong and merry lot, and for their status in life, very prosperous.

Beggars. The condition of no class varies so much as that of the mendicants. The professional beggars and religious mendicants such as *fakīrs*, *vaishnāvas*, and *sanyāsis* are often very well off. But there are a large number of homeless beggars, nearly all cripples or diseased persons, who derive a bare subsistence from charity and who have suffered very greatly from the recent rise in prices.

CHAPTER VIII.

OCCUPATIONS, MANUFACTURES AND TRADE.

BURDWĀN with its coal mines and factories is much less dependent on agriculture than the average Bengal district. The statistics obtained at the census of 1901 show that 58·9 per cent. of the total population are supported by agriculture, a figure much below the average for the division. The agricultural population in all numbers 902,000. Of these only 32 per cent. including 3,800 rent-receivers, 251,000 rent-payers and 36,000 labourers, are actual workers. The industrial population accounts for 16·7 of the total, of whom about half are actual workers including 22,000 miners, 4,500 potters, 9,000 cotton weavers, 20,000 rice pounders and 2,000 masons; goldsmiths, ironsmiths, sweetmeat makers, silk spinners and carpenters are also common. Commerce and the professions support a very small number, only 1·3 per cent. of the population being engaged in trade, while 2·3 per cent. are dependent on the professions for their livelihood: of the latter 43 per cent. are actual workers including 8,000 priests and religious mendicants, 2,700 male and female doctors, and 1,100 teachers. About 113,000 persons are earth-workers and ground-labourers, and 16,000 are herdsmen. The following is a brief account of the principal manufactures and industries of the district. OCCUPATIONS.

The coal industry is naturally much the most noticeable feature of the trade and commerce of the district. In spite of the difficulties caused by the scarcity of labour and the shortage of wagons the industry has made very rapid strides of late years, and the number of mines rose from 37 in 1881 to 160 in 1901. In 1903 there were 110 mines with an output of 2,759,000 tons, the number of work-people employed being 30,566, and in spite of the recent depression in trade the output has now (1909) increased to 3,414,628 and the number of work-people employed in the industry to 51,188. Most of the coal is sent by rail to Calcutta, and from there it is exported in large quantities to Colombo and Bombay. The miners are generally Bauris from Burdwān itself or Santāls, who have immigrated from the neighbouring districts. It is quite common for all the members COAL.

of a family to work in the same mine, and as a man's average wage is 12 annas a day the work-people are fairly prosperous. A full account of the Rānīganj coal-field is given in Chapter IX.

Factories. The discovery of coal and iron has naturally led to the establishment of factories in the neighbourhood of the collieries, and some of the most important industrial undertakings in Bengal are to be found in the Asansol subdivision.

The Bengal Iron and Steel Works, Barākar. The iron ore of the Rānīganj field consists mainly of a clay iron ore somewhat altered at the surface and occurs in considerable abundance in the iron stone shale group of the lower division of the Gondwana system. The proximity of good coking coal at Barākar led to the formation there in 1874 of a company under the title of "The Bengal Iron Company" to work the ore. The Company, however, collapsed after five years and the concern was bought over by Government. It was afterwards sold to the Bengal Iron and Steel Company. These works are situated on the grand chord line of the East Indian Railway, a few miles from Asansol. They consist essentially of blast furnaces and a foundry. There are three blast furnaces which are all of the same type, with cup-and-cone arrangement for feeding and closing the mouth, and the hot blast is supplied by five tuyēres to each furnace. The blast is heated by Cowper stoves, of which there are eight. The coke for the furnaces is at present largely obtained from Jherria, though it is seriously under consideration by the firm to make all their own coke so as to ensure uniformity of quality. The large percentage of ash in Indian coal and coke is one of the difficulties which beset the producer of pig-iron in this country. The ore is obtained over a considerable area in the Bengal coal-fields, and very different grade ores are obtained from the various workings. The ores all contain the iron in the form of Fe_2 and O_3 and some, *e.g.*, the Kalimati ores, are high grade and contain as much as 65 per cent. iron. The majority, however, contain a high percentage of silica, often as much as 20 per cent. With the present system of working, the various ores are mixed so as to feed the furnace with a material of constant proportions. The Company are, however, prepared to work with purer ore in one furnace so as to produce a hæmatite pig suitable for acid-hearth steel-making, if there is sufficient demand. The limestone used comes from Sutna.

The foundry which is close to the blast furnaces produces about 15,000 tons of castings per annum and is capable of making from 25,000 to 30,000 tons. The Barākar pig only is used for the foundries. The bulk of the castings are pipes and potsleepers, but a number of small and intricate castings are also made. At Barākar there is also a steel-producing and rolling plant (two 25-ton basic open-hearth furnaces and rolling plant to correspond) which was put up and commenced work in 1904, but was closed down and is now lying idle.*

The total quantity of iron produced during 1908 was 46,906 tons valued at Rs. 27,13,625. The average number of operatives, employed daily, was 2,934, and most of them were housed in coolie lines near the factory. The system of working is by shifts in the iron works and blast furnaces, and by midday stoppages in the foundry. About 1,700 persons are daily employed in iron mining, in order to procure a supply of the mineral for the iron and steel works at Barākar. The ore is found (1) in thin alluvial deposits and soil at a number of places, (2) as masses of hæmatite and magnetite in metamorphic rocks at Kalimati in Singbhūm, (3) in the ironstone shales of the Rānīganj coal-field. The alluvial deposits were at one time worked by natives. The Rānīganj ore is in the form of carbonate at depth, but it readily weathers and at the surface consists of hæmatite and limonite. The beds vary from 2 to 8 inches in thickness and form 1-17 of the whole series, which is 1,000 feet thick. About 50,000 tons of ore were won in 1901 from shallow trenches and pits. The success of the industry depends in a great measure on the coking qualities of the Bengal coal. The coke hitherto made in the Rānīganj coal-field is inferior in quality, but both Giridih and Jherria furnish a hard coke suitable for blast furnaces, though rather high in ash.

There is also a small branch iron works at Barākar established by Messrs. John King and Company, Engineers and Founders of Howrah. The outturn is very small and for 1908-09 was valued at Rs. 11,250 only.

Factories of Messrs. Burn and Co.

In connection with their pottery works at Rānīganj, Messrs. Burn and Company have opened lime-works at Andāl and brick and tile works at Durgapur. At the Rānīganj pottery, the only pottery in Bengal which is conducted on a large scale on western methods, the clays which are used are chiefly obtained from the coal measures of the neighbourhood and consist of decomposed shales. The works were commenced in 1866 by a Mr. Macdonald, and were taken over by Messrs. Burn and Company in 1869. The outturn in 1000 was valued at Rs. 3,18,467 and the number of operatives employed averaged 938. The work-people are for the most part housed in coolie lines near the factory, and the

* Monograph on Iron and Steel Works in Bengal, by G. R. Watson, Calcutta, 1907.

monthly wages paid for skilled labour vary from Rs. 15 for a potter to Rs. 20 for a fitter. The system of working is by mid-day stoppages. Glazed drain pipes, bricks, tiles and every variety of pottery is manufactured. The outturn of the lime-works at Andāl in 1909 was 138,381 maunds valued at Rs. 44,281, and 68 hands were employed, while at the Durgapur Brick and Tile Works the outturn for the same year was valued at Rs. 45,896. At present the average number of hands employed daily is 208.

The other important factories in the district are the Bengal Paper Mills at Rānīganj opened in 1891, which during 1909 employed 1,074 hands and made 5,394 tons of paper valued at Rs. 16,36,119, and the Bengal Dyers and Skinners Company. The latter Company in 1900 opened works at Bansra near Rānīganj and manufacture a tanning extract from myrobolams which is exported to Scotland. In 1909 the outturn was 293 tons valued at Rs. 35,160 and 76 operatives were employed. There are large railway works at Asansol and the Locomotive shop here employs on an average 113 hands. Finally there are seven oil mills in the district which are worked by mechanical power. The outturn during 1909 was 43,935 maunds of oil and 97,552 maunds of oil-cake valued at Rs. 7,42,787 and Rs. 1,54,563, respectively.

ARTS AND MANUFACTURES. Silk and Tasar Weaving. The silk-weaving industry, although a declining one, is still fairly prosperous, and during 1908-09 the total output was 70,000 yards of *tasar* and 48,430 yards of silk, valued at Rs. 75,000 and Rs. 37,679, respectively. It is carried on at Bāgtikra, Musthāli, and Ghoranāsh in the Kātwa subdivision and at Memāri, Jagdabād, and Pānchkolā in the Sadar. *Tasar* cocoons are not reared locally but are imported from the Santāl Parganas and from Orissa. The *tasar* cloth produced at Bāgtikra and Memāri is of excellent quality, and is exported as far as Madras and Bombay, where there is a considerable demand for it, but most of the cloth produced elsewhere is sold locally. The silk is made into pieces with embroidered edges which are used for *dhutis*, *sāris*, *chādars*, napkins and *mooka* (turbans). They are sold preferably to dealers of native firms who come round and the prices average about Rs. 8 or 9 for a piece of *garad* silk 10 cubits long and Rs. 7 or 8 for a piece of *tasar* silk of the same length. In some cases the *Mahājans* advance the money to the weavers to buy yarn from the dealers and then buy the silks when manufactured. A few of the weavers bring their produce into Burdwān and by thus avoiding the middlemen make better profits. The majority of the Kātwa silk goes to Calcutta where it is sold or exported. The Muhammadans of Madras who use long pieces 21 feet by 3 feet for their turbans are the largest consumers. The following account of the industry is taken from Mr. N. G. Mukerjee's Monograph on the Silk Fabrics of Bengal.*

"In the Kâlna subdivision no weaving is carried on, but cocoons are reared to a certain extent, and a good deal of *tasar* yarn is also manufactured. Cocoons are raised at Serampur, Kaknail and Khaiduttpara. Spinning is carried on at the above-mentioned villages, and also at Satni, Signbagh, Hamedpur, Gachee, Pathangram, Khanpur, Hat Tare, Nakdaha and Hapania. Employment is given to about 3,000 people, mostly engaged in cultivation, who eke out their agriculture by raising cocoons and by spinning the thread. By caste they are chiefly Satgopes, Chandâls, Gandhabanias or Mussalmans.

"The yarn costs about Rs. 15 to Rs. 16 a seer. This is manufactured into articles which sell at the rate of Rs. 8 or Rs. 9 per piece of 10 cubits, of which 2½ to 3 pieces can be manufactured in a month, and the average net income of a weaver would thus be Rs. 8 to Rs. 12 a month. *Garad* silk requires more skill and care than *tasar* silk but the wages obtained are quite as high. The cocoons cost Rs. 12, and Rs. 2 go to the women for making the yarn, and there are incidental expenses for dyeing, etc., which make the cost about Rs. 15 a seer, which is about the same as for *tasar* silk. The same quantity is woven, and pieces 7 cubits long are turned out to the number of three to four per month. It is said that a thoroughly energetic and skilful man could make Rs. 15 a month, but, on the other hand, the ordinary weaver's wages are nearer the lower limit than the higher.

"The caste rank of the weavers is fairly high, being inferior only to Brâhmans, Baidyas, and Kayasthas. Financially their position is not very high, and is sinking along with their industry. In the Kâtwa subdivision, *tasar* cocoon-rearing, silk-spinning and weaving are carried on in the following villages:—Bâgtikra, Goalkanigi, Madhatpur, Musthâli, Amdanga, Ghoranâsh, Panchberia, Jagadlanandapur, Chandal, Sribati, Multi, and Maygachi. Employment is given to about 5,000 families.

"Various castes take part in the growing and spinning, but the weavers are Tântis of the Navasak caste, which is only inferior to Brâhmans, Baidyas, and Kayasthas. No cocoons from which *resam* or *garad* might be manufactured are grown in this subdivision or imported: all importations are in the form of yarn. Cocoons for *tasar* silk manufacture are grown at Kâlna along the banks of the river, and are also imported from various places, of which Chaibassa in Singhbhûm is the most favoured. Sonamuki

*Calcutta, 1903.

in Bānkurā, Hunsongoon in Cuttack, and some places in the Santāl Parganas also send cocoons. These are imported by Uriya merchants and also by traders from Rājgrām, Bānkurā and elsewhere: at Kātwa there are also a few merchants who import.

"The cocoons are of various classes, viz.—

(1) *Daba*, the best quality, comes exclusively from Chaibassa in Singhbhūm; one *kahan* makes two seers of yarn. Its price is Rs. 10-8 to Rs. 12-8 for one *kahan* = 1,280 cocoons.

(2) *Bagai*, which also comes from Singhbhūm, produces 1¼ to 1½ seers of yarn per *kahan*, and its price is Rs. 7-12 to Rs. 9 per *kahan*.

(3) The *mugo*, which comes from Hazaribagh, produces 1¼ to 1⅜ seers of yarn per *kahan*, and its price is Rs. 7 to Rs. 8-8 per *kahan*.

(4) *Jaidui* or winter cocoon is a quality imported from various places in the cold weather: it produces only 12 to 13 chitaks of yarn per *kahan*, and is sold at Rs. 3 to Rs. 5 per *kahan*.

"Yarn for *tasar* manufacture is prepared in the following way:—

If the cocoons are not dead, they are hung in a cloth over boiling water until they become so. After being dried in the sun, they are placed in a vessel containing water, cattle-urine, and potash or *saji* water (the former being preferred at Kātwa, the latter in the Sadar) and boiled for about an hour. As they become soft they are taken out and peeled by the finger and placed in a stone vessel. The spinning is done by the women of the family, while the males weave or engage in other occupations. The spinner takes hold of the cocoon and pinches it and draws out the clue. The thread is wound on to a bamboo frame (*latai*) which is held in the right hand. The cocoons are kept on the left side of the spinner, and as the thread passes over the right thigh, it is twisted with the left hand before it passes on the *latai*. The women manage to weave about two seers of yarn a month, and they sell the best quality yarn for Rs. 12½ to Rs. 14 a seer. As the price at which they purchased the cocoons of the best sort was Rs. 10-8 to Rs. 12-8, their average monthly earnings are rather under Rs. 2. One anna a day is about the rate of wages prevalent."

Cotton weaving.

The cotton weaving industry, although declining rapidly as a result of European and Indian competition, still affords employment to a considerable number of weavers. The chief centres of the industry are Purbasthāli, Kālna and Manteswar, and in these three places nearly 2,000 persons were daily employed as weavers during 1908-09. There are also cotton weaving establishments at Ichagram, near Memārī and at Bāhādurpur, Baje, Itta, and Srikrishtapur in thana Jamālpur. At Ichāpur only coarse cloths and napkins are prepared, but at the other places mentioned very fine cloths are made. The produce is usually sent to Howrah, but there is some local consumption. The district outturn of cotton cloth for the same year was 2,585,400 yards, valued at Rs. 2,81,378. In 1898 the Collector reported as follows on this industry:—

"In the Kātwa subdivision the cotton industry is carried on principally by the weaver caste among the Hindus. On account of the wide use of European piece-goods, which are cheaper and finer in quality, the indigenous industry is gradually disappearing. Large numbers of weavers have abandoned their looms and have taken up other pursuits. Indeed, very few families are to be found now who are wholly engaged in weaving alone. Their present number does not admit of any appreciable comparison with that which existed in the past, and, as such, no endeavours have been made to collect figures indicating the numbers now engaged in this district."

These remarks still hold good. It is true that the Swadeshi movement has created a desire among the educated classes to support home industries. But economically it seems impossible that the hand-loom should ever compete successfully with machinery. There are 55 fly-shuttle looms in use at Kālna and they have also been introduced into the Asansol subdivision with some success. Elsewhere, although the looms have been introduced, they are not popular.

Iron utensils are made locally throughout the district. The most common type of blacksmith, the man who has not specialised in any branch of his trade, requires next to no tools or outfit. A hearth, a bellows to supply a blast to the fire, an anvil, a few pairs of tongs, a few hammers, and a cold chisel complete his outfit. His work is entirely carried on in a small shanty not more than 10 feet by 10 feet. The ordinary village blacksmith in Burdwān is usually paid by contract for repairing the agricultural implements of the village and often in kind, but for the manufacture of new implements he is paid in money and according to the price of the article. IRON-WARE AND CUTLERY.

The manufacture of cutlery is carried on in Burdwān town. The following is an account of the process of manufacture in what are probably the best cutlery shops in Bengal:*

"The blade of a knife, or scissors, is first of all fashioned by the blacksmith. His implements are an anvil, bellows, a hammer,

* Monograph on Iron and Steel Works in Bengal, by G. R. Watson, Calcutta, 1907.

chisel, and a pair of pincers. He heats the iron or steel in the furnace and beats it to the required shape and size on the anvil. A skilful blacksmith can thus fashion 72 knife blades during the course of the day, two inches to three inches in length, by a quarter of an inch in breadth. The blacksmith then hands the rough blades to the grinders and polishers.

"There are two kinds of hones for grinding, polishing, and sharpening blades. The first is of ordinary sand found on the banks of rivers and is used for rough work. The second is of very fine grit, obtained by crushing what appears to be a very close grained sandstone, called locally '*kruich pāthar*.' The solid wheel is about 15 inches in diameter, and its polishing edge is about a quarter of an inch in breadth. The cutler squats on his hems over the revolving polishing wheel, takes the knife or scissor blade in both hands and applies it to the revolving edge of the polishing and sharpening wheel, dipping the blade in cold water, whenever it becomes too hot to hold. The skilled artisan does the preliminary polishing and grinding on the sand wheel. He then makes over the blade to a confrere who proceeds to apply it to the '*kruich pāthar*' polishing and sharpening wheel. When the blade is sufficiently sharp and polished, it is handed over to another artisan, who fixes it in a vice, drills the necessary holes, shapes the brass, horn, or ivory for the handle, and fixes the blade thereto. The brass is in thin sheets, and is readily cut with a pair of steel shears made in the workshop. The horn, or ivory, is cut with a saw made locally or imported. It is shaped with a file and fixed to the blade. The horn or ivory is also highly polished by rubbing it in a mixture of brick dust, charcoal and oil. Finally, the knife is again polished on the '*kruich pāthar*' hone. In the case of a highly skilled artisan the polish is mirror-like, and equal to that of the imported article; the edge is also equally keen and fine. The operation in the case of a scissor blade is somewhat different. The blade and thumb-ring are polished and rounded on the revolving hones. The blade is then fixed in a vice, and the operator proceeds to polish the ring and the lower parts with an instrument called a '*maskolla*'. The holes for screws and nails are drilled with an instrument called a '*bhumar*'. This is a steel drill made in the workshop; it is 2 or 3 inches in length and is fixed to a round wooden handle about 8 or 10 inches in length. It is a pointed instrument, and when worked with a bow rapidly bores its way through brass, horn, ivory, iron and steel.

"In the case of the razor blade the process is identical. The blacksmith gives it birth on the anvil; it is then passed over to the polisher and the driller. But very few artizans make razors, and only one or two cutlers lay claim to be able to fashion razor blades of superfine quality. The brittle nature of the steel, and the delicacy of the blades, demand an exquisite judgment and gentleness of touch on the revolving hone. A good razor blade has also to be manipulated with great patience; the skilled artizan working from morning till evening cannot turn out more than two such blades a day: and his profit is not more than 4 annas per rupee. The price of these blades varies according to size and quality from Re. 1-4 upwards.

"The final polishing is done with brick-dust, charcoal and oil. The revolving hones last a month and a half in the case of the sand wheel and 3 months in the case of the '*kruish pāthar*' wheel. In large workshops half-a-dozen such wheels may be seen spinning, so that the blacksmith is frequently under the necessity of making fresh ones. Dies for stamping the artizan's name on the heel of the blade are made of steel locally; and I have no doubt that an unscrupulous artizan is able to forge the trade-mark and name of a European cutler."

The industry is not in a particularly flourishing condition and the occupation is said to be unhealthy. During 1908-09 the out-turn of cutlery for the district was 1,458 dozen.

BRASS. Brass and bellmetal ware is manufactured on a large scale in the district at Banpas in the head-quarters subdivision and at Dāinhāt and Begunkhotā in Kātwa. The brassware industry in the latter subdivision is however declining, as, owing to the silting up of the Bhāgīrathi, there is great difficulty in exporting the manufactured articles. The wares manufactured at Banpas are preferred for their superior polish and make. During 1909 the outturn was estimated at 6,401 maunds valued at Rs. 2,80,306.

OTHER INDUSTRIES. *Biris* are manufactured at Asansol and it is reported that they are gradually taking the place of cigarettes. Mats are made in considerable numbers in the neighbourhood of Purbasthāli and 220 persons were engaged in this manufacture in 1908. There are flour-mills in Asansol and Rānīganj, and ice and ærated water are manufactured for local consumption at Burdwān, Asansol, Rānīganj and Sītārāmpur. Earthen pots are made in every village for local consumption, and molasses and oil and oil-cake are also manufactured locally. At Dainhāt and Kātwa there are four families of sculptors who carve Hindu idols in black and white stone which is imported. The work is not of a high class. The finished articles are mostly sold locally, but are occasionally exported to Calcutta. At Nilpur, a suburb of Burdwān town, mosquito curtains of cotton thread are made by the

Muhammadan weavers, which are imported in some quantity to Calcutta. Indigo was formerly manufactured on a considerable scale in the Kālna and Bud-bud thānas, and so late as 1877 the area under cultivation was estimated at 16,500 acres and the out-turn at 1,640 maunds. Most of the Burdwān factories were under native management and as they failed to secure uniformity in the colour of their indigo, the price obtained for the dye in Calcutta was usually only between Rs. 100 and Rs. 200 a maund even in the best days of the industry. It has now practically died out entirely.*

TRADE. Excluding coal and iron the chief articles of export are rice, pulses of all sorts, rape-seeds, and oil and oil-cake, while the imports are English and Indian cotton piece-goods, salt, spices, kerosine-oil and castor-oil. The imports and exports are mostly to and from Calcutta, but there is a considerable export of grain to the west. The district is very well provided with communications and most of the important marts enjoy ample facilities for export and import by rail, road, or river. The chief centres of trade are the towns of Rānīganj, Asansol and Burdwān, and the railway stations at Memāri, Mānkur, Pānagar and Guskhāra which are important distributing centres. A considerable trade in timber is carried on in the towns of Burdwān and Rānīganj. The wood is brought from the forests near Chaibassa, Chakradharpur, and Maurbhanj by rail, and is chiefly *sāl*. The importance of Kātwa and Kālna, which were formerly regarded as the ports of the district, has declined since the opening of the East Indian Railway on which the great bulk of the trade is now carried. A small proportion, however, is still carried by river, and the sliting up of the Bhāgīrathi below Kātwa has affected the trade of that town seriously. The town is served by steamers for a portion of the year when there is sufficient water in the river. During the rest of the year its trade is carried by carts or country boats and a good deal is sent by the Ranaghāt-Murshidābād line. The Kātwa line from Hoogli, which is now under construction, will probably stimulate further developments. The internal trade of the district is mostly carried on by means of permanent markets and also by *hāts* and fairs.

WEIGHTS AND MEASURES. The steady extension of the coal industry and the industrial development which has resulted from it has naturally led to the standardization of weights in the district. In Asansol, Rānīganj and Burdwān, the three chief industrial centres, the only weight in use is the standard *seer* of 80 *tolās*. Elsewhere and for agricultural produce generally the *seer* commonly in use is the

* Statistical Reporter, April 1877.

so-called *kacha seer* of 60 *tolās*. This is used in Burdwān for agricultural produce and in most of the principal marts such as Ausgrām, Raīnā, Manteswar, Jamālpur, Khandagosh, Satgāchia, and Galsi. At some of the principal markets both *seers* are used; for instance, at Kāksa, Purbasthāli, Memāri and Sāhebganj coal and oil-cake are sold by the standard *seer* and agricultural produce, fish, and sweetmeats by the *kacha seer*. At Kātwa four *seers* are reported to be used of 5[illegible], 60, 80, and 82⅝ tolas.

The standard cubit (*hāth*) is now everywhere 18 inches. As regards Government lands it appears to have been converted from the old cubit of 20 inches by an order of the Board of Revenue in 1849. The cultivators however usually claim the old cubit of 20 inches called by them the *Sikandari hāth*, after, it is said, some long-armed Muhammadan of that name. Measurements, except in the Government estates, are very uncommon.

CHAPTER IX.

THE RANIGANJ COAL FIELD.

EARLY DISCOVERIES. THE first Englishman to discover the existence of coal in Bengal was probably Mr. Suetonius Grant Heatly who, in 1774, was the Collector of Chotā Nagpūr and Palāmau. In that year he and a Mr. John Sumner obtained from Warren Hastings a license empowering them to work coal mines in "Pachete and Birbhum." A Mr. Redferne subsequently joined the firm which as Sumner, Heatly and Redferne applied for and obtained the exclusive right, for a period of 18 years, to work and sell coal in Bengal and its dependencies. It addition to paying a Government royalty of one-fifth of the value of all the coal raised by them, they also agreed to supply Government with ten thousand maunds of coal a year for a period of five years. Under this agreement the firm in 1775 announced the arrival of 2,500 maunds or 19½ tons of Pānchet coal, and asked that it should be taken over. This appears to be the first occasion on which Bengal coal in any large quantity was brought into the market. The coal however was not taken over until 1777 when upon a second application from the firm the Commissary of Stores was directed to examine and report upon it.

In 1777 about the same time Farquhar and Motte asked permission "to bore cannon and to cast shot and shell in the district of Jherria, lying between the rivers Dammuda and Barākar." They gave as their reason for the selection of that locality that it "abounds in iron ore and is contiguous to the coal mine of Messrs. Sumner and Heatly." Unfortunately the coal Heatly produced was reported as being much inferior to that of England. In fact the Commissary of Stores, as the result of a series of experiments, came to the conclusion that it was only half as good as English coal and it was returned to the firm. This circumstance, together with the indifference of Lord Cornwallis to measures calculated to develop the internal resources or promote the external commerce of India, led to the neglect and apathy that characterised the first few years of coal mining in India. Mr. Heatly was afterwards transferred and it is doubtful whether any more of the coal was actually brought into the market. The mines first worked by him are said to have been six in number, three of which were at Aitūria, Chinakuri, and Damulia, and the others further west near the Barākar. In his Wild Sports in the East (1808), Williamson alludes to Indian coal, but says that the Company "finds it easier to send coal from England, as ballast, to their arsenals abroad, where quantities are occasionally used in fusing metals for casting ordnances." But none of the early European travellers in India make any mention of coal, prior to the first decade of the 19th century. This is abundantly exemplified by the silence of Milburn (Or. Comm., 1813) and of Macpherson (Hist. Europ. Comm. Ind., 1812), two authors who were certain to have had chapters on Indian coal and India's requirements in coal had these been questions of public importance at the time in which they wrote.

In 1808 the Indian Directors of the East India Company actually complained of the heavy charges involved by the indents for coal made by their Indian representatives, and they accordingly recommended an enquiry whether charcoal could not be substituted; and if not, they further recommended the transference of the ordnance works to England. The Earl of Minto, who was at the time Governor-General of India, directed that Indian coal should be submitted to actual tests by the military authorities in India, and further experiments were accordingly made by Colonel Hardwicke. His report however, was again very unfavourable, and the subject of coal for a time dropped out of notice. But in 1814 the Marquis of Hastings once more urged on the Military Board the desirability of ascertaining beyond doubt "whether the coal of India was of a quality calculated for the purpose of the forge." He also announced that a fully qualified person would be appointed to examine the mines, who would be furnished with the necessary apparatus to make borings and who would, for experimental purposes, procure a supply of coal from such a depth as to ensure that it would represent the average quality. Previous experiments were thus discredited owing to the coal used having been obtained from the surface and therefore much deteriorated.

By this time apparently coal was being regularly conveyed by boat down the Dāmudar river to Calcutta, and we hear of a Calcutta merchant having commenced to use Bengal coal notwithstanding the unfavourable reports published by the Military Board.*

* The Commercial Products of India: Sir George Watt, John Murray, London, 1908.

The expert deputed by Government was a Mr. Rupert Jones who was sent from England on purpose to examine the Bengal coal fields, and his report (written in 1815) will be found in the Asiatik Researches (1833, XVIII). Mr. Jones rediscovered Mr. Heatly's workings and also found the seam at Rāniganj which later in 1815 or 1816 he began to work on his own account. His report was on the whole favourable, and showed that Bengal coal might very well be used for many of the purposes for which English coal was being imported. But he did not himself realise the full value of his investigations. He foretold increased prosperity to Calcutta, through the coal he had discovered being a better and more economical fuel for burning the Sylhet limestone than the firewood then in use, but apparently he knew little of the great revolution steam was destined to effect, nor of the imperative necessity of an abundant and cheap supply of coal for commercial and industrial prosperity.

First Indian Company.

Mr. Jones received an advance from Government of Rs. 40,000, on easy terms, to enable him to work the seam discovered at Rāniganj, but in 1820 he came utterly to grief. Failing in other undertakings he was unable to repay the loan and his securities, Messrs. Alexander and Company, an agency house, were required to make it good. They accordingly paid the demand and in return took over the leases of the ground on which the mine was situated and became the owners of the colliery. This the Rāniganj mine, the first regularly constituted Indian mine under European supervision and capital in Bengal, was opened in 1820.

Formation of the Bengal Coal Company.

Other mines under European management were opened in quick succession. In 1823 the Chinakuri colliery was started by Mr. Betts on the site of Mr. Heatly's old workings. In 1824 Messrs. Jessop and Company opened the Damulia mine, and in 1830 Mr. Homfray of that firm opened the Chanch and Nuchibad mines. In 1835 Messrs. Alexander and Company failed and the Rāniganj mine with all the land and buildings passed into the hands of Babu Dwarkanath Tagore. The mine was then worked by the firm of Carr, Tagore and Company who in 1837 purchased the Chinakuri mine. In the same year Narayankuri, Chanch, and Nuchibad passed into the hands of Messrs. Gilmore, Homfray and Company, and in 1843 the concerns of Carr, Tagore and Company and of Gilmore, Homfray and Company were amalgamated into the Bengal Coal Company, which has retained the property ever since and which still owns many of the most extensive collieries in the Rāniganj field.

In 1839 the output was 36,000 tons, and by 1846 this had risen to 91,000 tons. Still little progress was made till the construction of the East Indian Railway in 1854 tapped the coal fields. But even then the progress was but slow until the jute mills and factories of Calcutta created a demand for the coal. In 1857-58 which was apparently the first year of especially recorded production, 293,000 tons were taken from the Indian mines and 92,000 tons imported. From that date the prosperity of the Bengal coal-field was assured. The demand for the coal which has aptly been termed "the direct expression of a rapidly expanding modern commerce" has increased by leaps and bounds. In 1868 the output was 459,000 tons; in 1878, 925,000 tons; in 1898, 4,608,000 tons; in 1904, 8,348,000 tons; in 1906, 9,783,000 tons; and in 1908, 12,149,000 tons, of which amount the Bengal mines supplied 11,559,000 or 95·15 per cent. In 1885 there were 95 mines, of which 90 were in Bengal; in 1900 there were 286 in operation, of which 271 were in Bengal; in 1906 there were 307 of which 274 were in Bengal; and in 1908 there were 583 of which 529 were in Bengal. The greatest development has taken place in the Rānīganj and Jherria fields, where the collieries are only 120 to 160 miles from Calcutta. For 1902 the output for the Rānīganj field totalled over three million tons from 155 mines employing 41,000 persons daily and by 1906 this had risen to 3,650,000 tons. The total output of coal from the mines in the district in 1909 was 3,414,000 tons and the number of work people employed in the industry was 51,000.* SUBSEQUENT DEVELOPMENT.

The railways consume one-third of the total output of Indian coal; and as Calcutta is the only important distributing port, the state of the Calcutta market is a true index to the state of the Indian coal trade. It can now be affirmed that India is rapidly approaching the state of being able to meet all her own wants for fuel. The imports of foreign coal into Calcutta were 70,000 tons in 1880, but by 1901 had dwindled down to 2,000 tons. The exports to foreign parts amounted to 8 tons in 1880, 26,000 tons in 1890, a quarter of a million in 1897, and more than half a million in 1901. English coal still competes with Indian coal at Bombay; for, although Indian coal can be bought in Calcutta for Rs. 7 per ton, the steamer freight and other charges raise its price to Rs. 15 at Bombay, and English coal of better quality can be bought for Rs. 17 per ton. Indian coal reaches Suez on the west and Singapore on the east, where it competes with Japanese coal. The imports into India generally have been shrinking steadily for years and in 1903-04 were one-fourth of the quantity

* (Report of the Chief Inspector of Mines for 1908.)

taken nine years previously. And of these imports Bombay—a province remote from the Indian mines—consumes by far the major portion, viz., 148,311 tons out of the total of 179,935 tons in 1905-06 England, Australia and Japan are the supplying countries. But a new trade has arisen, namely in coal exported to Indian Ocean ports—a traffic that it would seem is instantly stimulated and permanently strengthened by the strikes and other accidental causes which in Europe and Japan tend to raise the price of coal. A vivid conception of the present magnitude and importance of the Indian coal industry may be had from the circumstance that in 1908 the output came to over 12 million tons, while the outputs of both Canada and Australia were each under 9 million tons. But a still more significant fact may be added in conclusion, namely, that Indian coal is the cheapest in the world. The average pitmouth price was in 1902, Rs. 2-12 (3*s.* 8*d.*) and in 1906, Rs. 2-15 (3*s.* 11*d.*) per ton, while in the United States the corresponding average price was 5*s.* 8½*d.*, in Australia 7*s.* 9*d*, in the United Kingdom 8*s.* 2¾*d*, in Germany 8*s.* 10½*d.*, in Canada 9*s.* 3*d.*, and in New Zealand 10*s.**

THE RĀNIGANJ FIELD.

The most valuable of the coal fields in Bengal are patches of Gondwāna strata faulted into the Archaean schists and gneisses, and arranged as a band roughly east to west along the valley of the Dāmudar river. The easternmost of these fields, known as the Rānīganj field, being the nearest to Calcutta, and consequently the earliest to be connected by railway with the chief market for coal, was the first to be opened up, and is still the chief producer. Coal was worked in this field more than a century ago, but its output merely supplied local requirements until the East Indian Railway entered the field in 1854. The Gondwāna system is represented in the Rānīganj field by beds ranging from the Tālcher series to the Pānchets, the strata being so disposed, with a general southerly dip, that the oldest rocks are found resting on the Archaean gneisses on the northern boundary of the field, while the younger series follow in order as bands, with outcrops tending roughly east and west until in the south the Pānchets are found as irregularly shaped outliers. The coal is confined to the Dāmudar series, which in this field is divided into:—

		Ft.
1.	Barākar stage	2,000
2.	Iron-stone shales about ...	1,400
3.	Rānīganj stage about ...	5,000

* The Commercial Products of India: Sir George Watt, John Murray, London, 1908.

Coal seams occur in the Barākar and Rānīganj stages, and in this field about 69 per cent. of the total output is obtained from the younger or Rānīganj seams. The formation lying between is worked for its clay iron-stone nodules, which are used in the blast furnaces at the Barākar iron-works. Coal from the older Barākar seams differs from that raised from the Rānīganj stage in containing a smaller percentage of moisture and volatile hydrocarbons, with a larger proportion of fixed carbon. The distinction is specially constant in regard to the included moisture. Barākar coals yield very nearly 1 per cent. of moisture, while the average amount in a series of assays of samples from the lower seams of the Rāniganj stage is 3·81, and from the upper seam of the stage 6·86 per cent.

Composition of Rānīganj and Barākar coals.

METHODS OF WORKING.

The seams vary up to 95 feet in thickness, and the portions worked vary from 2 feet 6 inches to 45 feet thick. The systems of work differ, though all are of the pillar and stall type. As a rule a quarry is commenced at the outcrop; and as it pays to remove a large overburden from thick seams, a number of huge open excavations have been formed. When the cover overlying a seam is too thick to be economically removed, or when the seam is thin, galleries from 8 to 12 feet wide are driven both on the dip and along the strike of the seam leaving pillars of coal, which vary according to the caprice of the manager of the colliery, from 12 to 40 and occasionally 100 feet square, the larger pillars being left in the case of thick seams or thick cover. A system which provides for 12 feet galleries and 12 feet pillars yields at once three-fourths of the coal but the remaining one-fourth, which is left in pillars, can seldom be won. A system, allowing 12 feet galleries and 60 feet pillars, yields 30 per cent. of coal in the first working and 70 per cent. is left in pillars, but unless the seam be more than 20 feet thick a large proportion of this 70 per cent. can be obtained in the second working ("pillar working" or "broken working"). Pillar working is mainly attempted in European-managed mines. There is always danger of a fire breaking out in large areas of pillars.

In driving galleries it is usual to start in the top of the seam with a height of 6 feet, and after this drive has advanced some distance, to deepen it to the full height of the seam by cutting out the remainder of the coal in successive steps. At a few mines the galleries are commenced in the lower portion of the seam, and are heightened by dropping the coal left above. In the East Indian Railway collieries in the Giridih coal-field a whole "side of work" is extracted by a combination of the pillar and long wall methods. The lower portion of the seam is cut up into pillars 6 feet in height, and the latter are thinned down till they are only just able to carry the weight of the overlying coal. These thinned pillars are then blown down by dynamite, and the top coal (17 feet thick), which comes away readily from a strong sandstone roof, falls on the floor. When a large area of coal has been extracted, a rib of coal is left against the worked out portion of goaf, and a new set of workings formed from the goaf.

The systems of raising the coal to the surface vary from the primitive method of manual labour (*i.e.*, in baskets carried on the heads of coolie women) to hauling-sets of five or ten tubs on inclines provided with rails set to gauges varying from 1 foot 9 inches to 2 feet, or winding out of well-fitted shafts up to 640 feet in depth by direct acting engines. At one colliery double-decked cages with four tubs have been introduced. All three methods are in vogue in the chief coal fields.

LABOUR. A large number of the colliers are aboriginals, Sântals, Mundas, Oraons or Kols, and the rest are semi-Hinduized low castes among whom communities of Bauris, who are nominally *palki* bearers and cultivators, have been cutting coal for so many generations that they now regard it as the special function of their caste. The average output of coal per labourer is very low and in 1908 was only 101 tons as compared with 290 tons in the United Kingdom and 596 in the United States. "Handling a miner's tools is more a matter of skill than is generally supposed, and at present the Indian coal miner is a raw recruit and clumsy with his weapons."*

The underground work is performed at a fixed price per tub of coal by families or gangs of men, women and children, who choose their own hours of labour. The men cut the coal and the women and children carry and load it into tubs. As a rule they also push the tubs to the shaft or incline, but at one colliery 110 horses and ponies are employed to "lead" the coal underground. A man can cut about 2½ tubs (1¼ tons) of coal per day of eight hours, but he seldom works more than five days in the week, and strictly observes Pujas (religious festivals), while during the marriage season no work is done. "Apparently the Indian miner has not yet reached that stage of ambition when he wishes to increase his earnings. As by filling one tub per day he can obtain quite sufficient to meet all his needs it does not dawn upon him that by filling three he might be steadily placing himself beyond the risk of want." The coal cutters in Bengal can earn from 8 to 12 annas a day for underground work, while unskilled labourers on the surface earn only four

* (Report of the Chief Inspector of Mines for 1905.)

to five annas a day. Women may earn from 1 to 2 annas and as a result of this high total income of a family there is a general rise of labour rates around all mining centres. Electric lighting, electric blasting, and electric coal cutting are now being introduced into some of the Bengal mines. In a very few mines safety lamps are used, but in the great majority no appreciable quantities of fire damp are found. Accidents are also rare. There has been not only a very low death-rate from isolated accidents in Indian coal mines but also a general absence of those disasters which led in Europe to special legislation for the protection of the miners. During 1908, however, there was a serious falling off in this respect and the death-rate per 1,000 persons employed was 1·37 as compared with ·86 in the preceding year. In his report the Chief Inspector of Mines writes: "The desire to increase raisings, the frequent attempts to get easy coal regardless of safe conditions, particularly trespassing to rob pillars, the casual way in which work-people wander about the haulage roads in Bengal mines, and the large amount of untrained labour is responsible for much of the increase."

For purposes of inspection the district of Burdwān together with the adjoining district of Bānkurā is included in inspection circles Nos. 2 and 3. Circle No. 2 also includes all mines in the district of Mānbhūm east of Ādra and Gobindpur and all mines in the district of Hazāribāgh: it also includes all mines in Baluchistan, the United Provinces, the Punjāb, and Ajmer-Merwāra. Circle No. 3 includes the Sāntal Parganas, Bīrbhūm, Bombay, the Central Provinces and Madras. INSPECTION.

(Authorities.—The Commercial Products of India, Sir George Watt: John Murray, London, 1908. Statistical Account of Burdwān, Sir William Hunter. The Imperial Gazetteer of India, Vol. III. Report of the Chief Inspector of Mines for 1908.)

CHAPTER X.

MEANS OF COMMUNICATION.

FORMER ROADS.

THE earliest road, in the modern sense of the word of which there is any trace in the district was the magnificent Bādshāhi (royal) or military road, constructed by the Muhammadan conquerors, which ran from Midnapore through the town of Burdwān to Rājmahāl, whence it was continued to Monghyr. The remains still exist in perfection in what is now the Bīrbhūm district, just north of the Ajay. The road was an embanked one, 75 yards in width, planted with trees and was aligned in perfectly straight sections between certain points chosen for their natural features, such as river crossings, or great tanks. At every eight miles a mosque was built, with an assignment of lands for its maintenance. According to tradition the road was constructed by the Subāhdars of Bengal in the 15th century, when their seat of Government was either at Panduā or Gaur. In the Burdwān district no bridges survive on this road, and the waterways which it traverses are so wide that it is not likely that their bridging was ever attempted. District roads follow this great roadway from the Ajay through the police circle of Mangalkot to the metalled road from Guskhārā railway station to Nityanandpur on the Burdwān and Kātwa road, and from Karjāna, one of the mosque stations, to Burdwān. The Burdwān and Kātwa road also is maintained along it for eight miles, whilst south of Burdwān the metalled road from that town to Midnapore adheres to its line. In the latter localities its distinctive character has been almost entirely lost, and its sides have been so much encroached on by cultivation that the present roadway is with difficulty maintained. The best preserved section of this grand old road, in which its original proportions can be most fully appreciated, is the length of eight miles from Karjāna to its intersection by the Guskhārā metalled road.

The mosque at Burdwān may be identified with that still attached to the Pīr Bāhrām shrine. At Karjāna, eight miles north of Burdwān, the mosque has disappeared, though the site and its brick ruins are plainly visible. At Kalutanr or Sayir, eight miles further north, a very large mosque, still maintained in a dilapidated state by the Musalman villagers, marks the old station. It is an ugly building, with only a little stone work about its foundations, and the bricks of which it is built are large, coarse and modern looking. At Sarbakpur on the road to Uchallan, eight miles south of Burdwān, a similar building survives in much the same state. At Mangalkot the mosque stands on a mound and is a beautiful ruin, still in very fair preservation. It is built of basalt and fine small bricks, the basalt stones having obviously first done duty in a Hindu building. It has been conjectured by some observers familiar with the Gaya shrines that the Mangalkot mosque was originally a Buddhist erection. The *aimma* lands which served for the maintenance of these buildings were all resumed between 1819 and 1836. If the tradition that the road was constructed in the 15th century is correct it points to the great age of some of the immense tanks, with which the district is studded, inasmuch as the most frequent points, from which the straight sections of the road were laid down, are these tanks, to the existence of which the angles in its course are plainly due.

On the bank of the Ajay opposite Kātwa the village of Sankai stands in a rectangular mud fort, now intersected by the high road, which was subsidiary to that at Kātwa and served to defend the mouth of the river which, in its course through the district, formed the principal highway from the west up to the end of the last century. Three miles north of Sankai there stands in isolation on the plain a solid mass of masonry, comprising a Mughal bridge of three large arches, but the waterway, which it was meant to span, has disappeared. It is uncertain whether this bridge stood on the road from Hooghly to Murshidābād, along which Clive marched in 1757, or on the branch road from Kātwa to Nagar in Birbhūm. There is another old Bādshāhi road known as Takti Khan's Jangal which extends over thirteen miles from Rādhakantapur on the Satgāchia road near Satgāchia police station to the border of the district at Dastanpur in thāna Jamālpur. A portion of this road, about four miles in length, from mile 55 of the Grand Trunk Road to Jougrām has been restored by the District Board recently. The road has also been bridged though it is not metalled.

In a letter from the Judge and Magistrate, dated the 9th March 1802, we read that the "three grand and most useful roads leading to Hooghly, Cutwa and Culna, which may properly be termed the ports of the district, have been completely made." A fourth leading to Birbhūm was in a considerable state of forwardness, and the Magistrate proposed to commence another to join the military road leading to Midnapore. A new bridge had recently been constructed over the Bānka at an expense of Rs. 20,000. The roads, however, were very defective in bridges. Most of these roads were originally constructed and maintained by forced labour, convicts being employed on this work, but a considerable portion of the road to Kālna was made by the Mahārājā of Burdwān, that town being his country seat.

MODERN ROADS. The District Board now maintains in all 203½ miles of metalled and bridged roads, 298 miles of unmetalled roads and 652 miles of village roads. Of these the Grand Trunk Road which traverses the district for 100 miles running parallel with the railway, portions of the Rānīganj-Midnapore road and the Lithoria road near Sitārāmpur, are maintained by the Board with the help of a grant from Provincial grants. The more important roads are (1) the Grand Trunk Road which enters the district at the 51st milestone from Calcutta. This magnificent road, 40 feet wide in places, is metalled with laterite metal up to the 128th mile, and beyond with horneblende or iron stone, the metalled surface being 8 feet wide except for the last 20 miles before it leaves the district, where it is 16 feet wide. Throughout its length, except in the town of Burdwān itself, 150 feet of land has been acquired for the road. The road is bridged throughout, crossing the rivers Banka, Tamla, Singaran and Nunia, and the Bengal-Nāgpur Railway at Asansol, which here runs in a cutting, by an overbridge. There are level crossings of the East Indian Railway at Memāri, 56th and 59th miles; near Pānagar, 101st mile; on the 143rd mile where the road crosses the Luckipur branch line; and near Asansol, 156th mile. There are inspection bungalows at Bud-Bud, 96th mile; Rajband, 106th mile; Mohanpur, 119th mile; Chandmaree, 129th mile; and a dāk bungalow at Barākar. The road runs parallel with and close to the East Indian Railway throughout its entire length, and there is consequently little traffic on it except between Rānīganj and Barākar.

(2) Burdwān to Katwa, 34 miles 70 yards. The road is metalled and bridged throughout and there are inspection bungalows at the 8th, 15th, 29th and 35th miles.

(3) Memāri to Manisambati, 16 miles.

(4) Panduā in Hooghly to Kālna, 15 miles, of which the first twelve miles are in the Hooghly district and are maintained by that Board.

(5) Khāna junction feeder road to the Grand Trunk road, 1 mile 5 furlongs.

(6) Guskhārā to Nityanandpore, 14 miles 1 furlong. There is an inspection bungalow on the first mile at Guskhārā.

(7) Guskhārā to Mānkur, 14 miles 6 furlongs.

(8) Mānkur to Bud-Bud, 2 miles 2 furlongs.

(9) Pānagar to Elambazar, 14 miles. The Dulay-Kandore suspension bridge on the 5th mile has a 75 feet span and a waterway of 750 square feet. The river Kunur, crossed in the 7th mile, is generally fordable throughout the year, but is subject to sudden freshets which last only a few hours. The road ends on the right bank of the river Ajay and there is an inspection bungalow on the 2nd mile near Kaksa.

(10) Pānagar to the Dāmodar, 3 miles.

(11) Rājband to Gopālpur, 2 miles 3 furlongs.

(12) Rāghunāthchak Ferry Road, 6 furlongs.

(13) Rānīganj to Mangalpur, 2 miles.

(14) Rānīganj to the Ajay, 16 miles. The road is continued in Bīrbhūm to Suri. There is a ferry at the end of the road, on the river Ajay, in the Bīrbhūm district.

(15) Sītārāmpur to Nyāmatpur, 1 mile 4 furlongs.

(16) Barākar Feeder Road, 4 furlongs.

(17) Rādhānagar to Sanctoriā, 2 miles 7 furlongs.

(18) Rānīganj to the Dāmodar river, 3 miles 2 furlongs.

(19) Lithoria road—Nyamatpur to the Dāmodar river, 3 miles 2 furlongs.

Besides these first class roads there are several main roads of which portions are metalled. The more important are—

(1) Burdwān to Bānkurā, 10 miles 3 furlongs.

(2) Burdwān to Kālna, 33 miles 7 furlongs; an old road constructed by the Mahārājā of Burdwān and made over to the Road Cess Committee. The first 4 miles and the last 5 miles and 7 furlongs are metalled. The Mahārāja used to maintain staging bungalows at every eight miles along this road, but only two are now kept up—at Satgāchia and Kālna.

(3) Kātwa to Kālna, 33 miles 7 furlongs, of which the first five miles from Kātwa are bridged and metalled.

Besides these almost every railway station has its feeder road and these are for the most part metalled. There are also a number of unbridged roads constructed during the scarcity of 1874. The north Dāmodar embankment from Guhugram, 13 miles west of Burdwān, to below Chakdighi, where the river enters the Hooghly district, affords a high-level roadway passable by carts, and the Ajay embankments are much used as foot-paths.

The Burdwān, Rānīganj and Asansol Municipalities, as well as those of Kātwa and Kālna, also maintain a considerable length of metalled roads. In 1908 the Burdwān Municipality Municipal road.

kept up 23 miles of metalled road, while in the Rānīganj Municipality there were 5 miles of metalled roads. Kālna and Kātwa which are comparatively poor Municipalities maintain 18 miles of metalled road, while at Dāīnhāt 4 miles of metalled road are maintained.

Staging bungalows.

The District Board maintains staging bungalows on the Grand Trunk Road at Bud-Bud, Rājband, Midnapore and Chandmaree. It also keeps up inspection bungalows at Karjāna, Susandighi, Srikhand, Kātwa, Memāri, Guskhārā, Pānagarh, Oochalan, Satgāchiā, Kālna, Asansol, Banbahāl, Jaunagar and Kusumgrām. Dâk bungalows are also maintained at Barākar on the Grand Trunk Road and Burdwān, where half of the circuit house is now used as a dâk bungalow. Most of the bungalows have accommodation for two persons and contain the necessary furniture.

Bridges.

The network of rivers, creeks, and drainage channels with which the district is covered add very greatly to the cost of the construction and repair of its road communications. For instance the Grand Trunk Road, which traverses the district from end to end for nearly 100 miles, is carried over six rivers, including the Banka, Tamla, Singaran and Nunia. Two of the bridges over these have each a total waterway of 2,000 superficial feet, and the total waterway of the bridges on the road is 10,020 superficial feet. In the same distance there are one hundred and sixty-six brick arched culverts with a total waterway of 3,562 superficial feet. At Barākar, where the road leaves the district, the river of that name is spanned by a fine masonry bridge. Other important bridges are the Dulay-Kandore suspension bridge on the road from Pānagar to Elambazar, which has a span of 75 feet; the Singaran and Tumani bridges on the road from Rānīganj to the Ajay; the Victoria bridge over the Khusi Nala and the Karjāna bridge on the Burdwān-Kātwa road.

WATER-WAYS.

The chief waterway is the Bhāgīrathi, up which steamers ply to Kālna all the year round. Formerly all the coal exported from the Rānīganj coal-field was carried down the Dāmodar. An account of this traffic in 1852 is given in the report on the Dāmodar Valley by T. Oldham*.

"At present all the coal from this district is sent down to Calcutta in boats by the Dāmodar, a river, or rather torrent, which is only navigable for a few months in the year, and even then during floods only. At these times an immense fleet of boats may be seen starting from the several wharfs or ghats along the

* No. VIII of the selections from the records of the Bengal Government, 1852.

banks, and stretching in a continuous line for some miles in length. Should the flood continue these boats, with few exceptions, reach Umpta (where the river becomes sufficiently deep to be navigable at all seasons) in safety, but should the water fall, as often happens before they have accomplished this distance, they are left stranded on some *char*, possibly to get off again during some succeeding rise of the water but more probably to be destroyed at last." There is now practically no traffic on either the Ajay or the Dāmodar. Such as there is consists merely of timber rafts floated down when the rivers are in flood.

The trade on the Bhāgīrathi above Kātwa is now declining greatly owing to the silting up of the river bed. At certain seasons of the year the river is only with difficulty kept open for the passage of country boats, and it is only in the rainy season that the steamers from Calcutta can reach the town. This river was formerly the ordinary channel for Behar produce and in 1842-43 carried as much as 120 lakhs of maunds of produce, and even so late as 1876 carried 40 lakhs of maunds a year.* The competition of the East Indian and other railways however has reduced the traffic on it to a mere shadow of what it once was, and although this is now to some extent reviving owing to the demand in Calcutta for country produce, such as jute and vegetables, it forms but a minute proportion of the trade of the district.

There is a daily steamer service of Messrs. Hoare, Miller and Company's steamers to and from Kālna throughout the year, and to and from Kātwa on alternate days during the rainy season. The steamers carry both passengers and goods. The only other boat route of which much use is made is the lower reach of the Kharī river below Manteswar police-station. A large quantity of grain is brought down in country boats by this route from Nādanghāt, the principal rice mart of the interior.

The only canal in the district is the Eden canal, which was opened by Sir Ashley Eden in 1881. The canal receives its water from the river Dāmodar with which it is connected by the river Bānka. There are sluices at Jujuti some six miles west of the town of Burdwān. The canal starts from an anicut at Kānchannagar, immediately west of the town, and extends to Jamālpur where it joins the Kāna-Nadi and the Kāna-Dāmodar. It is never used for navigation, and was constructed partly for purposes of irrigation and partly in order to supply the Burdwān Municipality with a sufficient supply of water for the waterworks, and to clear the low-lying waterlogged villages on the right bank of the Dāmodar. Canals.

* (Statistical Register, April 1877.)

Ferries. The District Board maintains thirteen public ferries, the management of which has been made over to the Local Boards. The most important of these are the ferry over the Dāmodar at Ragunath Chak near Rānīganj on the Rānīganj-Midnapore road, those over the Bhāgīrathi at Mirzapur, Dewānganj and Uddhanpur, and the ferry on the Ajay on the Kātwa road at Sankhari. The ferry receipts are decreasing and in 1908-09 amounted to Rs. 9,300 as compared with Rs. 10,700 in the previous year. The decrease is attributed to the fact that most of the rivers are fordable during the greater part of the year. Besides the thirteen ferries managed by the District Board there are five ferries which belong to Government, viz., at Kālna, and Gayespur on the Bhāgīrathi, and at Sadar Ghāt and Kastha Golā on the Dāmodar within the town of Burdwān. The whole proceeds of the Kastha Golā ferry and half the proceeds of the Sadar Ghāt ferry have been made over to the Burdwān Municipality.

RAILWAYS. The East Indian Railway main line traverses the district, the loop and chord lines branching north at Khāna Junction, and Sītārāmpur. At Ondal (Andāl) Junction the line to Suri which crosses the Ajay by the recently constructed bridge north of Baidyanathpur station leaves the main line. The growth and prosperity of the district have been very intimately connected with the railway. Construction was started in 1851 and in 1855 the line was opened as far as Rānīganj, which was the terminus during the Mutiny. The rapid development of the coal industry which has transformed the Asansol subdivision from an unpeopled wilderness into one of the busiest industrial centres in the world soon followed. Formerly, as has already been noted, all the coal was sent down the Dāmodar in barges, an expensive and risky method of transport. Of late years many new branch lines have been constructed to serve the coal fields, and in the western portion of the Asansol subdivision there is now a network of lines and sidings leading to the collieries. The Ondal loop separates from the main line at Ondal and goes round the north of the coal fields, rejoining the chord line at Alipore north of Sītārāmpur, while there is an interior loop which serves Toposi, Ikhra, Jamuria and Chichuria stations with a branch to Domohāni. From Asansol a branch of the Bengal-Nagpur Railway connects with the main line at Sini. In 1907 the grand chord line between Gaya and Sītārāmpur was opened. The line crosses the Barākar river at Barākar by a fine viaduct and has considerably shortened the through route to Allahabad. Asansol itself has become one of the largest railway settlements in India, and the locomotive shops there are said to be the most extensive in the world. There are Railway settlements also at Andāl, Burdwān and Rānīganj.

Railway projects.

A line from Hooghly to Kātwa via Kālna is at present under construction and the land is now being acquired. The length will be 65·20 miles and the approximate cost is estimated at Rs. 61,72,000. It is proposed to eventually continue this line through Azimganj to Barharwa station on the loop line, with the object of tapping the more important villages and trading centres along the west bank of the Bhāgīrathi. A further extension of the line to Sainthia station on the Ondal-Sainthia chord line, or to Ahmadpur station, is also projected in order to link up this section of the line with the proposed Gaya-Koderma-Baidyanath and Ahmadpur branch, the survey of which was sanctioned by the Government of India in 1902. The construction of a branch line from Burdwān to Kātwa is also under consideration, but it is unlikely that this will be taken up for some time.

Light Railways.

There are no light railways or tramways in the district. In December 1901 Messrs. Martin and Company submitted a proposal to the District Board for a light railway (2′ 6″ gauge) from Memāri railway station to Chakdighi on the Dāmodar river, a distance of some 15 miles. The Board at first received the proposal favourably but, after further investigation, decided not to proceed with the scheme.

POSTAL COMMUNICATION.

In 1908-09 there were 183 post-offices in the district and 656 miles of postal communications. During the year 6,946,000 postal articles were delivered including 2,230,000 letters, 3,960,000, post cards and 350,000 packets and parcels. The value of money-orders issued in the same year was Rs. 31,79,000 and of those paid Rs. 25,07,000. Postal telegraph offices have been opened at Burdwān, Kālna, Kātwa, Samudragarh, Ukhra, Rānīganj, Kālipahāri, Asansol, Sitārāmpur, Barākar, Kulti, Nandi, Panuria, Charanpur, and Dishergarh.

CHAPTER XI.

LAND REVENUE ADMINISTRATION.

EARLY HISTORY.

IN the "Ain-i-Akbari" (1590 A. D.), Burdwān is mentioned as a *mahāl* or *parganā* of *Sarkār* Sharīfabād, and was, as then constituted, assessed at 46,903½ Akbarshāhi rupees of 175 grains troy of silver each. The present district area, however, at Todar Mal's settlement fell within various *sarkārs*, portions of which were afterwards amalgamated into one great zamīndāri, including also the whole of Bānkurā and Pānchet (Mānbhūm) together with parts of Hooghly and Bīrbhūm.

The settlement was revised in 1658 by Prince Shāh Shuja, the son of the Emperor Shāh Jahān, and again in 1722 by Murshid Kulī Khān, better known as the Nawāb Jafar Khān. In his statement Burdwān is mentioned as a '*chakla*,' comprising the *sarkārs* of Sharīfabād, Madāran, the greater part of Salīmabād or Sulaimanabād, and a portion of Sātgaon or Hooghly, and included the great estates of the Burdwān house, one-third of Bīrbhūm, and the whole of Bānkurā and Pānchet. The *chakla* contained 61 *parganas*, and was assessed at a revenue of 22,44,812 *sikka* rupees. On the 27th September 1760 A. D., Burdwān, which then contained an area of 5,174 square miles, and was described as being the most productive district within the whole Province or *Subah* of Bengal, was ceded to the East India Company, together with the districts of Midnapore and Chittagong, by Nawāb Mīr Muhammad Kasīm Khān, Governor of Bengal. By the Imperial *farman* which made the grant, the Company acquired the right of free perpetual tenure in the land, and these rights extended over the whole *chakla* of Burdwān. This great zamīndāri when ceded to the Company, was estimated to yield a net revenue of 31,75,391 *sikka* rupees but for many years afterwards the Company's officers had the greatest difficulty in collecting even a portion of this sum. The first "Superintendents" appointed by the Company were Mr. Johnstone, Mr. Hay and Mr. Bolts. Dissatisfied with the collections for 1760-61 they farmed out the estate at public auction for a period of three years with the result that the revenue was increased from Rs. 31,75,391 to Rs. 38,58,429, the total gross revenue from the district in 1765 being estimated at Rs. 44,84,049. The increase was however more apparent than real and it was not till 1771 that this revenue was realised in full.

A most interesting account of the early revenue history of the district under British rule is given in Mr. Sharistadar Grant's famous review of the revenues of Bengal, which is incorporated in the fifth report of the Select Committee on the affairs of the East India Company. After proudly comparing the zamīndāri of Burdwān, "the most compact, best cultivated, and, in proportion to its dimensions, by far the most productive in annual rent to the proprietary sovereign" with the "boasted Hindoo territory of Tanjore" and the great zamīndāri of Benares he goes on to point the moral of his comparison. "This pre-eminence of the ceded British territory in financial circumstances, hath been attained chiefly in a period of ten years by repeated *hustabood* investigation, and bringing to the credit of the exchequer the Keffyet or profitable increase discovered to have been privately realised from the country by the zamīndār and other intermediate Agents of Government, in addition to the jumma Ausil and Abwab already authoritatively established. The Company's management of Burdwān is approved of on all sides, and by the most enlightened of our English financiers held up as an example worthy of general imitation. The circumstances which distinguished it were briefly as follows.

In September 1760 the whole district, with all the other ceded lands, became subject to the British Government; it was rated proportionately, in the moment of transfer, by original and increased assessments, at a standard considerably higher than that of any other zamindary jurisdiction of the *saubah*; yet then or afterwards, no diminution of its rental, such as was suddenly effected by M. R. Khān in 1765, could even have been dreamt of. On the contrary, with the extension of local knowledge, the revenues were progressively improved, and always surpassed the share that should be proportionately forthcoming. When Bengal altogether was rated at or yielded the largest income to the exchequer, before the Company's acquisition of the Dewanny, Messrs. Johnstone, Hay and Bolts, were the first appointed English Superintendents. They appear to have acquired a minute and intimate knowledge of the resources and capacity of the country confided to their charge, in so much as to ascertain the portions of the country cultivated, uncultivated, alienated, and most productive lands. In their researches, though aided by uncommon universal intelligence, they probably obtained the most satisfactory information through the custom, which

First English Superintendents.

then was tolerated, of admitting European farmers. They held a considerable part of the district in their own hands and were accused of selecting for themselves the most profitable parganas leased.

"In violation of the financial practice of the Mogul Empire, the rents of Burdwān were let at public sale in 1169 A.B. (1762) for three years to irresponsible temporary farmers, from whose engagements, if fulfilled, a Keffyet or annual profit would have accrued to Government of 13 lakhs of rupees above the aggregate assessments of Ausil and Abwab. The needy adventurers who became contractors at the sale of course failed in their agreements, and to crown the measure of imputed mismanagement, an impost of 9 annas per bega was levied on all the Bazee Zemeen found in the district, to make good the deficiencies of the stipulated malgoozary. The territory thus alienated, and ascertained by Mr. Johnstone, after an arduous scrutiny by 70 persons for eight months, in 1763-64 A. D., was 568,736 begas, making near a fifth part of all the arable productive ground in the zemindary; which, estimated at 2 rupees per bega, being the valued medium rent of all the lands in Burdwān, yield an annual income to the possessors of 11,37,472 rupees. These possessors are, undoubtedly, for the most part, the official land-owner himself clandestinely, his minions, and the mutseddies of the Khalsa; whose acquiescence to such collusive benefices, under the sanctified appellations of religious or charitable gifts, at different times became necessary, as they were in their nature wholly fraudulent and sure to be resumed if made known to the Mussulman Government. Mr. Johnstone, who had the principal part in all these transactions, was subjected to all the opprobrium that could hence be attached to his public character by the suggestions of his powerful political enemies, and of the aggrieved multitude, and was soon afterwards for those reasons proscribed by his ruling countrymen. Finally Mr. Verelst, in 1172 A. B. (1765) appointed Supervisor of Burdwān, profiting by the errors and local information of his predecessors, his own financial experience matured by further *hustabood* investigations on the spot, restored the ancient system of managing the revenue, an adherence to which brought back the most effective standard of the collections regularly in 1778, to the full amount of the supposed inflated contract price of the three years' settlement in 1171 (1764) fixed on the impolitic ground of extra farming, and ultimately involving a real instead of the nominal Keffyet or improvement before mentioned of 13 lakhs." According to Mr. Grant's analysis the revenue of the zamīndāri when ceded to the British Government in 1760 amounted in all to *sikka* Rs. 31,75,391, after allowing for a deduction of *sikka* Rs. 51,543 on account of collection charges. This sum consisted of the "Ausil Jumma," the imperial revenue collected by Akbar and his successors which in 1722 amounted to *sikka* Rs. 23,07,277, and various *abwābs* or cesses imposed after that date by the Subahdārs of Bengal, amounting in all to Rs. 9,19,657. Of the latter the most interesting was the *chout marāthā*, a cess imposed by Ali Vārdi Khān on the pretence of raising the well-known tribute exacted by these marauders from the Mughal Empire. In the year 1771 the gross revenue was increased to 43,28,509 *sikka* rupees and in 1783 to 43,58,026 *sikka* rupees. On these figures Mr. Grant in 1787 estimated the annual net revenue at *sikka* Rs. 40,00,000 after deducting Rs. 3,30,000 on account of charges. These charges included the *Salānāh mushāharā*, or proprietary allowance made to the Mahārājā, which was estimated at 10 per cent. on the imperial revenue and amounted to *sikka* Rs. 2,30,000; *sikka* rupees 50,000 on account of collection charges; and *sikka* rupees 50,000 on account of embankment charges or *pulbandi*. This estimate was accepted as a basis for the permanent settlement, and in 1789 the Mahārājā executed an agreement to pay Government a land revenue of 40,15,109 *sikka* rupees and 1,93,721 *sikka* rupees on account of *pulbandi*, making a total of 42,08,830 *sikka* rupees. But in spite of the permanent settlement the affairs of the estate did not fully recover and the disastrous effects of the famine of 1769 and the bond of debt and arrears which it had left in its train were still felt. The estate fell into arrears. The disorganisation and mismanagement became so pronounced that Mahārāni Bishnu Kumāri, the mother of Mahārājā Tej Chandra, compelled him to execute a deed of sale assigning the entire estate to her. She was a woman of considerable business capacity and she might ultimately have succeeded in saving the whole estate if her life had been prolonged. Many of the lands had been parcelled out among a large number of farmers or *ijārādārs*—the settlements extending from five to ten years. Most of these *ijārādārs* withheld payment and the proprietor found it well-nigh impossible to realise his rents through the courts with the same punctuality with which he was compelled to pay this Government revenue. The inevitable result of this sub-infeudation was the accumulation of arrears in the Government demand. In 1794, we find the Collector referring to the Board of Revenue a letter from the Mahārājā complaining of his difficulties :—

"The difficulty I found in realizing the instalment (kist) of revenue for Agrahayan from the Mahārājā induces me to listen to his earnest request of representing to you the hardship he sustains from one of his renters, who, destitute of good faith, and availing himself of the delay that necessarily attends the institution of law process for the recovery of arrears of rent, is encouraged to withhold from him his just dues. The Mahārājā begs leave to submit for your consideration, whether or not it can be possible for him to discharge his engagements to Government with the punctuality which the Regulations require, unless he is armed with powers as prompt to enforce payment from his renters as Government has been pleased to authorize the use of in regard to its claim on him. He seems to think that it must have proceeded from oversight rather than from any just and avowed principle, that there should be established two methods of judicial process under the same Government,—the one summary and efficient for the satisfaction of its own claim; the other tardy and uncertain in regard to the satisfaction of claims due to its subjects,—more especially in a case like the present, where the ability to discharge the one demand necessarily depends on the other demand being previously realized."* The translation of the Mahārājā's protest which is annexed to the Collector's letter will show the difficulties with which he had to contend.

"The arrear of rent on account of pergunnah Baleya, to the end of Pouse 1200 B. S., amounts to *Sikka* Rupees 43,743, and the arrear on account of 1199, amounts to *Sikka* Rupees 3,900, in all 47,643, now due from Barranessy Ghose, farmer of that pergunnah, who absents himself, and fails in the performance of his engagements. I have many times represented his conduct to the Hazoor, and twice made application to the Adawlat; but without obtaining any satisfaction of the demand. I therefore request the case may be represented to the Board of Revenue, and application made to have the defaulter apprehended, and sent to the cutcherry, to discharge his engagements."

Creation of *Patni* Tenures. As a result of this reference Regulation XXXV of 1795 for better enabling individuals to recover arrears of rent or revenue due to them, and Regulations XXXVI and XXXVII of 1795 defining the powers of the Courts in relation to each other were passed, and the Governor-General in Council decided that the districts then comprised within the zilla of Burdwān should be formed into two districts with a separate Judge and Collector, for each. Those measures proved quite inadequate. The Mahārājā was summoned to attend the Board of Revenue, and was threatened with the forfeiture of his estates but to no purpose.

*Letter from the Collector of Burdwān, 9th May 1794.

Munshi, afterwards Rājā, Naba Krishnā Deb was appointed *kruk susawal*, or attaching officer, but could do nothing. Matters finally reached a climax when the Collector of Burdwān, despairing of realising the sums due, suggested the sale of the estate in lots as the only way of recovering the arrears of revenue, and in 1797 the Board commenced selling portions of the estate each lot consisting of several villages. The principal purchasers of the lots thus sold were Dwarka Nath Sinh of Singur, Chhaku Sinh of Bhastara, the Mukharjis of Janai and the Banarjis of Telinipara. Thus was laid the foundation of the landed aristocracy of Burdwān and Hooghly. The Mahārājā, alarmed at the dismemberment of the estate, himself bought up several lots in the names of his officials and dependants, and on the death of the Mahārāni, which occurred about this time, resumed the management of the estate. The difficulty experienced by the Mahārājā in paying his revenue suggested to him the advisability of binding his tenants to the same conditions to which he himself was bound by Government, and one of his first acts was the creation of *patnī* tenures or perpetual leases, a measure which ultimately proved the salvation of the estate.

The main conditions of this tenure are the hypothecation of the land as security for the punctual payment of the rent, and the liability of the tenure to summary sale in the event of default. The *patnī* system gradually extended, and by 1825, nearly the whole estate of the Mahārājā was leased out in this manner. The *patnīdārs*, finding how much trouble this mode of settlement took off their shoulders, created *dar-patnis*, or *patnis* of the second degree, upon the same terms and with the same rights over the land as they themselves had; and the *dar-patnidars* created *se-patnīs*, or *patnis* of the third degree. The subordinate tenure-holders possess their land upon the same terms and subject to the same liabilities as the original *patnīdār*. When the *patnī* system was first introduced, the Mahārājā used to let the land to the highest bidders at public auction, held in his Revenue Court. In case of arrears, the lands were publicly sold in the Court, and as much of the arrears was recovered as their sale fetched. These transactions were sometimes recognised and confirmed by the Board of Revenue, and sometimes ignored and set aside. The natural result was that great irregularity and confusion ensued. Under the permanent settlement the zamīndārs were declared to be entitled to make any arrangement for the leasing of their lands that they considered suitable. But by Regulation XLIV of 1793 such leases were subject to two conditions: first, that the rent should not be fixed for a period exceeding ten years and, second, that in a sale for arrears of Government revenue they should at once become void. Regulation V of 1812 rescinded the first restriction and Regulation XVIII of the same year distinctly declared that zamīndārs were entitled to grant leases fixing the rent in perpetuity. In practice such leases, which were really *patnī* leases, had frequently been given. Before the passing of Regulations V and XVIII of 1812, however, such leases were illegal and even after that date it was doubtful whether such as had been formerly created in contravention of the provisions of Regulation XLIV of 1793 were valid.

Ultimately, in 1819, at a suggestion by the Mahārājā, the Board of Revenue recognised all *patnī* tenures by a regular legal enactment, and Regulation VIII of 1819 was passed with this object. The preamble to the Regulation describes the history, incidents, and peculiarities of this tenure as follows.

"Furthermore, in the exercise of the privilege thus conceded to zamīndārs under direct engagements with Government, there has been created a tenure which had its origin on the estates of the Mahārājā of Burdwān, but has since been extended to other zamīndārs. The character of this tenure is that it is a *tāluk* created by the zamīndār, to be held at a rent fixed in perpetuity by the lessee and his heirs for ever; the tenant is called upon to furnish collateral security for the rent, and for his conduct generally, or he is excused from this obligation at the zamīndār's discretion; but even if the original tenant be excused, still, in case of sale for arrears, or other operation leading to the introduction of another tenant, such new incumbent has always in practice been liable to be so called upon at the option of the zamīndār. By the terms, also, of the engagements interchanged it is amongst other stipulations provided that in case of an arrear occurring, the tenure may be brought to sale by the zamīndār. And if the sale do not yield a sufficient amount to make good the balance of rent at the time due, the remaining property of the defaulter shall be further answerable for the demand. These tenures have usually been denominated *patnī tāluks*; and it has been a common practice of the holders of them to underlet on precisely similar terms to other persons, who on taking such leases went by the name of *dar-patnī-tālukdārs*; these, again, sometimes similary underlet to *se-patnīdārs*. The conditions of all the title-deeds vary in nothing material from the original engagements, executed by the first holder. In these engagements, however, it is not stipulated whether the sale thus reserved to himself by the granter is for his own benefit or for that of the tenant, that is, whether in case the proceeds of sale should exceed the zamīndār's demand of rent, the tenant would be entitled to such excess; neither is the manner of sale specified; nor do the usages of the country nor the Regulations of Government afford any distinct rules, by the application of which to the specific cases the defects above alluded to could be supplied, or the points of doubt and difficulty involved in the omission be brought to determination in a consistent and uniform manner. The tenures in question have extended through several districts of Bengal, and the mischiefs which have arisen from the want of a consistent rule of action for the guidance of the Courts of Civil Judicature in regard to them have been productive of such confusion as to demand the interference of the Legislature."

Section 3 of Regulation VIII of 1819 accordingly declared that 'the tenures known by the name of *patnī tāluks* as described in the preamble to this Regulation, shall be deemed to be valid tenures in perpetuity, according to the terms of the engagement, under which they are held. They are heritable by their conditions; and it is hereby further declared that they are capable of being transferred by sale, gift, or otherwise, at the discretion of the holder, as well as answerable for his personal debts, and subject to the process of the Courts of Judicature, in the same manner as other real property.' The Regulation also vested *patnī tālukdārs* with the right of letting out their *tāluks* in any manner they might deem most conducive to their interest, and the engagements so entered into by them were declared legal and binding.

Most of the district is now held in *patnī* from the Burdwān Rāj. There are also a large number of *aimmā* estates, and other revenue-free estates and rent-free tenures; but many of the old service holdings, *e.g.*, the *ghātwāli* lands, have been resumed. The land revenue demand of 30·58 lakhs is higher than that of any other part of Bengal, and is estimated at 25·15 per cent. of the gross rental of the district, the incidence per cultivated acre being exceeded only in the neighbouring district of Hooghly. Rents rule higher than in any other part of Bengal, except Hooghly. They are lowest in the poor paddy lands in the Rānīganj and Asansol thānas, and highest in the irrigated areas and in the rich alluvial soil further east, and range from Rs. 3-6 per acre in high lands to Rs. 9 in low lands, the average being Rs. 7-12-7. The following table shows the

Land revenue.

collections of land revenue, as compared with the total revenue, in thousands of rupees:—

	1880-81.	1890-91.	1900-01.	1908-09.
Land Revenue ...	30·45	30·13	30·50	30·68
Total Revenue ...	38·36	40·51	45·18	50·08

The subdivision of estates has gone on rapidly under British rule; and, notwithstanding the present greatly diminished area of the district as compared with what it was in the last century, the number of estates in 1870-71 had increased by 108 per cent. above the number in 1790, and the number of individual proprietors or co-sharers had increased by 134 per cent. within the same period.

The total number of estates in 1908 was 5,212 and the land revenue demand was Rs. 30,58,992 of which by far the greater part was paid by the Mahārājā of Burdwān. Of these estates 5,026 with a demand of Rs. 30,35,561 are permanently settled. Besides the permanently settled estates there are 153 estates of which Government is the proprietor, 120 with a demand of Rs. 6,457 having been leased to farmers for fixed periods, while 33 are under direct management. The former are mostly petty estates formed out of the surplus road-side land along the Grand Trunk Road and unimportant properties which have been bought in by Government at sales for arrears of revenue. The latter include alluvial accretions on the river Bhāgīrathi. There are also a large number of *aimmā* estates in the district. Some of these were originally granted free of revenue by the Muhammadan Government but they are mostly of the class described in section 9, Regulation VIII of 1793, as *malguzāri aimmās* which were originally granted for the purpose of bringing waste lands under cultivation. Such grants doubtless originated from the desire of the Muhammadan Government to establish colonies of soldiers and followers throughout the country. Some of the estates are now very profitable as the revenue assessed on them is very low; but they are usually subdivided among many co-sharers.

TENURES. The intermediate rent-paying tenures of Burdwān consist of properties held under the zamīndārs and comprise (*a*) *patnī tāluks* with their subordinate *se-patnī* and *dar-patnī* tenures; (*b*) *Mukarrarī tāluks,* (*c*) *istimrārī tāluks* and (*d*) *ijārās* including *dār-ijāras* and *zar-i-peshgī ijārās*. The following is a brief description of each of these classes.

This class of tenure was, as has already been described, created by Mahārājā Tej Chandra of Burdwān in 1799 when, after the death of his mother, he resumed the management of his estates. It is said that the design of granting perpetual leases was suggested by his son Pratap Chand who for some time acted as his regent. The measure, which from the landholder's point of view was most successful, was gradually extended throughout Burdwān, and Bishnupur until by 1835 almost the whole estates of the Mahārājā were leased out under these tenures. *Patni Tenures.*

A *patni* tenure is, in effect, a lease which binds its holder by terms and conditions similar to those by which a superior landlord is bound to the State. By Regulation XLIV of 1793 the proprietors of estates were allowed to grant leases for a period not exceeding 10 years, but this provision was rescinded by section 2 of Regulation 5 (V) of 1812; while by Regulation XVIII of the same year proprietors were declared competent to grant leases for any period even in perpetuity. Finally, as has been described above, Regulation VIII of 1819, known as the Patnī Sale Law, declared the validity of these permanent tenures, defined the relative rights of the zamīndārs and their subordinate *patni tālukdārs*, and established a summary process for the sale of such tenures in satisfaction of the zāmīndār's demand of rent. It also legalized under-letting on similar terms by the *patnidārs* and others.

Since the passing of the Patnī Sale Law, this form of tenure has been very popular with zamīndārs who wish to divest themselves of the direct management of their property, or part of it, or who wish to raise money in the shape of a bonus. It may be described as a tenure created by the zamīndār to be held by the lessee and his heirs or transferees for ever, at a rent fixed in perpetuity, subject to the liability of annulment on sale of the parent estate for arrears of Government revenue, unless protected against the rights exercisable by auction purchasers by common or special registry, as prescribed by sections 37 and 39 of Act XI of 1859. The tenant is called upon to furnish collateral security for the rent and for his conduct generally, or he is excused from this obligation at the zamīndār's discretion.

Under-tenures created by *patnidārs* are called *dar-patni*, and those created by *dar-patnidārs* are called *se-patni* tenures. These under-tenures are, like the parent tenures, permanent, transferable and heritable; and have generally the same rights, privileges, and responsibilities attached to them. They are usually granted on payment of a bonus. Section 13 of Regulation VIII of 1819 provides rules for staying the sale of a *patni*, if it takes place owing to the intentional withholding of payment of rent by the *patnīdār* with the object of ruining his subordinate tenure-holders. In such cases, the under-tenants are allowed the means of saving the *patnī* tenure and their own under-tenures, by paying into the Collector's office the advertized balance due to the zamīndār. The *patnī* tenure so preserved forms the necessary security to the depositors, who have a lien on it in the same manner as if the loan had been made upon mortgage. The depositors may then apply to the Collector for obtaining immediate possession of the defaulter's tenure; and the defaulter will not recover his tenure, "except upon repayment of the entire sum advanced, with interest at the rate of 12 per cent. per annum up to the date of possession having been given, or upon exhibiting proof, in a regular suit to be instituted for the purpose, that the full amount so advanced, with interest, has been realized from the usufruct of the tenure."

Mukarrarī tenures. These are hereditary tenures at a low rent fixed in perpetuity as the name itself, which is derived from the Persian *karār*, implies. Many of them were created by the operation of section 9 of Regulation XIX of 1793, which prescribes that resumed *lākhirāj* plots of less than 100 bighas existing before 1790 are to be settled in perpetuity at a fixed rent. At the creation of *mukarrarī* or *dar-mukarrarī* tenures the lessee usually pays a bonus or *salāmi*.

Dar-mukarrarīs are subordinate to *mukarrarīs* and are created by the *mukarrarīdār*. These tenures are also of a fixed nature and their rights and incidents are, in the absence of special provision, those of the parent tenure. *Dar-mukarrarī* tenures are not however common in Burdwān.

Ijaras. The status of *ijārādārs*, or farmers, and of their subordinate *dar-ijārādārs*, differs widely from that of the other intermediate tenure-holders described above. *Ijāradārs* hold farming leases, by which a definite amount of annual rent is fixed for a specified term, usually varying from 5 to 30 years. Such leases are granted not only by the zamīndārs or superior landlords, but also by subordinate *tālukdārs* or tenure-holders in an estate. The lessor cannot enhance the rent of an *ijārā* lease during its term; and on its expiry, the *ijārādār* is not entitled to renewal. If the latter is not specifically, by the conditions of his lease, debarred from creating an under-tenure, he occasionally creates a *dar-ijārā* tenure, the term of which cannot, of course, be longer than that of his own lease.

Another kind of *ijārā* is that known as *zar-i-peshgī ijārā*, *i.e.*, a lease granted in consideration of an advance of money

It may be granted for an unspecified term of years, and is usually made terminable on certain conditions, *e. g.*, when an estate is mortgaged as security for a loan, the term expires when the mortgagee has recovered the amount of debt and interest from the proceeds of the property. Such leases are much in vogue in this part of the country, where even the cultivators often give a *zar-i-peshgi ijārā* of their lands to the village *mahājan*.

TENANT'S HOLDINGS. The tenures held by actual cultivators comprise (*a*) *jamā* or *jot*, (*b*) *miādi jamā*, (*c*) *mukarrarī* and *maurasī jamā*, (*d*) *korfā* and *dar-korfā*, and (*e*) *bhāg jot*.

Jamā or jot. Cultivators' holdings, called *jamā* or *jot*, were generally, but not always, held without any written engagement. The lands have in many cases remained in the possession of one family from generation to generation and in most cases without any document of title. Written leases and agreements are now however usually taken and demanded when a new settlement is made. All these tenures are now governed by the Bengal Tenancy Act, VIII of 1885, as amended by Act I of 1907. In practice, a *jamā* is divided into as many parts as suit the convenience of the ryots who hold it, and the total rent contributed by the different holders thereof is paid by one of them to the *gomāshtā* or rent-collector.

Miādī jamā. The term *miādī jamā* is applied to the holding of a cultivator with only a temporary interest in his land, which he holds for a fixed term of years under a *pāttā* or lease.

Bhāg jot. Holdings for which the tenant pays a share (*bhāg*) of the produce as rent are known as *bhāg jot*. In some cases the arrangement is that the cultivator shall deliver a certain quantity of produce even although the crop should fail. Lands thus held are called *dhān thika* lands; but the payment of rent in kind in this manner is very rare in Burdwān. On the other hand holding in *bhāg jot* are very common and every well-to-do tenant usually holds a certain proportion of his land in *bhāg jot* generally from another tenant. Under-tenants also almost always hold their lands in *bhāg jot*.

Mukarrarī and Maurasī jamā. Some cultivaters hold land under leases called *mukarrarī* and *maurasī*, the chief stipulations of which are that the rent is subject neither to enhancement nor abatement, and that the tenure descends from father to son. These leases are generally granted on the payment of a bonus or *salāmi* by the tenant.

Korfā and dār-korfā. A sub-ryoti tenure subordinate to that held by an ordinary cultivator is called *korfā*. *Korfā* tenures are generally created verbally, and in some cases there are also *dar-korfādārs* or ryots holding under *korfādārs*.

SERVICE TENURES. When the *chakla* of Burdwān was ceded to the East India Company, there were four bodies of men employed in the protection of the country and in the collection of revenue. These were, first, a military force called *nagdis*, paid in cash, but since practically disbanded; they are now represented by the body-guard of the Burdwān Mahārājā, who, at the permanent settlement, received an annual remission of Rs. 50,000 for the support of this force; second, the *thānādāri* police; third, a body termed *grām saranjāmi pāiks*, who were at once village watchmen and collectors of rent; and fourth, *ghātwāls*, whose duty it was to keep the hill passes and roads free from robbers, and to protect travellers. These three latter classes were paid by assignments of land. The following is a brief account of each.*

Thānādāri Police. In 1790 the total strength of the Thānādāri police was 3,079 men, holding 14,491 acres of land. Under the provisions of Regulation XXII, of 1793, a portion of it, called the *sadar thānādāri*, consisting of 801 *thānādārs* and *thānā pāiks* and peons holding 4,652 acres of land, was abolished, and the lands resumed; while the remainder, consisting of about 2,200 *chaukidārs* or *phāridārs* in charge of *chaukis*, and *pāiks* and peons subordinate to them, holding in round numbers 10,000 acres of land, was retained. By 1837 this force had sunk to the level of the *grām saranjāmi pāiks*, and performed zamīndāri as well as police services.

Grām saranjāmi pāiks. In 1794, the total number of *grām saranjāmi pāiks* was reported to be 17,284 holding 46,236 acres of land. Their duties were 'to assist the farmer in collecting the rents, guarding the mufassal treasuries, conveying public money to the treasury of the District, and serving as guides to passengers.' In addition to these functions, 'they were considered as dependent on the authority of the thānādārs, and had to apprehend offenders, etc., and sometimes received a gratuity called *dwār mashahārā* for this service'† from the cultivators; engagements were also taken from them at that date to report offences. Since that date they have been known as *chaukidārs*, a curious instance of the degradation of a title: a hundred years ago the word meant the commandant of a *chauki* or post to which were attached several pāiks.

The numbers of the village police existing in the district, according to a report of the Collector dated April 1873, was as follows: *chaukidārs*, 8,978, of whom 66 were paid in cash;

* McNeil's Village Watch.

† Magistrate's letter, 22nd February 1793.

simāndārs (originally keepers of village boundaries), 2,138; *halshanas* (originally zamīndāri servants who kept the measurements of the cultivators' holdings), 36; *mirdhas* (originally peons who carried a measuring chain for surveyors), 2; *sardārs*, 5; *nagarchis* (originally drummers), 7; *ashtaprahāris* (originally watchers of the crops), 2.

From the *chākrān* registers of 1836-40 for the fifteen thānas then included in the district, it appears that there were at that time 71 *ghātwāli* tenures.. Subsequent transfers added to the number and some years later the total number of tenures of this class was reported to be 238, with a holding of 7,912 bighās. The word *Ghātwāl* as applied to this class of tenure-holders is a further instance of the degradation of a title. The *ghātwāls* proper were hill-chiefs who were partially subdued by the neighbouring zamīndārs and turned into feudatories. Their representatives are found only in Chotā Nāgpur and the districts of Monghyr, Bhagalpore and the Santāl Parganas. The *ghātwāls* of Bānkurā and Burdwān were, on the other hand, commandants of picquets created by the zamīndars. Their proper designation was *ghāt sardār* and their posts were *ghāts* and not *ghātwālis* which contain many *ghāts*. A *ghātwāl* was essentially a *Tālukdār*, who was bound to support *ghātwāli* police and from whom personal service was not demanded. A *ghāt sardār* was an actual police servant and the direct head of a body of watchmen. Ghatwals.

The original duty of the *ghātwāls* was nominally to protect the *ghāts* or hill passes, to keep open the roads and to protect travellers. Some of them held their lands free, others paid a quit-rent known as the *Panchaki* to Government and others to the zamīndārs. In Burdwān they were to all intents and purposes treated as part of the rural police, with the exception that they were exercised not within the village as such, but within an area roughly determined by immemorial custom and known as a *ghāt*. They were, however, for the most part practically useless for police purposes and, in November 1894, an amicable settlement of the *ghātwāli* lands was undertaken with a view to releasing them from police duties. Those operations have now been concluded. A full account of the history of these tenures up to the present time will be found in the Bānkurā Gazetteer.

The *chaukidāri chākrān* lands and the other allied service tenures mentioned above have also now been resumed and transferred to the zamīndārs under Act VI (B. C.) of 1870, the *chaukidārs* being now paid from the *chaukidāri* tax.

RENT-FREE TENURES.

Rent-free tenures form the last class of landed estates in Burdwān. These have always been very numerous and in 1763-4 A. D. the territory thus alienated and not assessed to revenue at all was estimated at 5,68,736 bighās. One of the first acts of the newly appointed British Superintendents was to restore this area to the rent-paying lands of the district. Between 1765 and 1788, however, grants to hold 6,600 acres revenue free under the names of *debottar*, *brahmottar*, etc., were given to 408 persons with a view to bringing waste lands under cultivation. In 1876 it was reported that there were 170,240 rent-free holdings of small plots of land included within the limits of permanently-settled estates. These are held rent-free of the zamīndārs; but Government revenue is paid by the proprietors on account of them. The tenures consist mainly of lands granted for religious purposes, such as *brahmottar*, *sivottar*, *debottar*, etc., by Hindus and *pīrottar*, *chirāgān*, *nazrat*, etc., by Muhammadans. Besides these, there are other rent-free tenures granted for charitable purposes, and numerous small rent-free holdings which do not appear to have been assigned for any special purpose.

CHAPTER XII.

GENERAL ADMINISTRATION.

In 1760 the district of Burdwān together with Midnapore and Chittagong were ceded to the East India Company by Mīr Kasīm Khān on the deposition of Mīr Jafar Khān. At that time Burdwān comprised the present districts of Burdwān, Bānkurā, and Hooghly and one-third of Bīrbhūm. West Burdwān was afterwards made into a separate district, and in 1820 Hooghly was also separated. Numerous minor transfers have been made to and from the district up to the year 1885, since when no change has been made. For purposes of administration the district is divided into four subdivisions with head-quarters at Burdwān, Asansol, Kālna and Kātwa. The sanctioned staff subordinate to the Magistrate-Collector at the district head-quarters consists of five Deputy Collectors and occasionally a Joint Magistrate is posted here. A covenanted Civil Servant, assisted by a Deputy Collector and Sub-Deputy Collector, is in charge of the Asansol subdivision. The Kālna and Kātwa subdivisions are managed by Deputy Collectors, who are sometimes assisted by Sub-Deputy Collectors. Public works within the district are in charge of the District Engineer, but the embankments and irrigation works are managed by the Executive Engineer, Northern Embankment and Drainage Division, whose head-quarters are in Calcutta. ADMINISTRATIVE CHARGES AND STAFF.

Excluding land revenue the principal heads of receipt are Stamps, Excise, Cesses and Income-tax. In 1907-08 the collections from these sources amounted (in round figures) to Rs. 19,40,000, of which Rs. 5,41,000 were realised from Stamps, Rs. 7,51,000 from Excise and Rs. 1,17,000 from Income-tax. REVENUE.

The total number of estates borne on the revenue-roll of the district in 1908-09 was 5,276 with a current demand of Rs. 30,58,992. Of this number 5,024 estates were permanently settled estates with a demand of Rs. 30,35,561; the number of Land Revenue.

estates in 1887-88 was 4,937. The actual collections of land revenue have only increased by Rs. 5,000 during the past 30 years; and in 1908-09 amounted to Rs. 30,68,999, of which Rs. 22,834 was realised on account of former years. The total land revenue demand is estimated at 25·15 per cent. of the gross rental of the district. There are 153 Government estates consisting mainly of the lands acquired on the side of the Grand Trunk Road, and of small and unimportant estates bought in at revenue sales. Of these 120, with a demand of Rs. 6,457, have been leased to farmers for varying periods, and 33 are under direct management.

Stamps. The receipts from judicial and non-judicial stamps increased from Rs. 4,07,000 in 1896-97 to Rs. 4,47,000 in 1900-01, and in 1907-08 amounted to Rs. 5,41,000. The expansion of industry and commerce, and the growing inclination towards litigation among the agricultural classes and petty landlords, is a sufficient explanation of the increase. Of the total receipts Rs. 4,14,000 or more than three-fourths, were realised from the sale of judicial stamps, including court-fee stamps; while non-judicial stamps accounted for Rs. 1,27,000, nearly the whole of this sum being realised from the sale of impressed stamps, which include besides general impressed stamps, salt and customs bonds, and bills of lading.

Excise. The receipts from excise rose from Rs. 2,75,000 in 1890-91 to Rs. 4,74,000 in 1900-01, and further increased in 1908-09 to Rs. 7,51,000, a figure which was only exceeded by three districts in Bengal, and which represents one-third of the total receipts for the entire division. The net excise revenue was Rs. 4,707 per 10,000 of the population, as compared with the provincial average of 3,191. More than two-thirds of the total excise revenue is derived from the sale of ordinary country spirit and *pachwāi*—the rice spirit which is consumed in large quantities by the Santāls, Bauris, and Bāgdis. In the same year the total receipts from these sources were Rs. 3,70,000 and Rs. 2,55,000, respectively. The manufacture and sale of country spirit is now carried on entirely under the contract supply system, a contract for the wholesale supply of spirit being given out to a firm of distillers. Local manufacture is prohibited and the contractors are forbidden to hold any retail licenses for its sale, but are allowed the use of distillery and warehouse buildings for the storage of the liquor. The right of retail vend is disposed of by separate shops, each of which is put up to public auction; and the retail vendors are forbidden to sell liquor except at the prescribed strengths, for which maximum prices are fixed. The returns for 1908-09 show that there are 82 shops for the retail sale of country liquor, or one shop for every $32\frac{3}{4}$ square miles and for 18,688 persons; and the average consumption of the liquor in that year was 32 proof gallons per 1,000 of the population, a figure far larger than that returned by any other district in the division. The excess in the excise revenue from Burdwān as compared with the other districts in the division is almost entirely due to the exceptionally large consumption of *pachwāi*. In spite of the abolition of 34 shops during the year the receipts on account of *pachwāi* amounted to Rs. 2,49,000, or nearly half of the entire provincial revenue from this source. The gross excise receipts per 10,000 of the population from spirits and fermented liquor amounted to Rs. 3,684, or more than twice the divisional average. The steady increase of recent years is attributed to the opening of new collieries and the consequent influx of highly paid labour.

The balance of the excise revenue is almost entirely realised from the sale of opium and hemp drugs. In 1908-09 the duty and licence fees on opium brought in Rs. 98,000, which represents an expenditure of Rs. 643 per 10,000 of the population. The receipts for *gānja* (*Cannabis Indica*) and the other hemp drugs amounted to Rs. 87,000, representing an expenditure of Rs. 571 per 10,000 of the population as compared with the divisional average of 396. Opium and preparations of the drug are much used as a preventive or cure for malarial fever.

Income-tax. In 1907-08 the total collections on account of Income-tax realised Rs. 1,17,000, which was paid by 1,242 persons. Owing to the unusual development of the coal trade in the district, a proposal has recently been made for the employment of a special assessment staff to revise the assessments in the colliery tracts in the districts of Burdwān, Mānbhūm and Hazaribagh. It is probable that such a revision might effect a very considerable increase of income from this source.

Registration. There are 16 offices in this district for the registration of assurances under Act III of 1887 (now Act XVI of 1908). The District Sub-Registrar deals as usual with the documents presented at the Sadar Office and also assists the District Magistrate, who is *ex-officio* District Registrar, in supervising the proceedings of the Sub-Registrars in charge of the other registration offices. The average number of documents registered annually during the quinquennium ending in 1903 was 44,428·80, but in the five years ending in 1908 it decreased to 44,245·80, the decrease being due to the conclusion of the settlement of the *chaukīdāri chākrān* lands. The following statement shows the number of documents registered, and the receipts and expenditure at each office in 1908:—

Office.		Documents registered.	Receipts.	Expenditure.
			Rs.	Rs.
Burdwān	...	4,279	14,822	11,865
Khandaghosh	...	2,174	2,156	1,839
Memāri	...	3,140	3,438	3,032
Jamālpur	...	1,315	1,888	1,926
Raina ...	...	3,681	4,047	2,285
Sahebganj	...	2,641	2,920	2,533
Mānkur	...	3,180	3,619	2,072
Guskhāra	...	2,171	2,432	2,825
Kālna	...	2,542	3,098	2,496
Purbasthāli	...	1,544	1,995	1,936
Manteswar	...	2,890	3,404	2,695
Kātwa	...	3,349	4,250	2,495
Ketugrām	...	3,152	3,533	2,176
Mangalkot	...	2,851	3,140	1,824
Rānīganj	...	4,447	6,547	2,464
Asansol	...	2,957	4,702	1,926
Total	...	46,318	65,551	45,889

ADMINISTRATION OF JUSTICE. The Civil Courts at Burdwān are those of the District Judge. There are five Subordinate Courts at head-quarters presided over by a Sub-Judge and four Munsifs, and an additional Sub-Judge is usually stationed here. There are also Munsifs at Asansol, Kālna, and Kātwa, who are subordinate to the District Judge. The Munsif at Asansol is at present assisted by an additional Munsif; the civil work here is increasing considerably and it is probable that the additional Munsif's Court will be permanently retained. Criminal justice is administered by the Sessions Judge, who is also the District Judge, and by the Magistrate of the district, the Subdivisional Magistrates stationed at Kālna, Kātwa, and Asansol, and their subordinates. Besides the Stipendiary Courts, there are benches of Honorary Magistrates at Burdwān, Rānigānj, Asansol, Kātwa and Kālna.

Crime. In the early days of the British rule the district had a very unsavoury reputation, and was overrun with dacoits who broke out from the wilderness of jungles and forest in the laterite country to the west to prey upon the unfortunate peasantry. In 1789 the Magistrate of Bīrbhūm estimated that there were 2,000 dacoits in Bīrbhūm, Burdwān and Rājshahi. These marauders, taking full advantage of the unsettled state of the country collected in large bodies, and on one occasion the officer charged with the duty of arresting one of their leaders asked for a battalion of sepoys and a howitzer

Frequently they were actively aided and abetted by the local zamīndārs or their servants. Of the dacoities committed in 1819 we read that one-half occurred in the estates of Mahārājā Pratap Chand Bahādur of Burdwān, "a powerful and contumacious individual". But in his estates not a single dacoit was tried or apprehended. And in the next year the pargana of Burdwān was actually attached by the orders of the Magistrate of Bīrbhūm, as the zamīndār would not appear to answer a charge of declining to aid the Police. A report of the Judge and Magistrate in 1802 shows the difficulty with which our officers had to contend in dealing with crime :—

"The Police establishments are certainly not adequate, the thānas are too few, and the establishments will not admit of the necessary detachments for the performance of the duties in the numerous populous villages under them, and little assistance can be expected from the zamindary Pikes (*sic*) and village watchmen as these are generally found to be the offenders. The crime most prevalent is dacoity or gang robbery, which is frequently accompanied with murder." Raina thāna was formerly a haunt of the Thags and in Bengal they were first found here in 1802. In 1817 it was estimated that their number was three hundred, including five Hindu and three Muhammadan women. Their descendants after the suppression of Thagi, according to popular rumour, turned to dacoity as a means of subsistence. Some of the stories still told about these robbers bear witness to their reputation for ferocity and strength, and show the terror in which they were held by the common people. One leader "could eat the raw flesh of three goats with two bottles of brandy and five pounds of bread a day." Another could fight single-handed with four soldiers. One woman of 35 years of age "twice plundered a big zamīndār's house with the assistance of her husband and a sword." Another, a Muhammadan widow, at the age of 46 could ride a horse "as cleverly as an expert Captain or Colonel could do," and on one occasion, with the assistance of her old father, killed ten men who attacked them. Dacoities are still fairly common in the district, and the detection of the offenders is very difficult. It is an easy matter for the members of the gangs to conceal themselves among the numerous up-country coolies employed at the many collieries in the Asansol Subdivision, where the population is constantly fluctuating. Running train thefts are also exceedingly common between Asansol and Burdwān, and petty thefts and burglaries are very common in the Asansol Subdivision, especially in the neighbourhood of Asansol itself.

Police.

The district is divided into 23 thānas with 9 outposts as shewn in the statement in the margin.

Police Station.	Outpost.
Sadar Subdivision.	
Burdwān.	Bara Bazār.
	Birhatta.
	Muradpur.
	Noutonganj.
	Keshabganj.
	Kānchannagar.
Sahebganj.	
Khāndaghosh.	
Rainā.	
Satgāchia.	
Jamālpur.	
Ausgrām.	
Galsi.	
Memari.	
Asansol Subdivision.	
Rānīganj.	
Kāksa.	
Asansol.	
Faridpur.	
Barākar.	
Kātwa Subdivision.	
Kātwa.	Dāinhāt.
Ketugrām.	
Mangalkot.	
Kālna Subdivision.	
Kālna.	
Purbasthāli.	
Manteswar.	

In 1908 the regular police force of the district consisted of the District Superintendent, and Deputy Superintendent, 8 Inspectors, 49 Sub-Inspectors, 68 head-constables, and 552 constables, a total force of 679 men representing one policeman to every 3·9 square miles and to every 2,257 of the population. The rural force employed in the interior consists of 162 rural *dafadārs* and 4,144 rural *chaukīdārs*, who are paid at the rate of Rs. 6 and Rs. 5 a month, respectively. Until recently there were still many watchmen called *phāridars*, *pāiks* and *ghātwāls* who held lands in return for police service. These men are survivals of the old village watchman, who was maintained by the village community in which he lived and whose duty was to guard the property and persons of his fellow-villagers from the attacks of dacoits, burglars and thieves. As a rule he himself belonged to some thieving gang and his engagement as watchman was simply blackmail. It is therefore hardly surprising to find that these watchmen were reckoned * "vile and abominable." The majority of these have now been replaced by paid *chaukīdārs* under Act VI of 1879 and the *chaukīdāri* and *ghātwāli* lands have been resumed and resettled with the zamīndārs.

There is a District Jail at Burdwān with accommodation for 271 prisoners, *viz*, 7 barracks for 195 male convicts and 1 for 19 under-trial prisoners, a female ward for 11 female convicts, 6 cells for male convicts, and a hospital with 36 beds for male convicts. There is also a female segregation ward with accommodation for four prisoners. The industries carried on are the manufacture of mustard oil, *daris* and carpets, *newār* tape, and wheat flour. The subsidiary jails at the 3 Subdivisional outstations have accommodation for 88 prisoners.

* Dr. Buchanan's report on Purneah, 1810.

CHAPTER XIII.

LOCAL SELF-GOVERNMENT.

EXCLUSIVE of municipal areas the area of the district is 2,669 square miles, inhabited by 1,438,443 persons, and within this the management of local affairs, such as the maintenance of roads, bridges, ferries, and pounds, the control of village sanitation and water-supply, and the provision of medical relief, is vested in the District Board with the Local Boards and Union Committees under it. The Burdwān District Board consists of 19 members including the Chairman, who is the Magistrate of the district. Of the remaining 18 members 6 are elected and 12 nominated by Government, 4 of whom hold their appointment *ex-officio*. The Board is thoroughly representative and at present 6 members are pleaders or mukhtars, 6 are Government servants, 4 representative of the landed interest and 3 are classified as miscellaneous. District Board.

For the period of ten years ending with 1902-03, the average annual income of the Board was Rs. 3,03,000; and by 1906-07 this had risen to Rs. 3,86,000. This income was mainly derived from the local rate (road cess) Rs. 1,62,000; pounds Rs. 9,000; ferries Rs. 9,000; and other sources Rs. 60,000, and included Rs. 1,44,000 contributed by Government. The Government contribution, however, includes the allotment for Government works executed by the District Board. Excluding the opening balance the receipts for the year 1907-08 amounted to Rs. 3,80,000, including Rs. 1,70,000 realized from road cess, Rs. 1,59,000 contributed from Provincial revenues as contribution to the Board and on account of Government works executed by it, Rs. 10,000 obtained from ferries, and Rs. 10,000 from pounds. Here, as elsewhere, the road cess is the principal head of receipt, but the taxation is not heavy, amounting to annas two per head of the population. Income.

The average annual expenditure during the ten years ending 1902-03 was Rs. 2,98,000, of which Rs. 1,88,000 was spent on civil works, Rs. 51,000 on education and Rs. 4,000 on medical relief. During the five years ending in 1906-07, it amounted Expenditure.

to Rs. 3,91,000, the chief heads being civil works (including Government works undertaken by the Board) Rs. 2,58,000, education Rs. 60,000 and medical Rs. 10,000. In 1907-08 the expenditure was Rs. 3,28,000, of which about two-thirds, Rs. 2,32,000, was expended on civil works (including Government works); education Rs. 55,035 and medical Rs. 12,857 being the other principal heads of expenditure.

The maintenance of communications is the heaviest charge on the income of the District Board, which now maintains 203 miles of metalled and 298 miles of unmetalled roads, in addition to a large number of village tracks with a total length of 654 miles. The cost of maintenance in 1907-08 was Rs. 327, Rs. 67 and Rs. 14 per mile for these three classes of roads, respectively. Besides these about 100 miles of Provincial roads are maintained by the Board, the cost being met from funds allotted by Government. The Board also maintains 8 Middle schools, and aids 78 Middle, 218 Upper Primary, and 1,005 Primary schools, and employs 14 Inspecting Pandits to supervise the management and expenditure of the schools. It also maintains a technical school at Burdwān, under its direct management, with annual contributions of Rs. 240 from the Burdwān Municipality and of Rs. 360 from Government. In all a little more than 6 per cent. of the ordinary income of the Board was expended during the year on medical relief and sanitation. Ten permanent dispensaries, and five temporary fever dispensaries are entirely maintained by it, and grants-in-aid are also made to four Municipal dispensaries. The expenditure includes the cost of special measures taken to provide gratuitous medical relief to the people on the outbreak of epidemic diseases. A veterinary dispensary is also maintained at Burdwān.

LOCAL BOARDS. Under the District Board there are four Local Boards in this district, which are entrusted with the maintenance of the village roads, pounds, ferries and primary education within each subdivision of the district. For these purposes they receive fixed allotments from the District Board. The Burdwān Local Board consists of 15 members, and the three other Local Boards of 9 members each. Of the members two-thirds are elected and one-third nominated by Government, the Chairman and Vice-Chairman of the Boards being elected by the members. At present the Chairmen of the Asansol, Kātwa and Kālna Local Boards are the subdivisional officers, who have been elected *ex-officio*, while the Chairman of the Burdwān Local Board is a non-official.

UNION COMMITTEES. There are at present six Union Committees in the district at Memāri, Mānkur, Srikhanda, Sribāti, Baidyāpur and Bāgnāpārā. The marginal table shows the area and population of each union. Each of these committees is administered by a Board of 9 members, and they are entrusted with the administration of the village roads within their jurisdiction. Hitherto the Union Committees have not displayed much activity and their income and expenditure has been in many years merely nominal. But the scope of work of the Union Committees has been much widened by the recent amendment of the Local Self-Government Act, and much useful work may be expected from them in the future.

Name of Union Committee.	Area in square miles.	Population.
Memāri ...	12	10,323
Mānkur ...	12	10,473
Srikhanda ...	8	8,500
Sribāti ...	10	11,800
Baidyāpur ...	10	6,922
Bāgnāpārā ...	10	7,160

MUNICIPALITIES. There are at present six municipalities in the district, Burdwān, Kātwa, Kālna, Dainhāt, Rānīganj and Asansol. The Burdwān Municipality was established in 1865; and the municipalities at Kālna, Kātwa and Dainhāt in 1869; that at Rānīganj was established in 1876, while the Asansol Municipality, which is now the second largest in the district, was established so recently as 1896.

Burdwān. The Burdwān Municipality covers an area of 8·4 square miles and includes 38,691 people, of whom 8,070 or 20·87 are ratepayers. It is administered by 22 Commissioners, 15 of whom are elected and 7 nominated by Government, 2 being appointed by virtue of their office. During the ten years ending in 1902-03, the average annual income and expenditure of the municipality was Rs. 1,02,000, and Rs. 1,14,000, respectively, and by 1906-07 they had risen to Rs. 1,32,000 and Rs. 1,32,000. In 1908-09 the income amounted to Rs. 1,29,000 the principal heads of receipt being the tax on houses and lands, which is here levied at 7½ per cent. Rs. 41,000; water-rate, Rs. 26,000; conservancy Rs. 18,000; and grants and contributions from Government and other sources Rs. 15,000. The incidence of taxation and of income per head of population was Rs. 2-8-9, and Rs. 3-5-6, respectively. During the same year the total expenditure amounted to Rs. 1,20,000, which was distributed mainly under the following heads: Establishment 7·41 per cent.; Lighting 4·46 per cent.; Water-supply 15·53 per cent.; Drainage 1·6 per cent.; Medical 11·8 per cent.; Public Works 15·07 per cent.; and Education 6·69 per cent. Burdwān, which was formerly considered one of the healthiest and most prosperous towns in the Province, suffered very severely from the epidemic of fever which ravaged the district between 1862 and 1874. It has been estimated that more than half of the inhabitants died or left the town during these disastrous years. Although the health conditions are now much improved, the town is still badly drained and, at certain seasons of the year, suffers severely from fever. The houses for the most part drain into the shallow tanks and depressions from which the materials for their construction were excavated and these tanks in many cases become veritable cess-pools, obstructing the natural drainage, and are a great source of danger to the public health. A surface drainage scheme which will cost some 6 lakhs of rupees has been prepared for the town. The Mahārājā has promised to contribute Rs. 50,000 towards the cost of the work and Government has promised to make a similar contribution. The municipal finances, however, are not very prosperous, and it is improbable that the scheme will be taken up soon.

The most successful feature of the municipal administration is the water-works. These were constructed during the year 1884-85 at a cost of Rs. 2,35,500. Of this amount Government contributed Rs. 50,000 as a grant, and Rs. 11,000 as the price of the old sluice at Jujuti, which was taken over from the Municipality, and the Mahārājā of Burdwān made a similar contribution while the balance of Rs. 1,24,500 was raised by loan in the open market. Most of the loan has now been repaid. The management is in the hands of a special sub-committee of the Municipality, which includes among its members the Chairman and Vice-Chairman, the Civil Surgeon, the District Superintendent of Police, and an Engineer of the East Indian Railway. The supply is drawn from the Dāmodar river. The pumping station is situated some 2½ miles north-west of the town and has four engines, three boilers, one intake with a roughing filter, five high level settling tanks, two low level settling tanks, five filter beds with a daily capacity of 875,000 gallons, and one clear water reservoir with a capacity of 285,000 gallons. The average daily consumption is 413,000 gallons or 12·9 gallons per head; and the total income and expenditure during 1908-09 was Rs. 26,000 and Rs. 18,000, respectively. Generally speaking the quality of the water supplied is good, but when the Dāmodar falls during the hot weather, the supply has occasionally to be taken from the Bānka. At this season of the year this river is practically an open drain and receives all the drainage of the villages on its banks, and in addition the supply of water is often very insufficient. In order to ensure a constant supply of Dāmodar water, it would be necessary to construct a weir across that river below the sluice. This project has frequently been proposed, but there are very serious engineering difficulties to be overcome and the cost would be prohibitive. In spite of this defect the water-supply has been of enormous benefit to the townspeople and is undoubtedly the chief cause of the recent marked improvement in their health. The only portion of the town which is not supplied with water is that lying to the south of the Bānka river and a project for extending the water-supply to this quarter is under discussion.

The total population of Rānīganj at the last census was 16,398 and of this number 1,692 or 10·3 are rate-payers. The Municipality is administered by 12 Commissioners, eight being elected and four nominated. The town is a busy centre of trade and contains, besides a small Railway settlement, Messrs. Burn and Company's pottery works which employ nearly a thousand operatives, the Bengal Paper Mills, and several oil and flour mills. Formerly it was the centre of the coal industry and the Bengal Coal Company still has its head office at Egara near the town and works several mines in the immediate neighbourhood. Some workings which have been made over to Messrs. Burn & Company are actually being carried under the town itself. The town is thickly populated: almost all the buildings are of brick and in good order, and the roads are well maintained. The water-supply is derived from a large number of wells, both private and public, and the Municipality has also leased several tanks in different parts of the town in order to provide water for the public as the present supply is inadequate. The income and expenditure for 1907-08 were Rs. 18,528 and Rs. 21,249. The income is principally derived from the rate on holdings, which is levied at 7½ per cent. on the annual valuation, and the conservancy rate. Nearly one-third of the expenditure is spent on conservancy, and about one-fifth on medical relief. For the past 15 years the income and expenditure have practically balanced each other and the Municipality has no funds to spare for new projects. Rānīganj.

The Municipality of Kātwa, which was established on the 1st April 1869, is administered by a Municipal Board composed of 12 Commissioners, of whom eight are elected and four nominated by Government, one of the latter being appointed *ex-officio*. The area within municipal limits in 1908 was one square mile, and the number of rate-payers was 2,385 or 30·03 per cent. of the whole population, with an average incidence of taxation of Re. 1-1-2 per head of the population. Kātwa.

During the five years ending in 1906-07, the average annual income and expenditure of the Municipality were Rs. 10,200 and

Rs. 10,800 respectively, and in 1907-08 the annual income excluding the opening balance amounted to Rs. 12,500. The chief sources of income are the tax on persons levied at twelve annas per cent. on the circumstances and properties of the rate-payers, from which Rs. 4,700 was realized in 1907-08, and the conservancy rate which brought in Rs. 2,100 in the same year.

The expenditure for the same year was Rs. 13,000, excluding Rs. 2,400 expended on the repayment of loans, advances and deposits, the principal heads being conservancy and medical, which accounted for 39·59 and 11·83 per cent. of the total expenditure. The Municipality maintains a charitable dispensary. The roads are mostly metalled, but very narrow and skirted by masonry drains. A drainage scheme, which is estimated to cost Rs. 77,000 has been prepared for the town and will be taken up as soon as funds permit.

Kālna. The Kālna Municipality was established in 1869 and is administered by a Board of 15 Commissioners, of whom ten are elected and five are nominated. The area within municipal limits in 1908 was two square miles, and the average incidence of taxation in 1907-08 was Re. 1-13-7 per head of the population. The average annual income and expenditure of the Municipality during the five years ending in 1906-07 were Rs. 14,000 and Rs. 13,900, respectively. In 1907-08, the income was Rs. 15,000; the chief sources being the tax on persons which brought in Rs. 4,900 and the conservancy rate which brought in Rs. 3,500. During the same year the expenditure was Rs. 14,000, of which sum Rs. 4,700 was spent on conservancy and Rs. 2,100 on road repairs. A drainage scheme for the town, which is estimated to cost Rs. 36,000, has been prepared under the supervision of the Assistant Sanitary Engineer. The northern portion of the town is thickly populated, and is better provided with roads and drains than the southern and interior portions. In these quarters the waste lands, and depopulated homesteads, the silted up tanks and depressions full of rubbish of all sorts bear eloquent witness to the decline of trade and the decay of prosperity. The trade is now, however, increasing, and the Municipality may expect better times.

Dainhāt. The Municipality of Dainhāt, which was established on the 1st April 1869, is administered by a Municipal Board composed of 12 Commissioners, of whom 8 are elected and 4 nominated by Government, 1 being appointed *ex-officio*. The area within municipal limits was nearly 4 square miles in 1908, several villages with a total area of 2 square miles having been included within the Municipality in 1900. The number of rate-payers is 1,270 or 22·6 per cent. of population, and the average incidence of taxation in 1907-08 was annas 7-10 per head. In 1907-08, the income aggregated Rs. 4,870 excluding an opening balance of Rs. 713. The income was mainly derived from the tax on persons, which brought in Rs. 2,379, and the conservancy rate which brought in Rs. 429. The expenditure in the same year was Rs. 4,743, the principal heads being general establishment, conservancy, medical and public works, which accounted for 15·6, 31·6, 24·3, and 11·2 of the total expenditure, respectively. The supply of drinking water is mainly from the river Bhāgīrathi and, when the stream dries up in the hot season, is very deficient. Most of the roads are unmetalled. The Municipality maintains a charitable dispensary.

Asansol is the second largest Municipality in the district and is administered by a Municipal Board composed of 12 Commissioners nominated by Government, of whom 7 are appointed *ex-officio*. The Municipality was established in 1896, and in 1904 an additional area of 1·48 square miles was included in it. The area within municipal limits at present is 3·73 square miles. The number of rate-payers in 1908 was 2,312, or 12·8 per cent. of the population, and the average incidence of taxation was Re. 1-2-1 per head of population. The average annual income during the five years ending 1906-07 was Rs. 19,000, and the expenditure was Rs. 18,000. In 1907-08, the income excluding the opening balance amounted to Rs. 24,000 and was mainly derived from the rate on holdings at 7½ per cent. on the annual value of the holding, which brought in Rs. 14,000, and the conservancy rate which brought in Rs. 4,900. The expenditure in the same year was Rs. 26,000, the principal items of expenditure being drainage, conservancy, and public works, which accounted for 12·04, 56·0, and 13·6, respectively, of the total amount. Drainage and water-supply schemes are awaiting adequate funds. **Asansol.**

CHAPTER XIV.

EDUCATION.

INDIGENOUS SYSTEM. UNDER the old Municipal system of the Hindus each village had its chief, its accountant, its priest, smith, carpenter, potter, barber, washerman, poet, doctor and last but not least its village or hedge school master, the *guru mahāsaya*, who presided over the village *pāthshālā*. In 1835 Mr. Adam calculated that there were more than 100,000 of these schools in Bengal and Behar. In 1802 the Magistrate of Burdwān reported "that there are few villages of any note in which there is not a school but the instruction in them is confined to the teaching of children to read and write." The children of Muhammadan parents usually received their education in the common branches from the village school masters. But in villages where Muhammadans were numerous the Hindu *pāthshālā* was usually replaced by a *maktab*. In the Hindu *pāthshālā* the teacher (*guru mahāsaya*) was a poor Kayesth or less often a Brāhman, who was usually paid in kind, or was given a contribution in cowries by each boy's family, and also got a small share of grain at harvest time. The school was held in his hut, and often in fine weather under some tree in the village. Here the boys were taught reading, writing and mental arithmetic. They practised writing with ink on palm or plantain leaves, or with chalk on the floor, and after they had learnt the Bengali alphabet, some small collections of verses were committed to memory. Particular attention was paid to mental arithmetic and mensuration, the boys learning by heart the verses of one Bhrigurām Dās, better known as the Subhankāri, which contain formulæ for calculating arithmetical figures, interest, land measurements, etc. Boys were sent to the *pāthshālā* in their fifth year and stayed there three to six years. In *maktabs*, the teacher (*ākhungi*) taught arithmetic and the rudiments of Persian or Urdu, the boys writing not only on leaves but also on country paper. The bulk of the pupils finished their education in these elementary schools, and then followed their hereditary occupations. Many of the Kayesths went on to the landlords' *kachāris* and learnt zamīndāri accounts, thus qualifying for employment as writers or *gumāshtas* (agents). A few read at home the vernacular versions of the epics or Purānas while Brāhmans studied the rudiments of Sanskrit under some *pandit* in the neighbourhood, and thus qualified themselves for the priesthood.

The more ambitious of the Brāhmans, however, were not so easily satisfied and studied at one or other of the educational centres in Bengal containing *tols* or Sanskrit colleges. The most famous of these were at Nadiā and in its neighbourhood, but there were smaller circles at Bhāngāmodā in this district, Bhatpārā in the 24-Parganas, and in Howrah at Bally. The students resided in the house of some learned *pandits* and were treated as members of the family, doing domestic work, and if they had means, contributing to the cost of the household. Every pupil learnt grammar in the first instance for some years, and then read some easy literary works. After this he selected some special subject for study, usually higher literature, *nyāya* or logic, and *smriti* or law. The whole period of learning lasted usually from eight to sixteen years. After finishing the course, many went on tour to complete their studies, visiting Mithila (Darbhanga) to learn *darshana* or philosophy and law, and Benares for grammar, rhetoric and the Vedas. On returning home, many of them set up small *tols* in their own houses.

Well-to-do Musalmans sent promising boys to Madrasas, which were established at nearly all the head-quarters of the local Governors. These institutions date back to the beginning of Muhammadan rule in Bengal, for we find that Muhammad-i-Bakhtyār Khilji and his Amirs set up Madrasas at Lakhnauti, and in 1313 A. D. Zafar Khān built one at Tribeni. They were usually attached to some mosque and were often liberally endowed. The students had lodging and boarding free, though contributions were frequently made by those whose parents were better off. The pupils were taught the Koran and Persian classics by maulvis, while special instruction was also given in the Hādis or Musalman law and in Arabic literature. In the old correspondence reference is made to several such institutions. For instance, in September 1818 we find the Collector reporting concerning a religious institution and school at which 5 or 6 scholars were entertained, the cost being met by a pension of Rs. 6 a year, granted by Government to the principal. In

1819 there is a reference to a Madrasa attached to a mosque, possibly that at Bohār, and in July 1823 the Board reported an endowment for a college in Burdwān of 254 sicca rupees per annum.

No special arrangements appear to have been made for female education. Hindu girls of tender age often attended *pāthshālās* but few were permitted to go there after seven or eight years of age. The Muhammadans were stricter and apparently did not permit them to go to any *maktab*, but many of the more affluent allowed their girls to be taught at home. Among the Kayesths and Brāhmans, a few managed to learn Bengali or Sanskrit at home. The Vaishnāvas were more liberal-minded, allowing girls, and even elderly ladies, to read and write; indeed, there were several poetesses among them.

PROGRESS OF MODERN EDUCATION.

The first attempt to improve on this system of education was made in 1816 when Captain Stewart, a servant of the East India Company, established two vernacular schools in the district, in connection with the Church Missionary Society. In two years the number of schools had increased to ten containing a thousand children and costing Rs. 240 a month. Captain Stewart at first encountered considerable opposition, and the Brāhman school masters, who saw their occupation threatened, circulated rumours that he designed to kidnap all the children and send them to England. One instance even is said to have occurred, in which a father exposed his child to prevent the possibility of his being educated by Captain Stewart. The introduction of printed books also caused some alarm. Formerly nothing but manuscripts had been used and it was remarked of the village school masters: "If you put a printed book in their hands they are unable to read it without great difficulty and are still less able to understand its contents." Besides the rudiments of Geography, Astronomy, and History Captain Stewart caused instruction to be given in some few of the preambles of the East India Company's regulations with the object of instructing the people in the benevolent intentions of the Government. These schools became so celebrated that the Calcutta Society sent its Superintendent for five months to Burdwān in 1819 to learn Captain Stewart's system, as it was found that he educated a greater number of children with fewer teachers and at half the cost of the old system and when Mr. Adam made his enquiry into the state of education in 1837, he reported that Burdwān was the best educated district in Bengal. The educational work of the mission continued to prosper. Under the Revd. J. J. Weitbrecht (1830-1852) the Mission managed 14 schools scattered over an area of 40 miles with an attendance of a thousand boys, a girls' school, and one of the first High schools in Bengal with a hostel for Hindu students attached to it. Of these schools four in Burdwān were supported by the subscriptions of the European residents in the station, who contributed Rs. 60 a month for this purpose. Besides the vernacular schools maintained at and near Burdwān elementary schools had also been opened before 1834 at Kālna and Kātwa, the latter being managed by the Baptist Missionary Society.

In his third report on the state of education in Bengal Mr. Adam gives a detailed description of the schools and colleges then existing in the district. There were in all 629 Bengali elementary schools, one village containing as many as seven, and seventy-nine containing two or more. Of these schools nine were supported by the Missions and one by the Rājā of Burdwān. The teachers were mostly Kayesths, Brāhmans, Sadgops or Aguris by caste, and many of them eked out their professional income by engaging in farming, money-lending, trade, weaving or service. The total number of scholars was found to be 13,190 of whom 13 were Christians, and 769 Muhammadans, and the average period passed at school was estimated at about 11 years. They were drawn from all classes and castes, but in the Mission schools a far larger proportion of low caste boys were taught. In addition to these elementary schools there were 190 Sanskrit schools with 1,358 students. The subjects commonly taught in these were Grammar, Lexicology, Literature, Law, Logic, Medicine and Mythology. And besides these there were 93 Persian and 8 Arabic schools, of which two were supported by the Mahārājā of Burdwān. There were also four girls' schools at Burdwān, Kātwa, and Kālna. All the schools were managed by Missionaries, and the number of girls taught in them was 175, of whom 36 were Christians, and one a Muhammadan. The standard of instruction given in most of the elementary schools can be judged from the fact that out of the total number of scholars no less than 7,113 had not advanced beyond writing on the ground, and only 2,610 had learnt to write on paper.

State of education in 1837.

In the next thirty years a great advance was made and by 1868 ten aided and two unaided High schools, and twenty-two Middle English schools had been established. The Church Missionary Society, besides its High school and hostel at Burdwān, which was in a flourishing condition, had opened a High school at Memāri, and another had been established by the Free Church of Scotland Mission at Kālna. In these three

State of education in 1868.

schools alone the number of boys taught was 518. In addition the High school maintained by the Mahārājā of Burdwān, which had been established as an Anglo-Vernacular school in 1817, had increased largely and at that time was attended by 500 pupils. Another High school known as the Burdwān Preparatory School had been started in the town and was doing well. A free High English school had been established at Chakdīghi by the trustees of the will of the late Babu Sāradā Prasād Singh Rai, and aided High English schools, under native management, had been started at Kātwa, Kulingrām, Okersha, Belgona, Bāgnāpārā, and Badla. Besides these Government Middle Vernacular schools had been established at Amadpur, Barākar, and Galsi. Two schools for European and Eurasian children, the first in the district, had also been opened in 1866-67.

Female education. The first school for girls was started by the European ladies at Burdwān in connection with the Ladies' Society at Calcutta some time before 1834, and by 1837 there were altogether four girls' schools in the district. All these schools were under the management of the various Missionaries. The Ladies' Society of Calcutta supported those at Japat near Kālna and in Burdwān itself, and these schools were under the mangement of the Rev. Mr. Alexander. Another in the premises of the Church Missionary Society at Burdwān was supported and managed by the Rev. J. J. Weitbrecht, while the school at Kātwa was managed by the Rev. W. Cary and supported by the Calcutta Baptist Society for promoting native female education. In the schools supported by the Ladies' Society a sum of Re. 1-8 a month was allowed for providing refreshments for the children. And three female messengers were employed to bring the children to school and to take them home. If the messenger brought ten scholars a day for a month, she was paid Rs. 2, but it was not necessary that the same children should always be brought, and only the number was regarded. It is therefore hardly surprising to find Mr. Adam writing of the schools that the progress of the children was slow and their attendance irregular. The number of girls taught in these schools was 175 and the instruction was largely religious. Of this number 36 were Christians, and only 1 a Muhammadan, while Mr. Adam reports that out of the total number of scholars, 112 could read but could not write. In 1868 there were altogether 9 girls' schools and the Deputy Inspector reported that a desire for the education of girls was steadily progressing.

If Burdwān is no longer the best educated district in Bengal it compares very favourably in this respect with the rest of the Province. Out of a total population of a little over one and-a-half millions, 130,000 persons, or one in every 12, were returned at the last census as literate, that is, they could read or write some language, while 16,658 or a little more than one in every 100 persons, could read and write English. This proportion is considerably larger than that returned for the Province as a whole. Of the persons who were returned as literate, males, as might be expected, predominate enormously, the percentage of literates among them being 16·2 as compared with the provincial average of 10·4; while among females 8 out of every thousand were literate—a proportion which is the average for the division and is considerably higher than that returned for most districts. In respect of English education, also, the district stands high. Approximately 1 man in every 50 and 1 woman in every thousand were able to read and write English—a figure which is exceeded only by the metropolitan districts, that is, Hooghly, Howrah, and the 24-Parganas. It is only the higher castes such as Baidyas, who to judge by the census returns are much the best educated caste, Kayesths and Brāhmans who have any knowledge of English. Among the lower castes who form the great bulk of the population there are practically none who have any acquaintance with it. Present state of education.

It is difficult to estimate with any accuracy the progress in education, owing to a change in the system of recording the census. On former occasions the population was divided into literate, learning and illiterate, but in the census of 1901, the only distinction made was between the literate and illiterate. It is certain that a good many persons who would have been entered as "learning" under the old rule have in the last census been shewn as illiterate, and it is therefore impossible to base any accurate estimate of the advance in education on a comparison of the returns. A rough approximation can however be arrived at by taking all persons over 15 years of age who were entered as "learning" in 1891 as "literate." Such a comparison was made in the census report for 1901. The results obtained for the district show that in 1891, 19 per cent. among males over 15 years of age were literate and five per thousand among females. The corresponding figures for 1901 were 20 per cent. among males and 10 per mille among females. There are now in the district no less than 1,470 schools of which 1,457 with 53,483 pupils are public institutions, and 13 with 330 pupils are private institutions. Of the former

26 schools, attended by 1,138 pupils, are under public management, 16 being managed by Government and 10 by the District or Municipal Board; while 1,431 schools, attended by 52,344 pupils, are under private management, 1,207 being aided and 225 unaided. The number of boys at school as compared with the number of boys of school-going age, is steadily increasing and is now 46,718 out of a total of 114,711, which represents a percentage of 40·7, the district in this respect standing tenth among the districts in the Province. The inspecting staff consists of one Deputy Inspector of Schools, 3 Additional Deputy Inspectors of Schools, 9 Sub-Inspectors of Schools, 3 Assistant Sub-Inspectors of Schools and 16 Inspecting Pandits.

COLLEGIATE EDUCATION.

The only college in the district is that maintained by the Burdwān Rāj in the town of Burdwān. This institution, which is entirely maintained by the Mahārājā, was founded in 1817 as an English Vernacular school. In 1868, by which time it had become a High school, there were 500 boys on the rolls, and in 1881 it was finally recognized as a second grade college. The number of pupils on the rolls has of late years steadily declined and in 1909 was only 53 as compared with 203 in 1904. The principal causes of the decrease are reported to be the establishment of the Wesleyan Mission College at Bānkurā and the recent imposition of tuition fees. Twenty-five boys were sent up for the F. A. examination of 1908, of whom 14 passed, one passing in the 1st division and nine in the 2nd. At the supplementary F. A. examination of the same year 5 students passed, of whom 1 stood first and another seventh in order of merit. The returns for 1907-08 shew that the total receipts from fees amounted to Rs. 2,287, and from endowments to Rs. 7,232, the total expenditure being Rs. 9,500 which represents an average of Rs. 144 for each student a year. Attached to the college is a collegiate school also maintained by the Rāj. The number of pupils on the roll in 1909 was 258 including 12 Muhammadans. The Rāj also maintains a High school at Kālna.

SECONDARY EDUCATION.

The number of secondary schools in the district is 135 including one for girls with an attendance of 11,639 boys and 69 girls. Of these schools 28 are High schools, of which 17 were aided and 11 unaided. There are 3 High schools at Burdwān—the Burdwān Municipal School which is supported by the Municipality with a grant-in-aid, the Burdwān Rāj Collegiate School, the cost of which is entirely borne by the Rāj, and the Burdwān Albert Victor School, which is the largest in the district, having 394 boys.

The following statement gives the high schools during the year 1909-10 :—

Aided schools.	Unaided schools.
1. Burdwān Municipal.	1. Burdwān Rāj Collegiate.
2. Bhailā.	2. Burdwān Albert Victor.
3. Memāri.	3. Gopālpur.
4. Nasigrām.	4. Sankāri.
5. Mānkur.	5. Torkona.
6. Raina.	6. Chakdīghi.
7. Badla.	7. Kālna Rāj.
8. Bāgnapārā.	8. Putsuri.
9. Patuli.	9. Mathrun.
10. Purbasthāli.	10. Ukhra.
11. Kātwa.	11. Ethora.
12. Dainhāt.	12. Siarsol.
13. Okersha.	
14. Rānīganj.	
15. Asansol Railway.	
16. Sanktoria (Disergarh).	

Besides the High schools there are altogether 85 Middle English schools in the district, of which 4 are under the direct management of the District Board, 61 are aided and 20 unaided. Of the 22 Middle Vernacular schools 4 are under the District Board, and 16 are aided. The number of pupils in the secondary schools is rising and in 1909 was 11,700 against 11,200 in the preceding year. Of this number 4,200 or 37 per cent. belonged to the secondary stage. The total expenditure on the schools amounted to Rs. 1,79,000 of which Rs. 22,000 was derived from public funds and Rs. 1,56,000 from private sources. Of the expenditure, Rs. 44,000 or more than one-fourth was in the Primary department, Rs. 2,000 being derived from Government, Rs. 3,000 from the District Funds, Rs. 22,000 from fees, and Rs. 21,000 from private sources. During the same year the total contribution from Provincial revenues for secondary education amounted to Rs. 8,000, and the total receipts from fees to Rs. 93,000. The annual average cost of educating a boy in a High school, Middle English school, and a Middle Vernacular school was Rs. 20, Rs. 11 and Rs. 12, respectively.

PRIMARY EDUCATION.

The number of boys' Primary schools in the district is 1,138, of which 221 are Upper Primary and 917 Lower Primary schools. Of these, 8 schools attached to the 8 Guru Training schools are managed by Government and one by the Municipal

Board. The rest are under private management, 972 being aided and 157 unaided. Of the aided schools there are 8 colliery *pāthshālās* in the Asansol subdivision, which in 1908-09 received grants from an assignment of Rs. 800 made by Government for the education of the miners' children, 4 schools were aided from the receipts from Government estates, 28 were aided by the various Municipalities, and 721 by the District Board. The number of pupils attending the schools during the year 1908-09 was 36,000 of whom 9,000 were in the Upper Primary schools. The Gurus in charge of the schools are now paid a small subsistence allowance and a further allowance at the end of the year, which is only given if their schools satisfactorily pass the tests imposed by Government. The total expenditure for 1908-09 on Primary schools was Rs. 88,249, and the average annual cost of an Upper Primary school was Rs. 135-8 and of a Lower Primary school Rs. 63-8. Most of the Primary schools are badly equipped with furniture and teaching appliances, the only equipment prescribed by the District Board for an Upper Primary school being a school house, 3 wall maps (the World, Bengal and the District), a black board and a chair or stool. And at least ninety per cent. of the Lower Primary schools possess no school house, a private house or a shed attached to some temple being generally used for that purpose. In 1906-07 Government placed a grant of Rs. 1,600 at the disposal of the District Board for the construction of buildings for the Primary schools, but it was found impossible to raise a sufficient amount by local subscription and no buildings have as yet been erected.

GIRLS' SCHOOLS. In 1908-09 there were 76 girls' schools in the district of which 7 received grants-in-aid from Government, 59 were aided by the District Board and 3 by the Municipalities, and 7 were unaided. Two Model Girls' schools have been opened by Government at Paraj and Amadpur, which are now under the control of the Education Department, and all the other schools receiving Government aid are under the management of Missionaries. Excluding boys the total number of pupils under instruction in the girls' schools in 1908-09 was 1,998, of whom 7 belonged to Middle English schools, 71 to Middle Vernacular schools, 175 to Upper and 1,754 to Lower Primary schools. The only secondary girls' school in the district is the Asansol Mission Girls' Middle Vernacular school, which was formerly a Middle English school but has recently been reduced. The expenditure on secondary and primary schools for girls amounted in the same year to Rs. 13,000 as compared with Rs. 11,500 in the preceding year. Of this sum Rs. 1,800 was contributed by Provincial revenues and Rs. 1,900 and Rs. 330 by the District Board and the Municipalities, respectively. Fees are charged in very few of the schools and the receipts from this head only amounted to Rs. 142. Female teachers are employed in the schools under Missionary management and in that maintained by the Burdwān Rāj at Burdwān, but generally speaking almost all the girls' schools are taught by male teachers who are drawn from some boys' school in the locality. Most of the schools send up their pupils for the examinations conducted by the Uttarpārā Hitākāri Sabha.

EUROPEAN SCHOOLS. There are three schools for Europeans in the district. These are the Railway school at Asansol for boys and girls, and the St. Patrick's boarding school for boys and the Loretto Convent school for girls which are maintained at Asansol by the Roman Catholic Mission. The Railway school is maintained by the East Indian Railway Company and is aided by Government. The other schools are unaided.

TECHNICAL SCHOOLS. There are two technical schools in the district—the Burdwān Technical School at Burdwān, which is managed by the District Board, and the Kharsoli Industrial School, attached to the Wesleyan Mission at Rāniganj. The Technical school at Burdwān was started sixteen years ago. It is at present divided into an apprentice department and an artizan class. In the apprentice department the course of training corresponds exactly to that in the first and second years' apprentice classes of the Sibpur Engineering College, and after two years' training the pupils are sent up for the Sub-Overseer's examination of that College held under the Joint Technical Examination Board. In the artizan class practical carpentry and blacksmith's work is taught. No fees are charged in this class and the Burdwān Rāj provides 3 scholarships, each of the value of Rs. 30 a year, tenable for two years, for artizans under training. There were 61 pupils on the rolls in 1908-09 and the total expenditure in the same year amounted to Rs. 4,600, of which Rs. 2,800 was contributed by the District Board, Rs. 240 by the Municipality, and Rs. 60 by the District Board of the 24-Parganas, while the income from fees amounted to Rs. 1,200. The Kharsoli Industrial school is attached to the Wesleyan Mission at Rānīganj and was founded in 1897. Lower primary education and a training in simple carpentry is given to the pupils, who are all boarders in the Mission orphanage.

SPECIAL SCHOOLS. There are 78 *maktabs* and Koran schools in the district with 2,566 and 265 pupils attending them. Of the Koran schools the Raigrām Madrasa receives Rs. 48 a year out of a special grant of Rs. 400 sanctioned by Government for the encouragement of Muhammadan education in the district, and 62 *maktabs* are aided from public funds, receiving in all Rs. 1,680 from the District Board, Rs. 142 from the Municipalities and Rs. 300 from Provincial revenues. There are also 13 unaided indigenous schools which have not accepted the standards of the Education Department, including *tols*, *maktabs*, and Koran schools with 330 pupils.

There are 43 night schools, *i.e.*, primary schools attended by adult labourers and cultivators in the evening after their day's work, which were attended by 836 pupils. For training *gurus* or primary school teachers there are 8 training schools with 8 practising schools attached to them, working on an upper primary basis. The number of pupils was 113. Ten hostels for male students and one for females are maintained, which are all under private management. There are also 8 lower primary schools specially intended for the children of Santāls and other aboriginals.

Miscellaneous. There are five public libraries in the district, the Burdwān Rāj Public Library, the Kālna Mayo Library, the Kātwa Shyām Lal Library and a public library at Rānīganj. Of these the Burdwān Rāj Library is the largest and most important. It was established in 1881 and in 1908-09 was visited by 70,435 persons. It is entirely supported by the Mahārājā. The Kālna Mayo Library is partially supported by the Municipality and those at Kātwa and Rānīganj are maintained entirely by public subscriptions. Four newspapers are published in the district, the Burdwān Sanjibani, the Pallibashi, the Ratnakar, and the Prosun and there are four public printing presses at Burdwān, two at Asansol and two at Rāniganj. There are printing presses also at Kātwa and Srikhando in the Kātwa subdivision, and at Kālna.

CHAPTER XV.

GAZETTEER.

Agradwīp.—A village in the Kātwa subdivision situated on the Bhāgīrathi. The sacred river at Kātwa has for Hindus an especial sanctity rivalling in that respect the Ganges at Benares. According to tradition the great Vikramāditya used to transport himself from his palace at Ujain in Rājputānā daily in order to bathe in the river. Agradwīp is a famous place of pilgrimage and contains a temple of Gopinath at which some ten thousand pilgrims gather every April.

Andāl.—An important junction on the East Indian Railway, situated some ten miles east of Rānīganj in the Asansol subdivision. There is a large railway settlement here and the station which is known as Ondal station is the junction for the Ondāl Loop line which serves the north of the Rānīganj coalfield, and also for the recently constructed line to Sūri in the Bīrbhūm district.

Asansol Subdivision.—The north-western subdivision of the district lying between 23° 25′ and 23° 53′ N. and 86° 48′ and 87° 32′ E. with an area of 618 square miles. A hundred years ago the whole of this tract was a wilderness of forest and jungle, dotted at long intervals with tiny clearings and settlements. For centuries it had been a sort of debateable land between the Jharkhand, or great western forest, inhabited by the aboriginal tribes whom the Hindus classed indiscriminately as Chuars, and the settled country to the east; and even at the end of the eighteenth century it was the haunt and refuge of bands of broken and outlawed men who, taking advantage of the unsettled state of the land, ravaged and plundered the country-side. The tract contains the famous Rānīganj coal-field. It is now one of the busiest centres of industry in the Indian continent and its coal and iron fields are filled with a throng of busy and prosperous miners and artisans. It is bounded on the north by the Santāl Parganas and the Ajay which separates it from Bīrbhūm, on the east by the Burdwān subdivision, and on the south and west by the Dāmodar and Barākar rivers which separate it from Bānkurā and Mānbhūm.

Until 1906 in which year the subdivisional head-quarters were transferred to Asansol, the subdivision was known as the Rāniganj subdivision. The north-western part consists of a rocky undulating country, which merges in the south and south-east in the alluvial plain stretching along the Dāmodar. Its population was 370,988 in 1901, compared with 310,273 in 1891. It contains 2 towns: Asansol, its head-quarters and a great railway centre (population 14,906), and Raniganj, its former head-quarters (15,841) and 811 villages. The subdivision is now the most progressive part of the district, but the density of population, 600 persons to the square mile, is still slightly less than that of the Kātwa subdivision. It differs from the rest of the district, which is entirely agricultural in character; the alluvial soil here changes to laterite, and rich coal and iron fields have of recent years caused a continuous increase in the number and prosperity of its inhabitants. The subdivision contains numerous collieries and also the Bengal Iron and Steel Works at Kendwa near Barākar, the potteries of Messrs. Burn and Co., and the Bengal Paper Mills at Rānīganj, and Messrs. Burn and Co.'s Lime and Brick Works at Andāl and Durgāpur.

Asansol.—Head-quarters town of the subdivision of the same name, situated on the East Indian Railway, 132 miles from Calcutta, in 23° 41′ N. and 86° 59′ E. Population (1901) 14,906. The head-quarters of the subdivision have recently been transferred from Rānīganj to Asansol, which is situated in the centre of the coal-field and is now one of the most important railway centres in Bengal. In 1881 the town was a rural tract. In 1891 its population was returned at 11,000, and in 1901 at 14,906. There is a large European community connected with the railway and the bazar is growing rapidly. The town is situated in the middle of the Rānīganj coal-field, and since coal of a better quality is obtainable here than further east it has practically taken the place of Rānīganj as the centre of the coal industry. There is a junction here with the Bengal-Nagpur Railway and the railway station and workshops have recently been much enlarged and improved; the locomotive shops are said to be the largest in the world. Asansol was constituted a Municipality in 1896 and the Municipal Board consists of 9 Commissioners; the area within municipal limits is 3·73 square miles. The Grand Trunk Road runs right through the town, which lies on either side of it for a distance of some two miles. The subdivisional offices and the civil courts are situated on the south of the road on high ground beyond the Bengal-Nagpur line, some two miles west of the town. The East Indian Railway

Volunteers have their head-quarters at Asansol, and in 1901 head-quarters were constructed here for the newly raised "B" troop of the Chota Nagpur Mounted Rifles. A Roman Catholic Mission in the town maintains a church, convent, and schools, and a Methodist Episcopal Mission supports a leper asylum, orphanage, and girls' school. The town contains the usual public offices. There are also several emigration depôts where coolies who have been recruited from other districts halt before they are despatched to the tea-gardens in Assam. The town contains a very large railway settlement and a handsome Institute and extensive recreation grounds have been provided for the employés.

Ausgrām.—A village in the Burdwān subdivision situated some five miles north-west of Guskhārā Railway Station. It contains a charitable dispensary, which is maintained by the District Board, a police-station, a middle class English school and a branch post-office. There is also a Sanskrit *tol* in the village. On the road to Ausgrām there is an old fort called Panchaganga which is intersected by the metalled road from Guskhārā to Ausgrām. The population of Ausgrām according to the census of 1901 is 1725.

Bagnapārā—A village in the Kālna subdivision containing a Siva *lingam* temple known as Gopeswar. The place is identified with Chaitanya and his followers, the Vaishnabs, visit this temple in considerable numbers on the occasion of the *Shibarātri* festival.

Banpās.—A village in the head-quarters subdivision with a population, according to the census of 1901, of 1,425 persons. The village is noted for its manufacture of brass and bellmetal ware, and gives its name to a railway station on the loop line of the East Indian Railway, though situated at some distance from the line.

Barākar.—A village in the Rāniganj subdivision of the district, situated on the left bank of the Barākar river in 23° 45′ N. and 86° 49′ E., about 143 miles from Calcutta. The population of Barākar proper in 1901, was 385 but the name is ordinarily understood to include the villages of Beguniā, Ladna, Manberiā and several small collieries with a total population of nearly 5,000. Kendwa, some two miles from Barākar, is the site of the Bengal Iron and Steel Works, which employ nearly 3,000 hands daily and had a total output in 1903 of 18,900 tons valued at 27 lakhs. The works were originally managed by Government but in 1889 were handed over to Messrs. Martin and Co., Calcutta. A full account of them will be found in Chapter VIII. The opening of the grand chord line of the East

Indian Railway has placed Barākar on the main line, and it is at present one of the busiest industrial places in Bengal. The roads are thick with coal dust, and the country round is studded with collieries and factories, and covered with a network of railway sidings. Two fine bridges carrying the Grand Trunk Road and the new railway line span the Barākar river, and the town is thus in direct communication with the Jherriā coal-field. There is an old dâk bungalow on the Grand Trunk Road at the approach to the bridge over the Barākar river, which was formerly an important halting-place. The town also contains some very fine old stone temples. The following description of these is condensed from that given in the Archæological Survey Reports, Volume VIII (1878):—There are four temples whose towers are in entire preservation. Of these two consist of a simple cell each, surmounted by a tower roof, but there are traces of a *mandapa* in front, of which all but the foundations have disappeared. Apparently the temple consisted of a cell with its doorway: an *antarala*, formed in the thickness of the back walls of the *mahamandapa:* and a *mahamandapa* about thirteen and a half feet square. The towers are richly indented. There is an inscription at the doorway of one of the temples. It is in two distinct pieces both of which are in a variety of the Bengali character. From the style of the characters the temples do not appear to date beyond the Muhammadan conquest, or at the utmost to just before. The inscriptions are not dated. One of them mentions the erection of the temple by one Harishchandra for his beloved: but who Harishchandra was or when he built the temple is not mentioned. The temples are particularly interesting as being the finest existing examples of their type. They face east. In the cell of the inscribed one is a *Ganeça* on a pedestal in front of which is an oblong *argha* with three *lingam* holes cut into it. A peculiarity of these temples, and not of these alone but of the entire series of temples of this type to be found in Mānbhūm, is the sunk position of the floor of the sanctum. Temple No. 3 stands by itself. Its features are much like those of the temples already described but unlike them it faces west. The object of worship inside is the figure of a fish lying flat, serving as an *argha* to five *lingam* holes cut in it. This sculpture is especially interesting as proving that the fish is essentially a representation of the female powers of nature, a character which it bears in the mythology of other nations, but which appears to have been overlooked or forgotten in Indian mythology, where it, and a similar symbol, the tortoise, are dissociated from the *lingam*. Close to this temple and facing it stands temple No. 4. It is now partially enclosed within a courtyard: but the walls of this enclosure are evidently later additions, as they cover up the mouldings of the temple outside on the sides. Divested of this wall the temple consists of a cell and an *antarala* or vestibule. It does not appear to have ever had a *mahamandapa* in front. The object of worship is a *lingam* placed in a great *argha* 4 feet 7 inches in diameter. Externally the tower differs considerably from those of the other temples, and though in bad order, surpasses them in beauty and richness, though the sculptured details are not so profuse or minute. The temples are surmounted by urns and not, as usual, by cylinders or spires, or cones. Four miles north of Barākar under the Hadla hill there is a beautiful stone shrine to Kalyaneswari, the Lady of Fulfilment, a place of pilgrimage for barren women, which is said to be 400 or 500 years old. According to tradition the shrine and the group of temples attached were erected by an ancestor of the Pānchet Rājā, who is said to have married the daughter of a Rājā Lau Sen of Senpahāri. The story is that a Rohini Deoghar Brāhman once saw a jewelled arm rise out of the waters in the adjacent nala. He went and informed Rājā Kalyāna Sinha of Kasipur of Pānchet who came himself and saw the prodigy. At night the goddess herself appeared to him in a dream and pointing to an irregular stone, somewhat like a rude *argha*, said, "This is my *murti*; worship it." The Rājā built the temple and the stone having been duly inscribed was installed in it.

Bārul.—A village in the Asansol subdivision situated in 23° 44′ N. and 87° 7′ E. The population according to the census of 1901 was 532. Bārul is situated in the middle of the iron ore tract and has given its name to the surrounding iron ore field. About 1,700 persons are daily employed in iron mining and practically all the mineral iron is despatched to the Iron and Steel Works at Barākar, where pig iron, pipes, and various kinds of castings are turned out. The ore is found in the alluvial deposits and soil at a number of places, as masses of hematite and magnetite at Kālimati in Singhbhum, and in the iron stone shales of the Rānīganj coal-field. The Rānīganj ore is in the form of carbonate at depths, but it readily weathers and at the surface consists of hematite and limonite.

Budbud.—A village situated on the Grand Trunk Road, some 22 miles from Burdwān, in 23° 24′ N. and 87° 34′ E. It was formerly the head-quarters of a subdivision and the station of a Munsif. In 1879, however, when the present districts of Burdwān and Bāukurā were constituted, the head-quarters of the subdivision was removed to Bishnupar in the latter district. Two of the three thānas of the old Budbud subdivision, Budbud and Ausgrām, were included in the head-quarters subdivision of the Burdwān district, while the third, thānā Sonāmukhi, was transferred to Bānkurā. The Munsifi was abolished shortly afterwards, and in 1898 the police-station was removed to Galsi. Budbud is now a place of little importance. According to the census of 1901 the population is 938.

Burdwān Subdivision.—Head-quarters subdivision of the district, lying between 22° 56′ and 23° 37′ N. and 87° 26′ and 88° 14′ E. and extending over 1,268 square miles. The subdivision is bounded on the north by the Kātwa and Kālna subdivisions, on the east by Hooghly, on the south by Hooghly and Bānkurā and on the west by the Asansol subdivision. It contains the thānas of Burdwān, Sāhebganj, Khandaghosh, Raina, Satgāchia, Galsi, Ausgrām and Jamālpur and the outpost of Memāri. The subdivision for the most part consists of a flat alluvial plain, covered with rice crops, which is a part of the delta formed by the Ajay, the Bhāgīrathi and the Dāmodar. In thānā Ausgrām, however, the soil becomes laterite, and a tract of about 100 square miles in this thāna is covered with forest of bastard *sāl*. The principal rivers are the Dāmodar, which separates the thānas of Khandaghosh and Raina from the northern portion of the subdivision; the Bānka and the Kharī, which are tributaries of the Bhāgīrathi. The Eden canal also runs through the subdivision. Its population in 1901 was 679,412 as compared with 619,868 in 1891. It contains one town, Burdwān, the head-quarters of the district and 1,688 villages. It is less densely populated than the rest of the district supporting only 536 persons to the square mile. Brass and bellmetal ware and cutlery are manufactured at Banpās and Kānchannagar, and silk *dhotis* and *saris* at Memāri; a large annual fair is held at Kānchannagar a suburb of Burdwān town. A considerable *tasar* silk industry is carried on at Mānkur, which is also an important trade centre.

Burdwān.—Principal town and administrative head-quarters of the district situated in 23° 14′ N. and 87° 51′ E. on the Bānka river and the main line of the East Indian Railway. The population according to the census of 1901 is 35,022 (excluding 3,669 persons returned as living within railway limits) of whom 25,453 are Hindus, 9,441 Muhamadans and 128 others. The town really consists of 93 villages stretching over an area of nine miles, and the greater part of it is rural in character. In 1814 the population was estimated at 53,927 and for a long time the town was regarded by the residents of Calcutta as a sanatorium. From 1863 onwards however it suffered very severely from the Burdwān fever and, though the more virulent type of the disease has now completely disappeared, the town is still very unhealthy at certain seasons of the year. Since the construction of the water-works, however, the health of the town has much improved. It was the head-quarters of the Commissioner of the Burdwān Division from 1854 to 1871 and again from 1884 to 1896. The Commissioner's head-quarters are now at Chinsura in Hooghly.

The town has been indentified by M. de St. Martin with the Parthalis or Portalis which, according to the Greek geographers, was the royal city of the Gangardæ or Gangarides. According to Colonel Waddell one of its suburbs was the capital of the old Kingdom of Karna Suvarna which lay to the west of the Bhāgirathi and under the Gupta Kings in the seventh century comprised the present districts of Burdwān, Bānkurā, Murshidābād, and Hooghly. Mr. Beveridge, however, places the capital of Karna Suvarna at Rangamati in Murshidābād, and this is probably the more correct view. Burdwān city is first mentioned in Muhammadan histories in 1574, in which year, after Daud Khān's defeat and death at Rājmahāl, it was captured by Akbar's troops. Subsequently it is mentioned as the country residence of Sher Afgan, the first husband of the famous Mihr-ul-nissa, afterwards the Empress Nur-Jahān ("light of the world"), who was treacherously attacked and slain just outside the town by the Emperor's foster brother Kutb-ud-din, who was then Subāhdar of Bengal. Jehangir subsequently married Mihr-ul-nissa and there is little reason to doubt that her first husband was murdered by his orders. Kutb-ud-din himself was killed in the encounter, the scene of which is still pointed out near the railway station, and his grave and that of Sher Afgan are still to be seen in the town.

Burdwān was again besieged and taken by prince Khurram, afterwards the Emperor Shāh Jahān, in 1624 and by the rebels Subha Singh and Rahim Khān in 1695. Subha Singh was killed by a daughter of the Rājā of Burdwān whom he attempted to outrage, and Rahim Khān was eventually defeated and slain just outside the town by Azim-u-Shān the Emperor's grandson. After his defeat of the rebels Azim-u-Shān continued to reside in the town for some three years, during which time he built the great mosque which still bears his name.

There are several ancient tombs in the town, the most interesting being those of Pir Bahrām Shāh, Khoja Anwār Shāh, Sher

Afgan and Kutb-ud-din. Of the two last an account has already been given. The following reference to Pir Bahrām occurs in the memorandum book of Khusgo:—"Hajrat Haji Bahrām Sekka was a native of Turkestan. He belonged to the Bayet sect of Musulmans." He is also noticed in the memorandum book of Nudrat: "During the reign of Emperor Akbar, Bahrām Sekka came to Delhi and was, for his piety, taken into the good graces of the Emperor, who placed implicit confidence in him, but owing to the machinations of Abdul Fazl and Faizi who held important posts in the court of Akbar and who had grown jealous of him, Bahrām Sekka left Delhi in disgust and came to Burdwān. He however died here within three days of his arrival. It is also stated that when Bahrām Sekka arrived at Burdwān he heard of a famous hermit named Jaipal and made his acquaintance. The latter, however, very much impressed with the miracles performed by this Muhammadan saint, became his disciple. The garden where the grave of Bahrām Sekka lies formerly belonged to Jaipal, who having made over all his belongings to Bahrām Sekka, fixed his residence in the corner of the garden. When the news of the death of Bahrām Sekka reached Akbar, he, through the Nawāb Nazim of Bengal, allotted the revenues of certain villages to the perpetuation of his memory. The tank and garden were repaired and an allowance of two rupees a day was made for daily charity." The lands assigned have been resumed, and Government has granted a monthly allowance of Rs. 42-2-3 to replace the income from them. It is further related that Bahrām Sekka was a Hāji of Mecca and Medina and he afterwards became a water-carrier in the streets of Mecca and Najaf. It was his duty to offer water to every thirsty wayfarer and this act was considered highly virtuous. Bahrām Sekka wrote in his works: "Shaikh Sadi was a water-carrier for forty years." The translation of the Persian inscription on the tomb is as follows:—"When I wished to know the date of his death, methinks I heard a voice from the seat of God saying 'My Bahrām Sekka was a wonderful fakir.'" Died 970 Hijri. Khoja Anwār Shāh fell in battle near the town and his tomb was built by the Emperor Ferokh Shāh in consideration of his services. The date on the tomb is 1127 Hijri.

About 2 miles from the town, at Nawāb Hāt, is a group of 108 Siva *lingam* temples which stand in a rectangle planted with trees and containing some well-kept tanks; these temples were built and consecrated in October 1788 by the Mahārānī Adhiswāri Bishtu Kumāri Bibi, wife of Tilak Chandra and mother of Tej Chandra. This series of temples is exactly similar to that at Kālna, of which a full description is given in the article on that town. Near the temples, and probably intended to guard them is the spacious fort of Tālitgarh which formed the refuge of the Burdwān family and its retainers during the Marāthā invasions of the 18th century. The fort stands in an open plain. It is almost circular in form and is a space of over half a square mile in extent, defended by a lofty earthwork rampart, with bastions at regular intervals, and encircled by a wide and deep moat. There are still traces of masonry at the northern gateway, and in the citadel and some of the bastions. The interior forms the cultivated lands of a village which has grown up within it and in the main street of which a twenty-four pounder gun was visible in 1888, half buried in the soil. The fort was constructed by the Rājās of Burdwān expressly as a place of refuge against the periodical incursions of the Marāthās, and though never completely armed must, when defended by a numerous body of men, have been impregnable against the attacks of horsemen unprovided with artillery. The cannon, mostly twenty-four pounders, with which it was mounted, were very numerous and are now kept at Burdwān. There is a similar fort at Kulingrām, about six miles south of the Memāri railway station.

Within the town itself the principal places of interest are the palaces and gardens of the Mahārājā, which are in the centre of the town. The Dilkusha, which is surrounded by spacious and well-kept grounds, is situated some two miles west of the railway station: here there is a small zoological garden maintained by the Mahārājā, which is well worth a visit. There are also some fine old tanks among which may be noticed the Krishnā-sāgar tank constructed by Krishnā Rām Rai, and the Rānīsāgar tank excavated by Rānī Brojo Kishori in 1709 A. D. According to tradition Krishnā Rām Rai was assassinated while bathing in the tank which bears his name. The only modern monument of any importance is the Star of India arch erected by the present Mahārājā at the entrance to the town, to commemorate Lord Curzon's visit. Cutlery is manufactured at the suburb of Kānchannagar and there are two oil mills in the town; a large annual fair is also held at Kānchannagar. Burdwān was constituted a Municipality in 1865 and the Municipal Board consists of 22 Commissioners, of whom 15 are elected. The area within municipal limits is 8·4 square miles. Water-works, constructed at a cost of Rs. 2 lakhs, were opened in 1884, the Mahārājā of Burdwān contributing half a lakh, and the remainder being borrowed from or contributed by Government;

the health of the town has since greatly improved. The town possesses the usual public offices. The district jail has accommodation for 256 prisoners, the chief industries being *surki* pounding and the manufacture of oil and *newār*; carpets are also made and indigo dyeing is carried on on a small scale. The most important educational institutions are the Burdwān Rāj College, maintained by the Rāj, and a technical school affiliated to the Sibpur Engineering College, maintained by the District Board, with a contribution from the Municipality. The Church Missionary Society early fixed on Burdwān as a centre from which to carry on its work and in the early half of the last century had established a prosperous and well-managed mission under the Rev. J.J. Weitbrecht. The fever epidmic of 1864—72, however, compelled the society to transfer most of its institutions elsewhere, and the mission is now a purely evangelistic one.

Culna.—*See* Kālna.

Cutwa.—*See* Kātwa.

Chakdīghi.—A village in the head-quarters subdivision, some thirteen miles south of Memāri station. It is the residence of one of the leading zamīndārs of the district. The village contains a free High English school which was established in 1863 by the trustees of the will of the late Bābu Sārada Prasād Singh Rai and a charitable dispensary.

Churulia.—A village in the Asansol subdivision lying round a ruined stone fort on the Ajay in *pargana* Shergarh. The village is occupied by Muhammadan *aimmādārs* who have built their houses and mosques from the stones of the fort. They have no tradition of how they came there. The fort is said to have been built by one Rājā Narottam and is known as Rājā Narottam's fort, but nothing is known of this Rājā and no one can even say to what caste he belonged. It is possible that the fort may originally have belonged to the Pānchet Rājās as Mr. Oldham has suggested.

Dainhāt.—A town in the Katwa subdivision, situated on the right bank of the Bhāgirathi in 23° 36′ N. and 88° 11′E. According to the census of 1901 the population is 5,618. Brass and bellmetal work is manufactured in the town, and weaving is carried on; there is also some trade in salt, jute, grain, English cloth, cotton and tobacco. The town, which lies between Kātwa and Kālna, was formerly considered one of the principal ports of the district. But the river is gradually receding from it and its prosperity has long been declining. It is now of little commercial importance. The remains of the Rājās of Burdwān from Abu Rai, the founder of the house, to Jagat Rām Rai, are preserved here. Dainhāt was constituted a Municipality in 1869. The area within municipal limits is 4 square miles.

Dīgnagar.—A village in the Burdwān subdivision of the district, situated in 23° 26′ N. and 87° 42′. E. Population (1901) 2,717. It is a local market for grain and sugar and is noted for its brass and bell-metal ware. Shellac and lac-dye are manufactured here. The village is described by Jacquemont as a place of some importance.

Faridpur.—A village situated on the Grand Trunk Road near Oyaria station. It is the head-quarters of a police thāna. It is important from a police point of view as it is situated in the centre of the jungle area which lies to the north of the Grand Trunk Road.

Gopbhūm.—A large *pargana* lying on the eastern slopes of the Asansol watershed. This was the name given to the tract of wooded upland forming the cape or headland of the promontory from Central India which juts out into the district. The neck of this promontory is Shergarh, lying between the Ajay and Dāmodar. Between it and Gopbhūm in the same formation are the recently formed *parganas* of Salīmpur and Senpahāri, which probably belonged to Gopbhūm. The actual headland is formed by Gopbhūm with the delta, not only fencing it in on the west but coming round it on the south and edging in on the north. Gopbhūm, which is still covered for the greater part of its surface with *sāl* forest, was by universally current tradition the seat of a Sadgop dynasty of which some traces are still extant. The only Rājā of the race whose name survives was Mahendranāth or, as he is locally called, Mahindi Rājā. The ruins of his fort at Amrārgarh near Mānkur, and of other forts at Bharatpur and Kāksa, which apparently belonged to cadets of the house, are still visible. The remains at Amrārgarh do not appear to be very ancient, and the Sadgop kingdom of Gopbhūm apparently existed till almost modern times, first as subject to the Mughals and then under the shadow of the Burdwān house itself. But by 1744 Raja Chitrā Sen of Burdwān had occupied Gopbhūm and had constructed his forts at Rājgarh at Kāksa and near Gorangapur.*

Gorangapur.—A village in the Asansol subdivision situated on the Ajay in *pargana* Senpahāri. The name is derived from one of the names of Chaitanya, the great Vaishnavite reformer—Goranga or Gouranga the fair limbed. The village contains a beautifully built brick temple, a landmark for miles far and wide, still in fine preservation though deserted, and evidently

* Oldham, Some Historical and Ethnical Aspects of the Burdwān District.

more than a hundred and fifty years old. The building is known as the temple of Ichhay Ghose, and tradition says that Ichhay Ghose was a devout person who constructed the temple in honour of the goddess Bhagabati. He is said to have been killed in battle by a Rājā called Lau Sen who, according to tradition, was a descendant of Ballal Sen, the king of Bengal. It is very probable however that this supposed Lau Sen is no other than the Burdwān Rājā Chitra Sen Rai, who conquered Gopbhūm in the middle of the 18th century. Close to Gorangapur on a small tableland overlooking the Ajay, which is clothed with dense forest, on the very confines of Bīrbhūm and Pānchet (Shergarh), stands the fort constructed by Chitra Sen Rai to overawe Gopbhūm and Senpahāri, in which his cannon with his name in Persian characters deeply engraved on them lie to this day. Another account makes Ichhay Ghose the architect or artificer of the temple.

Guskhārā.—A large village in the head-quarters subdivision situated on the Loop line of the East Indian Railway. Since the opening of the railway station the village has grown largely and it is now a rice mart of considerable importance. It contains a sub-registry office, a sub post-office, a Sanskrit *tol* and a District Board bungalow. Guskhārā is now an important distributing centre and cultivators come from a distance of fifteen or sixteen miles to it to sell their rice and paddy. A *hât* is held twice a week on Tuesday and Fridays. The population in 1901 was 2,172.

Jamālpur.—A village situated some eleven miles south of Memāri railway station on the east bank of the Dāmodar river. The village is an important trading centre and contains a sub-registry office, a police station, a sub-post office, a lower primary school and a Public Works Department inspection bungalow. The Dāmodar here is connected with the Eden canal by a sluice from Halara to Jamālpur. Population (1901), 795.

Kāksa.—A village and police station in the Asansol subdivision, situated about half a mile north of Pānagar railway station on the main line of the East Indian Railway in 23° 27′ N. and 87° 30′ E. According to the census of 1901 the population amounts to 2,244. Kāksa is historically interesting on account of its connection with the Sadgop dynasty which, according to universally current tradition, formerly ruled in Gopbhūm and Senpahāri. The south-western extremity of this kingdom, now *pargana* Salimpur, was apparently held by two Sadgop kinglings, probably mere cadets of the house of Gopbhūm—one stationed at Bharatpur on the Dāmodar, and the other at Kānkeswar or

Kāksa. The fort at Kāksa was stormed and the Rājā was slain by a Muhammadan leader from Bokhān named Sayad Sayad Bokhāri, whose descendant Sayads, hold the Kāksa lands in *aimmā* to this day. The date of the occurrence is very uncertain for while it is possible that Sayad Bokhāri may have been a leader during the earliest invasion into Bengal, it is equally probable that he was a soldier of fortune in later times. A similar fate probably overtook the Bharatpur chief. The remains of the tiny fort at Kāksa can still be seen and in the small tank below it figures of Hindu deities carved in basalt are still occasionally found. In addition much stonework of Hindu workmanship may be traced in the ruins of the mosque which is known as the Rājā's mosque close to the fort. Bharatpur overlooks the Dāmodar some four miles south of Kāksa and is only interesting as being traditionally identified with the princes of the Sadgop dynasty. Four miles north of Kāksa lies the fort of Rājgarh, which was constructed by Chitra Sen Rai of Burdwān to overawe his conquest of Gopbhūm. Local tradition now connects this stronghold and that at Churuliā on the Ajay with the Marāthā invasions of the 18th century, but this is contradicted by history and by the probabilities of the case. They lie in the path which the wild jungle tribes of the west, the Chuars of the Jharkhand, followed in their descents on the settled country of Bengal, and within the forest tract which possessed no attraction for the Marāthā freebooters. They are not provided with moats as a defence against horsemen and would have been easily assailable by well equipped troops, although they presented serious obstacles to naked hillmen armed only with bows and arrows. Moreover, the ghātwāli posts attached to them show that they were permanent stations for defence and not mere places of refuge. The country round Chiruliā is now open though bare, but the fort stands on a rocky promontory in such dense forest that it is difficult to make out its shape. A temple to Syāmarupa is still maintained in the citadel and near it lie seven dismounted five-pounder cannon of English manufacture, all of which have been carefully spiked. The Rājgarh fort is a handsome ruin forming a rectangular fortification without a moat, standing just clear of the forest and surrounded by a rampart, which on the west side is still about 40 feet high, with bastions at the corners and along the faces. Much of the masonry of the southern and northern gateways, and also of an interior residence, still remains. Outside the southern gate are the remains of an outwork or barbican, with polygonal towers at the corners built of small excellently moulded bricks. It commanded both the highway along the Ajay and the road from Suri or Nagar *viâ* Ilambazār to Bishnupur.

Kālna Subdivision.—The south-eastern subdivision of the district lying between 23° 7′ and 23° 36′ N. and 88° 0′ and 88° 25′E., with an area of 399 square miles. The subdivision is bounded on the north by the Kātwa subdivision, on the east by the Bhāgīrathi, and on the south and west by Hooghly and the Burdwān subdivision. The principal rivers are the Bhāgīrathi, which separates it from Nadiā, the Bānka, and the Kharī which joins the Bhāgīrathi a little above Kālna. The subdivision like the adjoining subdivision of Kātwa, is flat and alluvial and the eastern portion along the bank of the Bhāgīrathi is waterlogged and swampy, that river in its progress eastwards having left long loops of disused channels along its banks. The subdivision for many years suffered very severely from the Burdwān fever and is still very unhealthy. It contains the thānās of Kālna, Mantes-war, and Purbasthāli. Its population in 1901 was 233,269, the density being 585 persons to the square mile. It contains one town, Kālna, its head-quarters, with a population of 8,121 and 698 villages. Nādanghāt in the interior has a large trade in rice and is one of the principal agricultural marts of the district.

Kālna.—Head-quarters town of the subdivision of the same name, situated on the right bank of the Bhāgīrathi in 23° 13′ N. and 88° 22′E. The area of the town is two square miles and it lies on a long narrow strip of high land overlooking the river. According to the census of 1901 it has a population of 8,121 persons. Kālna was a place of great importance in Muhammadan times and the ruins of the old fort constructed to command the river can still be seen. It was formerly one of the principal ports of the district in the days when the river was the main channel for trade, but the river has silted up considerably, the East Indian and other Railways have diverted the traffic, and the prosperity of the town has long been declining. For several years also it was the focus of the terrible Burdwān fever, which ravaged the district between 1862 and 1874, and even after the disappearance of the disease was for many years extremely unhealthy. The town is falling into decay and many of the brick-built houses in the bazar are now in ruins. Kālna was formerly a favoured seat of the Burdwān house and most of the places of interest in the town are closely connected with that family. The Mahārājā still keeps up a palace here and near it are a series of 109 Siva *lingam* temples similar to those at Nawāb Hāt in Burdwān. The temples at Kālna were constructed and consecrated by Mahārājā Tej Chandra Bahādur in 1809. The temples, which are all dedicated to Siva, are arranged in concentric circles, the outer circle consisting of 66 temples containing black and white *lingams* alternately, while the inner circle has 42 temples containing white *lingams* only. The temples touch one another except where spaces are left for entrance into the centre. Each temple is a circular domed cell with the *lingam* in the centre. The worship of an hundred and eight phallic emblems of Sivā is mentioned in the *Tāntras* as productive of great religious merit. It is said to have special efficacy in averting certain dangers such as social degradation, loss of caste, extinction of one's race, or fatal disease. The number 108 has a great significance. The temples represent the beads in a rosary, and these symbolize the letters in the Sanskrit alphabet. The fifty letters counted from beginning to end and again the other way give us the figure 100., To this is added "8" as representing the groups (a, ka, cha, ta, tha, pa, ya, ça) into which the letters are arranged. There is yet one more bead called the *meru* or pole which serves to separate the two terminal beads and which, by its peculiar shape, apprises the votary that the full tale of the beads has been told off. Accordingly there is an 109th temple standing outside the temple grounds, typifying the *meru* or the polar bead. It may be interesting to note that the word "*aksha*", which is a Sanskrit synonym of rosary, is a compound of the two letters "*a*" and "*ksha*" (respectively the first letter and the *meru*). Among the other temples in the grounds of the palace are a very fine one of carved brickwork dedicated to Siva, two temples dedicated to Krishna, and several smaller ones erected and consecreted by the maidservants of the Rāj. The Samāj Bāri which contains tombs of all the Mahārājās and Mahārānīs of Burdwān is also attached to the palace. There is a separate building for each Mahārājā or Mahārānī, in which is kept the bones remaining from the funeral pyre, together with all the personal belongings of the deceased. But the remains of the late Mahārājā and Mahārānī are kept in the palace building which the Mahārājā used to occupy during his lifetime. The cooking and eating vessels of the Mahārānī, used by her in her lifetime, with her umbrella, fans, scent-holders, etc., are placed round her remains. The remains of the late Mahārājā Māhtab Chānd are dressed in the clothes which he used during his life, which are changed three times a day. They are regarded as if the Mahārājā was living himself and are placed on a velvet state cushion with silver salver, tumblers, *hookahs*, and *atar* holders, just as the late Mahārājā used to sit with all the paraphernalia of state about him. They are surrounded by his utensils, chowries, walking stick and all the articles daily used by him in life; in another room is shown his office table with the inkstand, pens, waste paper basket, etc., used by him; and in another the bed which he used. The meals which they used to take in life are offered to the remains daily and are then distributed to the poor. In front is a shed where shows and dances are given for their entertainment. The bones of the Mahārājās before Kirti Chand, from the founder of the family, Abu Rai, are similarly kept at Dainhāt. The only other historical remains of interest in the town are the tombs of Majlis Saheb and Badr Saheb, who are regarded as the patron saints of Kālna. Majlis Saheb and Badr Saheb, according to tradition, were brothers who came to Kālna some 400 years ago to spread the creed of Islam. They have taken their place as "*pirs*" in the public faith and their tombs, which are still shown, are worshipped by Hindu and Muhammadan alike. The most common offerings are small clay horses, though fruits, sweets and flowers are often presented at the shrines. It is said that between the two tombs which are almost a mile apart on the river bank a man is safe from any accident and even crocodiles will not attack him. Kālna is also intimately connected with the great religious reformer Chaitanya. It was often visited by him and according to popular tradition was the scene of one of his many transformations. There are many fine old mosques in the town but almost without exception these are now in ruins. Just south of Kālna and in its suburbs stand the ruins of a mosque said to be of very great antiquity. The superstructure is of brick but the basement is of basalt stone work, which, as in many similar edifices in Burdwān, bears manifest traces of having been carved for Hindu uses. The bricks are large and coarse and the antiquity attributed by tradition to the mosque most probably applies to an earlier building of either Hindu or Musalman construction.

Kālna was constituted a Municipality in 1869; the Municipal board consists of 15 Commissioners of whom two-thirds are elected. The area within Municipal limits is two square miles. The town contains the usual public offices; the subsidiary jail has accommodation for 14 prisoners. The Rāj maintains a High English school and a dispensary. There is also a hospital maintained by the United Free Church of Scotland Medical Mission. The town is served by Messrs. Hoare, Miller & Co.'s.

steamers which run daily throughout the year and which compete not unsuccessfully with the railway for both goods and passenger traffic. Its trade is now increasing owing to the increased demand in Calcutta for country produce; and when the railway which is at present under construction is completed, it will probably develop rapidly.

Kātwa Subdivision.—North-eastern subdivision of the district. lying between 23° 26′ and 23° 50′ N. and 87° 44′ and 88° 17′ E., with an area of 404 square miles. The subdivision consists entirely of a flat alluvial plain being a portion of the Gangetic delta, and in the east along the banks of the Bhāgīrathi the soil is water-logged and swampy. It is bounded on the north by Bīrbhūm and Murshidābād, and on the south by the Kātwa and Burdwān subdivisions. On the east the Bhāgīrathi separates it from Nadiā. The principal rivers are the Ajay, which for the last fifteen miles of its course runs through the subdivision, and the Kunur. Its population in 1901 was returned at 248,806 compared with 230,227 in 1891, the density being 616 persons to the square mile. It contains two towns Kātwa, its head-quarters, having a population of 7,220, and Dāinhat, and 445 villages. Large annual fairs are held at Agradwīp and Dadia. The manufacture of *tasar* silk is an important industry in the subdivision.

Kātwa.—Head-quarters town of the subdivision of the same name, situated at the junction of the Bhāgīrathi and Ajay rivers in 23° 39′ N. and 88° 8′ E. According to the census of 1901 the population is 7,220. The fine strategical position of Kātwa soon attracted the notice of the Muhammadan conquerors of Bengal and it was one of their earliest seats. During the period of the Marāthā invasions it was considered the key to Murshidābād, and was frequently used as a base by Ali Vārdi Khān in his operations against the invaders. In 1742 he defeated the Marāthās in a pitched battle outside the walls of the fort. In 1757 Clive, in his march up the western bank of the Bhāgīrathi before the battle of Plassey, seized the fort of Kātwa which was abandoned by the garrison at the first assault. The English army encamped in the town and it was here after an hour's meditation in a grove near the town, that Clive, disregarding the opinion of the council of war which he himself had called, formed the momentous decision that gave Bengal to the East India Company. The old fort which was a simple earthwork and mounted fourteen guns, now lies in the heart of the town and forms its poorest quarter entirely inhabited by Muhammadans. It is situated on a tongue of land at the confluence of the

Ajay and Bhāgīrathi and is still distinctly defined by a deep and wide moat except on the north side. A large mosque in very fair preservation still exists within it. It was built by Jafar Khān, better known as Murshid Kuli Khān, the founder of Murshidābād and Subāhdar of Bengal from 1702—1725. Kātwa is held sacred by the Vaishnabs as having been the place where their apostle Chaitanya entered upon the life of an ascetic. Steamers used to ply all the year round to the town, but owing to the silting up of the Bhāgīrathi and the opening of the East Indian Railway the commercial importance of the place has declined; the new railway line from Hooghly to Kālna will however by carried on to Kātwa and should lead to a revival of its trade. Kātwa was constituted a Municipality in 1869. The town contains the usual public offices; the subsidiary jail has accommodation for 24 prisoners.

Khāna.—A village in the head-quarters subdivision of the district, situated in 23° 20′ N. and 87° 46′ E. The population in 1901 was 1,600. Khāna is an important junction on the East Indian Railway where the loop line branches off from the chord line.

Khandaghosh.—A village in the head-quarters sub division of the district, situated in 23° 12′ N. and 87° 44′ E., 8 miles from Burdwān on the road to Sonāmuhki and Bānkurā. According to the census of 1901 its population was 4,201 and it is one of the largest villages in the district. It contains a police-station, a dispensary, a sub-registry office and a Middle English School.

Kulingrām.—A large village in the Burdwan subdivision situated some six miles south of Memāri railway station. The village is by common rumour a very ancient settlement. In the month of *Magh* a fair is held here in honour of the village deity Gopal and some thousands of people gather yearly to see the image of the god. There is a District Board dispensary here, and a branch post-office. The population according to the census of 1901 was 1,149.

Māhta.—A village in the Burdwān subdivision situated some seven miles from Guskhārā railway station. The village contains a District Board dispensary, a Sanskrit *tol*, a middle English school, a vernacular *pāthshālā* and a branch post-office. A fair is held here twice a week. Māhta is a very old village and was formerly a well-known centre of Sanskrit education. A religious fair is held here yearly at the beginning of *Magh* in honour of the village god Gobinda Ji.

Mangalkot.—A village situated on the banks of the river Kunur in the Katwā subdivision. It contains a police station.

a charitable dispensary maintained by the District Board, a Madrasa maintained by the local Muhammadans and a branch post-office. The sub-registry office named after the village is situated in Natunhât about two miles off. There are according to the last census 623 houses in the village containing a population of 2,335 souls. Mangalkot was formerly a great Muhammadan settlement and there are many ruined mosques in the village and in those adjoining it. The Muhammadan population still predominates though most of them are poor. It is also rich in Hindu remains of an earlier date and may possibly have been one of the outposts of the Sadgop kingdom of Gopbhūm.

Kogrām or Ujani, a neighbouring village on the other side of the river Kunur was the birthplace of the famous Vaishnab poet Lochan Das and is said to be one of the many places which received the fragments of *Sati's* corpse when it was cut into pieces by the wheel of Vishnu. It is also connected with Srimanta Saudagar whose voyage is described in the *Chandi* of the poet Kabi Kankan. A large number of pilgrims resort to the place on the anniversary of Lochan Das' death when a large fair is held.

Mānkur.—A village in the head-quarters subdivision of the district, situated in 23° 26′ N. and 87° 34′ E. The population in 1901 was 7,206. Mānkur is a station on the chord line of the East Indian Railway, 90 miles from Calcutta, and has a considerable trade; it is also the chief seat of the local silk weaving industry. The Church Missionary Society maintains a Medical Mission here with a hospital and dispensary with 3 European ladies in charge and an efficient staff of workers under the Church of England Zenana Society. Eleven thousand patients were treated in 1901. Mānkur is famous for its sweetmeats and its confectioners are noted for their *olā*, *khājā* and *kadmā*. Amrārgarh, a mile north of the railway station, is by tradition identified as the seat of Mahendranāth or, as he is locally called, Mahindi Rājā, the only prince of the Sadgop dynasty of Gopbhūm whose name still survives. The long lines of fortification which enclosed his walled town are still visible just where the laterite plateau juts out into the alluvial land of the delta. They consist of a ruined earthwork rampart and ditch enclosing a square of about a mile in area.

Manteswar.—A small village in the Kālnā subdivision situated on the east bank of the Kharī river. The village is the head-quarters of a police station, and contains a sub-registry office and a branch post-office. There are some very old temples here one of which is dedicated to Siva under his name Manteswar.

Memāri.—A village in the head-quarters subdivision of the district, situated in 23° 10′ N. and 88° 7′ E. The population in 1901 was returned as 1,674. Memāri is a station on the East Indian Railway and an important trade centre; silk *saris* and *dhotis* are also manufactured. The village contains an independent police outpost and a Sub-Registry office.

Nādanghāt.—A village in the Kālna subdivision, situated on the Kharī in 23° 22′ N. and 88° 15′ E The population in 1901 was 916. Nādanghāt is the principal rice mart in the interior of the district and large quantities of grain are brought down by country boat from the village to the Bhāgīrathi.

Ondāl.—*See* Andāl.

Rainā.—A village in the head-quarters subdivision of the district, situated in 23° 40′ N. and 87° 56′ E., south of the Dāmodar river. It is the head-quarters of a police-station and in the early part of the 19th century was notorious for its *thags*, who were first found in Bengal here in 1802. According to popular rumour the people of Rainā thāna are particularly fierce and warlike. After the suppression of *thagi* the descendants of the *thags* are said to have taken to dacoity as a means of subsistence. Some of the stories told of the most famous of these robbers among the country-people are worth recording. One of their leaders "could eat the raw flesh of a goat and drink three bottles of brandy at a meal". Another, a woman, could ride a horse "as cleverly as an expert colonel or captain would do" and on one occasion with only the help of a sword and her husband robbed a zamīndār's house in spite of his numerous men servants and armed retainers. Another woman with her old father put to flight and killed ten armed men who assaulted them.

Rānīganj.—A town in the Asansol subdivision, situated on the north bank of the Dāmodar river in 23° 36′ N. and 87° 6′ E. The population in 1901 was 15,841. The town, which is situated on the East Indian Railway, owes its importance to the development of the coal industry. Extensive potteries give employment to 900 hands, the value of the outturn in 1909 being estimated at 3·18 lakhs; paper mills employ nearly 1,100 hands and in 1909 made 5,394 tons of paper, valued at Rs. 16·36 lakhs; and three oil-mills were also at work. There is also a considerable trade in rice and oil. The town contains a police-station and sub-registry office. A Wesleyan Methodist Mission maintains a leper asylum, and an orphanage and day schools. Rānīganj was formerly the head-quarters of the subdivision, but in 1906 the subdivisional Magistrate's Court was removed to Asansol.

According to Homfray "the name is derived from the proprietary rights of the collieries having been vested in the late Rān of Burdwān."* A few years before the mutiny the portion of the town which now forms its centre, was an uninhabited plain covered with brushwood and jungle, and in the quarter now known as Khāntsuli there were only a few huts occupied by eight poor families of goālās and Muhammadans: whilst the village of Kumārbāzār or Kumār Rāmchandrāpur, now within municipal limits at the eastern edge of the town, was a pretty agricultural hamlet. During the mutiny Rānīganj was the terminus of the East Indian Railway, and a cantonment for the troops who had to detrain here on their way up-country was established temporarily at Khantsuli, which was afterwards better known as Gorābāzār or "the white soldier's market." After the opening of the railway the prosperity of the town was assured. Before the extension of the line the criminal court, police-station, post office and lock-up were located in Mangalpur, some two miles from Rānīganj; and the Munsif's court was at Ukhra, eight miles to the north, which was then in the district of Bīrbhūm. At that Rānīgānj was included in this district for purposes of revenue administration only, the criminal administration being under Mānbhūm. Rānīganj was formerly considered the centre of the coal industry and the Bengal Coal Company still has its head office at Egara, near the town. The quality of coal obtainable is not, however, so good as that received from the mines further west, and Asansol has now taken the place of Rānīganj as the centre of the trade in this district. Most of the houses in the town are of brick and the roads are well kept. The climate is very hot in summer but is dry and healthy.

Sāhebganj.—A large village in the head-quarters subdivision situated some seven miles north-east of Guskhārā railway station. The population in 1901 was 495. According to tradition the village owes its name to a Mr. Cheek (possibly the well known Mr. Cheap of Bīrbhūm) who started a trading centre here. It was formerly an important distributing centre but since the opening of the railway station at Guskhārā has greatly declined in importance. A market is held here twice a week.

Salimābād.—A village in the head-quarters subdivision of the district, in 23° 4′ N. and 38° 8′ E. It is the head-quarters of a police-station and in the seventeenth century was called Sulaimānabād, and was the revenue and executive centre of the Mughal Sarkār of that name.

* The coal-field of the Damudah. Journal of the Asiatic Society of Bengal, 1842.

Salīmpur.—A small *pargana* at the south-west edge of Gopbhūm which, according to current tradition, formed a part of that kingdom under the Sadgop chiefs of Kāksa and Bharatpur until it was wrested from them by the Muhammadans. The name is said to be a contraction of Sulaimānpur, after one of the kings of Bengal.

Satgāchia.—A village in the head-quarters subdivision of the district about 20 miles due east of Burdwān town. It is the head-quarters of a police-station. Close by at Bohār is a fine Madrasa which was constructed at the close of the last century. It is an extensive brick building enclosing a quadrangle with cloisters, chapels, dormitories and class rooms. Originally it contained accommodation for 700 students, but owing to the terms in which the *farman* constituting the *aimmā* grant for its maintenance is worded, the hereditary *mutwāli* is under no control, and the building is not fittingly maintained, while its character as a teaching institution has been entirely lost sight of.

Senpahāri.—A *pargana* on the eastern slopes of the Asansol watershed. The *pargana* was formed by Rājā Chitrā Sen Rai of Burdwān after his conquest of Gopbhūm, and is called after himself and the stronghold which he built near Gorangapur on a hill over-looking the Ajay.

Shergarh.—A large *pargana* in the Asansol subdivision which is practically conterminous with the Rānīganj coal-field. It is that part of the promontory of Central India which lies between the Ajay and the Dāmodar, a stretch of rolling rocky country parts of which are still covered with forest. Owing to its physical character and situation it was for many centuries the high road and harbour of the Chuars of the Jharkhand —the jungle tribes generally—in their descents upon the settled country to the east. It thus became a sort of debateable land the possession of which was contested by all the great houses lying upon its borders. It was ultimately conquered by Rājā Chitrā Sen Rai of Burdwān about 1742 A.D. It contains two old forts. That at Churulia on the Ajay is of stone and is said to have been built by Rājā Narottam. But tradition and history are alike silent as to this Rājā and no one can even say to what caste he belonged. The oldest residents of Churulia are the Muhammadan *aimmādārs* who live under the fort and who have taken its cut stones for their mosques and houses. Mr. Oldham conjectures that the *aimmādārs* may be descendants of Muhammadan soldiery who stormed the fort as in the similar case at Kāksa, which is not improbable. The other fort is an earthwork at Dihī Shergarh, the old capital of the *pargana* on the Dāmodar.

It was erected by and still belongs to the Rājput house of Pānchet, who were the proprietors of Shergarh until Rājā Chitrā Sen Rai wrested it from them. The Pathān sovereigns of Bīrbhum also at one time possessed part of the *pargana.* *

Sitārāmpur.—A village in the Asansol subdivision, situated on the main line of the East Indian Railway. It is an important railway junction, the chord line to Mokameh branching off here from the grand chord which goes on to Gaya. Sitārāmpur is one of the principal subsidiary centres of the Rānīganj and Barākar coal-fields, and there are many large collieries in its neighbourhood.

Ukhra.—A village in the Asansol subdivision situated on the railway line connecting Andāl and Suri. Ukhra is one of the largest villages in the district and contains some 4,000 inhabitants. There is a high English school here, a dispensary, a grain bank, and several interesting temples. The village is the seat of the an ancient family of zamīndārs to whose generosity and public spirit it owes most of the institutions mentioned above.

* Oldham. Some Historical and Ethnical Aspects of the Burdwān District.

INDEX.

A.

B.

C.

D.

E.

F.

G.

H.

L.

M.

B. S. Press—1-12-1910—4635J—538—J. L. C.